Economics, 3rd Edition
Part II

Professor Timothy Taylor

THE TEACHING COMPANY ®

PUBLISHED BY:

THE TEACHING COMPANY
4151 Lafayette Center Drive, Suite 100
Chantilly, Virginia 20151-1232
1-800-TEACH-12
Fax—703-378-3819
www.teach12.com

ISBN 1-59803-128-7

Timothy Taylor

Managing Editor, *Journal of Economic Perspectives*
Macalester College, St. Paul, Minnesota

Timothy Taylor is managing editor of the *Journal of Economic Perspectives*, an academic journal published quarterly by the American Economic Association. He was originally hired to help launch the journal in 1986, and it has since matured into the most widely distributed and widely read journal in academic economics. The purpose of the journal is to encourage communication and cross-fertilization across the many fields of economics.

He was born in Urbana, Illinois, and grew up in Bethlehem, Pennsylvania, and Saint Paul, Minnesota. He received his bachelor of arts degree from Haverford College in Pennsylvania in 1982 and a master's degree in economics from Stanford University in California in 1984. He then worked as an editorial writer for the *San Jose Mercury News* for two years, before taking the job of starting the *Journal of Economic Perspectives* in 1986.

He has taught economics in a number of contexts. In 1992, he was winner of the award for excellent teaching in a large class (more than 30 students) given by the Associated Students of Stanford University. At the University of Minnesota, he was named a Distinguished Lecturer by the Department of Economics in 1996 and voted Teacher of the Year by the master's degree students at the Hubert H. Humphrey Institute of Public Affairs in 1997. Professor Taylor has also been a guest speaker for groups of teachers of high school economics, visiting diplomats from Eastern Europe, radio talk shows, and community groups. The U.S. Department of State sent him to Japan in 1999 and to South Africa in 2003 to discuss trade and globalization issues with government and business leaders.

From 1989 to 1997, he wrote an economics opinion column for the *San Jose Mercury News*, and many of his columns were disseminated nationally over the Knight-Ridder-Tribune wire. In 2000, he co-authored *Updating America's Social Contract: Economic Growth and Opportunity in the New Century*, with Rudolph G. Penner and Isabel V. Sawhill. He has also written articles for *The Public Interest*, *Milken Institute Review*, and other publications. He has recorded several courses for The Teaching Company, including *Economics: An Introduction*, *Legacies of Great*

Economists, A History of the U.S. Economy in the 20th Century, and *Contemporary Economic Issues.*

Table of Contents
Economics, 3rd Edition
Part II

Economics, 3rd Edition

Scope:

The wisdom of economists is nearly proverbial, but in a negative sort of way, rather like the honesty of politicians, the verbal fluency of sports heroes, or the lips of chickens. Yet in the face of this prejudice, I maintain that economics does have useful lessons for understanding the world around us. My wife claims that I only hold to this belief because I am an evangelist, with economics as my religion. Perhaps so.

But I have also been asked many times, at conferences and cocktail parties, to recommend "just one book" that would explain economics. These requests often come from people who have just met me, but they have discovered that I edit an academic economics journal or that I teach economics classes. They aren't looking for a conservative lecture that defends the beauty of markets, nor for a liberal lecture about the need for government intervention in certain parts of the economy.

They are seeking a basic level of sophistication in economic matters. They have their own views on politics and policy, but they are self-aware enough to recognize that at least some of those views are built on a shaky or nonexistent understanding of economics. They want an overall view of what the U.S. economy looks like and how it is interconnected. They want to know how economists perceive the advantages of free markets and how economists reconcile a belief in markets with the problems of the world around them, such as poverty and pollution. They want to know why a budget deficit matters and what the Federal Reserve is and does. They want to know what economists think about international trade, how the exchange rate works, and what the "current account balance" actually is. They are skeptical about accepting all that economists have to say, as they would be skeptical about anyone who claims to have lots of answers. But they have not surrendered to cynicism; they are willing to accept that the study of economics does have some insights to offer.

The cynical view, I suppose, is that these people found themselves trapped at a dinner party with an economist (the horror! the horror!) and simply pretended an interest in the subject, hoping that I would go away. But I have an understandable preference for a more optimistic interpretation. These lectures are given in the firm belief that a body of concerned and interested citizens would like to know more about the subject of economics.

The conceptual pattern of this course follows the standard pattern of the introductory economics course offered at most colleges and universities. However, while the college course would present much of this material in a graphical and mathematical form, with an emphasis on solving the kinds of problems that will be on the exam, these lectures will focus instead on intuitive and verbal explanations of the underlying concepts.

The first 18 lectures of this course focus on *microeconomics*, which is the analysis of the economic behavior of individuals and firms. Thus, microeconomics encompasses how individuals and firms interact in markets for buying and selling goods, in markets for working and hiring labor, and in markets for saving and investing financial capital.

After Lecture One introduces the topic of economics, Lectures Two through Five discuss how the forces of supply and demand determine the prices charged and the quantities produced in markets for goods. Lecture Six applies this same structure of supply and demand to markets for labor, while Lectures Seven and Eight consider, first, the demand for financial capital by firms that want to make investments in new plant and equipment, followed by the supply of financial capital from households that are thinking about how to invest their savings.

The course then turns to a number of practical and policy issues that arise in microeconomics. Lectures Nine through Eleven discuss the competitive environment for firms, ranging from situations with many competitive firms to situations with a single monopoly producer. Government may have a role to play in encouraging competition or in regulating industries in which little competition exists.

Lectures Twelve through Fourteen turn to the policy problems that arise when a good or service is produced and sold—but the production of the good has effects on third parties who were not involved in the transaction. These external effects, or *externalities*, may be negative effects, such as pollution, or positive effects, such as the benefits of new technology or a better educated workforce.

Lectures Fifteen and Sixteen consider policy problems that arise in labor markets, including issues related to poverty and welfare reform, inequality of incomes, labor unions, and discrimination.

Lectures Seventeen and Eighteen consider issues that arise in financial capital markets, with a particular focus on the issue of who controls the decision-makers in large corporations and why markets for insurance—such as health or car insurance—often seem so costly and controversial.

In the second half of the course, starting with Lecture Nineteen, the focus shifts to *macroeconomics*. If microeconomics is the bottom-up view of the economy, looking at the actions of individuals and firms, then macroeconomics is the top-down view of the economy. Lectures Twenty through Twenty-Three introduce the most important patterns to describe an overall economy, which include gross domestic product (GDP), the rate of economic growth, periods of recession and economic upswing, unemployment, inflation, and the balance of trade.

Lectures Twenty-Four and Twenty-Five then introduce the aggregate demand and aggregate supply model of macroeconomics. Aggregate demand includes all demand in the economy for consumption, investment, government, and foreign trade. Aggregate supply focuses on total production of goods and services. The forces of aggregate demand and aggregate supply, and how they shift over time, will provide a framework for understanding the commonly observed macroeconomic patterns.

Lectures Twenty-Six through Twenty-Eight turn to government taxing and spending. These lectures describe the common patterns of taxes and spending, then discuss how government tax and spending policies will affect aggregate demand and aggregate supply and, thus, affect economic growth, unemployment, inflation, and the balance of trade.

Lectures Twenty-Nine through Thirty-One then turn to monetary policy, which in the U.S. economy, is conducted by the Federal Reserve. These lectures describe the economic role of money and the banking system, how the Fed controls the supply of money and credit in the economy, and how Fed policy affects the macroeconomy.

The course then closes with a set of lectures on international economics. Lectures Thirty-Two and Thirty-Three explain why most economists strongly believe that international trade offers benefits to all nations—but also review the arguments and counterarguments for limiting such trade. Lectures Thirty-Four and Thirty-Five discuss international financial movements, including issues that arise from exchange rates and even national financial crashes. Finally, Lecture Thirty-Six offers an overview of the global economy and where it is headed.

Skeptical listeners may wonder whether the economics in these lectures is slanted toward the policy conclusions of liberal Democrats or conservative Republicans. The answer is that professional economists of all political leanings use the tools and concepts taught in this course. The subject of economics is not a clear-cut set of answers but, rather, a structured framework for pursuing answers. Thus, although I hope the lectures will at some points challenge your own political beliefs, whatever they are, I also hope that the lectures will give you language and structure for articulating your own beliefs more clearly—and for becoming a more sophisticated participant in the economic disputes of our time.

Lecture Thirteen
Positive Externalities and Technology

Scope:

The previous lecture focused on negative externalities, in which the market produces too much of a negative item, such as pollution. This lecture turns the tables and discusses positive externalities, in which the market produces too little of some good things, such as scientific research, innovation, and education. Patents and copyrights have been the traditional tools for encouraging innovation. However, other policy tools would include direct government support or tax credits to industry.

Outline

I. Many people tend to identify free markets with innovation. But in a truly free market, it's possible that very little innovation would exist.

    A. Imagine a company that thinks about investing money in research and development.

        1. If the project fails, then the company will have a lower rate of return than its competitors and may be driven out of business.

        2. If the project succeeds, however, in a perfectly free market, the competitors will simply steal the idea.

        3. The result is a heads-you-lose, tails-I-win scenario that will discourage innovation.

    B. *Appropriability* is the term that economists use to describe the ability of a producer to reap the benefits of an investment or an invention. For many famous inventions, from the cotton gin to the laser, appropriability has been low.

    C. In conceptual terms, technology is just the opposite of pollution.

        1. In the case of pollution, those who are external to the transaction, not involved in buying or selling a good, suffer the costs of pollution.

        2. In the case of technology, some of those who are external to the transaction between the firm that invented the product and the eventual consumer of the product benefit from the new technology that was created, but do not pay for those benefits.

II. Intellectual property rights are a mechanism for giving inventors an exclusive right to use their inventions, at least for a time, and thus, to earn higher-than-normal profits as a return on those inventions.

    A. A *patent* is an exclusive legal right granted by government to make, use, or sell an invention for a specific and limited time.

    B. *Copyright* is a form of legal protection against copying original works of authorship, including literary, musical, and other works.

    C. A *trademark* is a word, name, symbol, or device that indicates the source of a good and, thus, helps the seller establish a reputation.

    D. A *trade secret* is a formula, process, device, or item of information that gives a business an advantage over competitors, that is not generally known or easily discovered, and that the business makes reasonable efforts to keep secret.

    E. Even with patents and copyrights in place, it is commonly estimated that an innovating company manages to get only 30–40% of the new value of what it creates, while the rest is captured by other firms. Thus, the incentive to innovate is less than the social value of innovation.

III. Government has a range of policies available to subsidize innovation more directly.

    A. One alternative is direct government funding of research through universities, private research organizations, or firms.

Research and Development in 2003
(by source of funds)

	R&D spending	Percent of total
Industry	$180 billion	63%
Federal government	$ 85 billion	30%
Universities and colleges	$ 11 billion	4%
Other nonprofits	$ 8 billion	3%
TOTAL	$284 billion	100%

Source: National Science Foundation

B. Another approach is to provide tax credits to business for research and development. This is a less centralized approach for the government than administering particular research grants.

C. Government can also provide support for research and development through subsidizing the spread of information across organizations, across the country through such methods as helping to build the Internet, and across international boundaries.

IV. There is controversy over whether some inventors may be receiving too much protection; after all, the ultimate goal of subsidizing innovation is to benefit consumers, not to make it easier for firms to earn long-term higher-than-normal profits.

A. The U.S. Patent Office grants about 200,000 patents a year, many of them after only a few days of consideration.

B. By their nature, patents block competition. But in some cases, they can become a large and nearly permanent block to other competitors and a potential hindrance to additional innovation.

C. Remember, the ultimate goal here isn't to be nice to innovators; it is to encourage a steady stream of innovations that can increase the standard of living of the U.S. economy.

Essential Reading:

Linda Cohen and Roger Noll, "Privatizing Public Research: The New Competitiveness Strategy," in *The Mosaic of Economic Growth*, pp. 305–333.

A. Michael Spence, "Science and Technology Investment and Policy in the Global Economy," in *The Mosaic of Economic Growth*, pp. 173–190.

Supplementary Reading:

National Science Foundation, *National Patterns of Research Development Resources: 2003*, www.nsf.gov/statistics/nsf05308/pdfstart.htm.

Nathan Rosenberg, "Uncertainty and Technological Change," in *The Mosaic of Economic Growth*.

Questions to Consider:

1. Make a list of policies that could stimulate research and development. Consider both policies that would encourage private-sector R&D and university and public R&D. Which of these policies has the highest public cost? Can you think of ways to focus any necessary public spending in a way that will get the most R&D bang for the buck?

2. Can you think of some other goods or services, besides technology, that may provide positive externalities? (If you're having trouble, some will be discussed in the next lecture!)

Lecture Thirteen—Transcript
Positive Externalities and Technology

The previous lecture focused on negative externalities, where the market produces too much of a negative item like pollution. This lecture turns the tables and discusses positive externalities, where the market produces too little of some good thing, like scientific research and innovation. Many people tend to identify free markets with innovation, but in a truly free market, it's possible that very little innovation would exist. Conflict between markets and innovation arises because of a "heads, you win; tails, I lose" kind of problem.

Let's imagine a company that's planning to invest a lot of money in research and development on some new invention. There are two possibilities. First, maybe the project fails. If it fails, then the company will have lower profits than its competitors, and maybe it'll even have losses and be driven out of business. The other possibility is the project succeeds. If the project succeeds in developing the new innovation, in a perfectly market, competitors will just steal the idea. The result will be that the innovating company had higher expenses—because it had to develop the new innovation—but it has no special gain in revenues. It will still have lower profits than all of its competitors, and it may still be driven out of business. Heads, you lose; tails, I win.

Thus, the key element is a company's ability to appropriate a substantial share of the economic gains from its investment in research and development. If a company innovates, how much of the profit can it keep? Economists have a term for this—economists have a term for everything, right? It's *appropriability*. Appropriability is the ability of a producer to reap the benefits of an investment or an innovation. If there's no appropriability, then businesses won't invest in new products because they fear they won't be able to get a reasonable rate of return.

There are a lot of famous examples of where appropriability didn't work out very well. For example, Thomas Edison's very first invention was an automatic vote-counting machine. Although it seemed to work perfectly well, he found that he couldn't sell it. The story is, that he then vowed in the future to only make inventions that people would actually buy.

A more recent example is the invention of the laser. A man named Gordon Gould came up with the idea behind the laser in 1957. We know he came up with the idea because Gould actually had his research notebooks for November 1957 notarized, so he could prove when the idea had come to him, and that he had actually written it down and he knew he had it. But Gould put off applying for a patent on the laser because he mistakenly believed that you needed to have a working prototype before you could apply for a patent. That's not true. But by the time Gould did apply for a patent on a laser, other scientists had some laser inventions of their own. A long, long legal battle resulted in which Gould spent more than $100,000 of his own money on lawyers and stuff before he eventually did get a patent for the laser in 1977, about 20 years later. Even then, he didn't get very much for his patent.

If you think about it, the laser has had an enormous range of uses. It's used in manufacturing compact disks; it's used in eye surgery, and in removing tumors; it's used for precision scientific measurement; it's used in navigational instruments; in chemical research; in spectroscopy for laser printers; it's used for cutting tools in textiles and metal working industries. Perhaps most of all, the laser has revolutionized telecommunications and computer networks by allowing so much more information to be carried over fiber optic cable than could have been carried over the old copper wires. So, compared to the enormous social benefits of the laser, Gould received really relatively little financial reward.

Of course, Gould wasn't the only one working on the laser. Many of the other scientists who worked on the science that led up to lasers in the 1940s and 1950s, as well as scientists who have worked on the practical development of how to use lasers since then, have received essentially no special benefit other than their normal salaries.

In conceptual terms, new technology is just the opposite of pollution. In the case of pollution, those who were external to the transaction, not involved in buying or selling the good, suffered the costs of pollution. But in the case of new inventions, like the automatic vote-counting machine or the laser, those who were external to the transaction, between the firm that invented the product and the consumer using it, are benefiting without needing to compensate the inventor.

A positive externality means that some economic actor, some firm or inventor, is providing benefits for third parties and not being compensated for those benefits. Because the inventor is not being compensated fully, the firm will provide less innovation than it otherwise would.

In the situation of negative externalities, like pollution, the appropriate policy response was to find a way to make someone pay the social costs of pollution. In the case of positive externalities, like developing new technologies and new innovation, the appropriate policy response is to help those who provide the social benefits of innovation get compensated for those benefits.

How do you do this? How do you provide appropriability? How do you allow inventors to be compensated for their innovations? Well, intellectual property rights are a mechanism that society uses to give inventors some exclusive right to use their invention, at least for a period of time. Since they have an exclusive right and can avoid market competition, they'll be able to earn higher-than-normal profits for a while, and get a rate of return on their invention.

The whole notion of intellectual property rights goes way back in U.S. history. In fact, it goes to the Constitution of the United States, which specifies in Article 1, Section 8, "The Congress shall have the power to promote the progress of science and useful arts by securing for limited times, to authors and inventors, the exclusive right to their writings and discoveries." Congress took that power in the U.S. Constitution and used that power to create the U.S. Patent and Trademark Office, as well as the U.S. Copyright Office.

So let's talk about these patents and copyrights in more concrete terms and what they mean. A patent is an exclusive legal right, granted by the government, to make, sell, or use an invention for a specific and limited time. In the United States, the exclusive patent right typically lasts for 20 years, although there are some specialized rules for particular industries in the fine print. Copyright, on the other hand, is a form of legal protection against copying an original work of authorship, which includes literary, musical, and other kinds of works. Or more specifically, according to the U.S. Copyright Office, "copyright protects dramatic, musical, architectural, cartographic, choreographic, pantomimic, pictorial, graphic, sculptural, and audio-visual creations." It protects all the stuff that people could be authors of.

When you have copyright, what that essentially means is, no one can reproduce or display the work, or perform the copyrighted work without the permission of the creator, of the author. The copyright protection now ordinarily lasts the life of the author, plus 70 years.

Roughly speaking, patent law covers inventions and copyright protects books, and songs, and art. But in certain areas, like the invention of new software, it's been unclear over time whether that was an invention—so that patent law should apply—or whether it was a work of authorship, in which case, copyright protection ought to apply. The law has gone back and forth on how to apply those two.

There are other kinds of intellectual property protection besides patents and copyrights. A trademark, for example, is a word, or a name, or a symbol, or a device that indicates the source of a good, and, thus, helps the seller establish a reputation. Common examples of trademarks would be: Chiquita bananas; or Chevrolet cars; or the Nike "swoosh" that appears on shoes and athletic gear. There are nearly 800,000 trademarks registered with the U.S. government.

The notion behind trademarks is that they help to build and facilitate competition, because it helps firms build a reputation for a certain kind of product, and then consumers can react to that reputation; firms can then compete more easily because their reputation is out front. A firm is allowed to renew its trademark over and over again for an unlimited period of time as long as the trademark remains in active use. If the product, whatever it is, stops being used, then the trademark eventually could expire over time.

A final form of intellectual property rights is called trade secrets. A trade secret is more or less what it sounds like. A trade secret is a formula, a process, a device, or an item of information that gives a business an advantage over its competitors that is not generally known or easily discovered, and where the business makes reasonable efforts to keep it secret.

What would be some good examples of a trade secret? Probably the most famous trade secret is the formula for Coca-Cola, which is not protected under copyright law, and is not protected under patent law, but is simply kept more or less secret by the company—although in a couple of books, they've published the formula for Coca-Cola, if you look back in the appendices. But it's still thought of as a trade secret.

Let me give you a couple of famous cases of trade secrets, to give you a sense of how they work. In 1995 out in Silicon Valley, a number of employees left a software firm that was called Cadence Design Systems, and they started a new competing software firm that was called Avant!. Did these employees leaving the one firm and starting another firm violate trade secret law?

Well, as the court case evolved, the answer turned out to be yes. The key evidence was that experts testified in court that the software from Avant! contained, in various places, the exact same error messages as the Cadence software did. In 2001, Avant! actually pleaded no contest to stealing trade secrets. Apparently, the departing employees had more or less taken the Cadence software out the door with them. They ended up paying millions of dollars in fines and served jail time for doing that.

A more famous case—at least among economists—is in 1969, there were two photographers in Beaumont, Texas. They hired a plane and flew over a chemical plant that DuPont was building to produce methanol with a new industrial process. Does hiring a plane, and flying over a construction site, and taking photographs violate trade secret law? The answer the court found was yes. The court found that DuPont had taken reasonable precautions to protect its new manufacturing process—it had built a fence around the construction site, that sort of thing. Taking photos from the airplane was an improper method of discovering the trade secrets, even if the flight itself was at a perfectly legal height and a perfectly legal distance. The court wrote, "This is a case of industrial espionage in which an airplane is the cloak and a camera is the dagger."

Even with patents, and copyrights, and trademarks, and trade secret law all in place, it is commonly estimated that an innovating company manages to get only 30–40 percent of the new value of what it creates. The rest of that value is captured by consumers or by other firms who buy its products.

Perhaps the most famous story of a firm not being able to capture what it created is the story of Eli Whitney. As many of you probably learned long ago, Eli Whitney invented the cotton gin, for separating seeds out of cotton. He patented it; it was the one of the first patents issued by the U.S. Patent Office. But as it turned out, Whitney's patent was not enforced by the Southern courts in all the cotton states. Other people just made cotton gins based on his patent, and then they used them. When he sued in the court in Georgia, or Alabama, or different places, the Southern court basically said, "We're not going to pay you vast sums of money just because you invented the cotton gin."

Whitney's comment was, "An invention can be so valuable as to be worthless to the inventor." The cotton gin was such an important invention that, in effect, society decided—or Southern courts decided—that they just weren't going to enforce his patent rights. In fact, Whitney never attempted to patent any of his later inventions; he just gave up on the patent process, even though later on, Whitney essentially reinvented American manufacturing as a whole by inventing the idea of mass production. The notion was that, even if you had unskilled workers, if you had lots of interchangeable parts, unskilled workers could assemble those interchangeable parts, and make some product like rifles. You can only imagine what the patent right would be to own the right for everything that's made with interchangeable parts. But Whitney didn't even try; it just didn't seem worth it.

The basic bottom line here: the incentive to innovate, even with all of the intellectual property rights in place, is typically less than the social value of the innovation. So, if we want to encourage innovation, and encourage people to provide the amount of innovation that would benefit society, we need to think of other policies beyond intellectual property rights that we might use to encourage research, and development, and innovation. Indeed, government has a range of other policies beyond intellectual property rights that are available to subsidize innovation more directly.

One example is direct government funding of scientific research. It can happen through universities, or private research organizations, or through businesses. The National Science Foundation, each year, collects data on spending for research and development for the economy as a whole. According to the NSF data in 2003, the U.S. economy as a whole spent $284 billion on research and development. Sixty-three percent of that was spent by industry; 30 percent of it was spent by the federal government; and the remaining seven percent was universities, and colleges, and other non-profits. Much of that would be state-level support, through state universities and colleges. So it's fair to say that, for the economy right now, most R&D is being paid for by private industry.

I don't know what the right proportion is of how much R&D should be paid by private industry and how much should be paid by the government; but I do know that over time, the government share of total R&D spending has been gradually sliding lower, and lower, and lower. Back in the 1960s, the federal government funded about two-thirds of all research and development in the U.S. economy. But toward the end of the 1960s and early 1970s, there was the end of the space program, which involved a lot of R&D spending and there was a big slowdown in military budgets at the end of the Vietnam War, which drags down a lot of aerospace and defense-related R&D spending. As the government level of R&D spending went down and down, the private industry share began to rise and rise. So it used to be two-thirds government; now it's almost two-thirds industry.

The concern here is that firms focus on a particular kind of research and development. They're going to focus on applied research and development that has a real short-term or near-term payoff. Government, on the other hand, is going to focus on big-picture basic research that might provide fundamental changes that stretch across the entire economy, like research on particles, or research on things like the laser, where the payoff to really understanding those things might be extremely large, but it isn't going to be even figured out for perhaps several decades into the future.

Another rule about government research is often that if the government paid for the research, then the results should be broadly available throughout the economy. So, when you have research which is all financed by firms, and the firms are patenting that research, then the firms are locking up that research inside the firm for whatever the 20 years is until the patent runs out. If the government funds more research, then a lot of that research disseminates through the economy more quickly, which can certainly be more helpful in terms of encouraging economic growth. So, one possibility for encouraging research is to have the government pay for it directly.

Another approach is to provide tax credits for businesses for research and development. There's actually something in the tax code called the R&D tax credit. How it works is a little bit complex, but basically, it's a tax credit which says, for every dollar a firm spends on research and development that is above a certain base amount, the firm gets to take 20 cents off its tax bill.

Now, the nice thing about an R&D tax credit is that it's relatively flexible. One of the concerns about the government spending money on R&D directly is that government also determines what the projects are, and the government's going to sit down and say, "You get a grant for this; you get a grant for that." But there's no reason to believe that the government knows exactly what all the right research projects are. If you just give firms a tax credit for R&D, that lets firms track down things that perhaps the government research panel or the National Science Foundation wouldn't necessarily have given tax money for.

The R&D tax credit has been a funny part of the tax code. It was originally put in place in 1981, but it keeps being put in place for just a few years at a time, which seems odd, if you think about it, because you would like businesses to be able to plan on it for the long term. I've heard some cynics say that, actually, Congress likes having it in place for just a few years at a time because then firms have to lobby for it to be reenacted again, which means more contributions for political campaigns every few years. But it's not a very pricey tax break. It reduces the taxes paid by corporations by a total of about $5 billion a year. So that's real money, but not in federal government terms.

Another way that the government can support R&D is to subsidize the spread of information across organizations, and even across the country, through methods like helping build the Internet, or across international boundaries as well. Let me try and give you a couple of examples.

In 1993, there was something called the National Cooperative Research and Production Act. What it allowed companies to do was to form jointly funded research and development institutions. Now, the problem for companies in the past had been that if they all got together and did common research and development, they might get attacked under the antitrust laws for getting together and acting like a cartel. When companies work together in one of these collaborative research and development things, they share the expenses of research and development, and they also share any discoveries that result. Such joint agencies offer a way for firms to share the risks of R&D, and also to share the benefits of research and development, rather than facing the risk that one winner-take-all innovator will discover the patent and lock up the market for the next 20 years.

Before this law passed, antitrust authorities might have challenged joint research efforts on antitrust grounds, but the new 1993 law removed that threat; since then, there have been a bunch of these joint research and development organizations that have been set up. Two of the ones I'm most familiar with are the one doing semiconductor research, and the one doing research on new batteries. Especially in Japan, there are a whole bunch of these organizations for doing jointly shared research.

The U.S. government has tried to come up with a lot of other ways, going beyond patents, and copyrights, and intellectual property, to subsidize research and development in a direct way. In fact, there is some controversy over whether, in some cases at least, inventors might be receiving too much protection, and might be receiving too large a benefit from this combination of tax breaks, and government spending, and intellectual property law. After all, it's worth remembering here, the ultimate goal of subsidizing innovation is to benefit consumers. It's to benefit the economy as a whole. It's not to make it easier for firms to earn really large profits for a long time.

So let's think about how it might be possible that inventors could receive too much protection. Let's first of all talk about some nuts and bolts of how patents are granted. The U.S. Patent Office grants about 200,000 patents a year. Think of that for a moment—they grant 200,000 patents a year, many of them after relatively little consideration. It usually takes, on average, about three years to get a patent. The patent examiner—the person in the office who sits looking at whether or not to grant the patent—on average, spends about 18 hours deciding whether to grant the patent.

But still, in the mid-2000s, there was a backlog of about 750,000 patent applications that was piling up, even though people are taking two working days to decide whether to grant one. Something like 85 percent of all patent applications eventually result in a patent, even if they have to change the patent, or change what was being applied for, along the way. But when you think about how many of those patents are important, one measure is that only about one-tenth of one percent of the patents that are granted are ever actually litigated in trial. The overwhelming majority of patents that are granted end up having essentially zero economic value, but a very small number of them end up having extremely large economic value.

This process ends up with some weird patents being granted, some patents that you look back on in retrospect and think, "I'm not sure how much sense that made." For example, the firm called Priceline.com—they sell airline tickets, and travel items, and a lot of other stuff—they actually got a patent on the idea that people could buy items by submitting bids over the Internet. Now, it's just not clear—at least to me—that that is an invention that should be patented somehow, the idea of submitting bids over the Internet.

The online retailer, Amazon.com, got a patent for the idea of being able to buy something on the Internet by clicking a mouse one time. I don't know. I'm just not sure that that's an idea that deserves a patent, as opposed to just a way of doing business.

One firm even got a patent that seemed to cover peanut-butter-and-jelly sandwiches with their crusts cut off. They were producing a product that was a peanut-butter-and-jelly sandwich with the crusts cut off, and they managed to get a patent on it, and they actually sued some other small sandwich shops for making peanut-butter-and-jelly sandwiches with the crusts cut off.

Patents block competition, but is it really necessary to block competition in these kinds of ways? In some cases, if a patent is blocking competition, it can become a large—and even in some cases, a permanent—block to other competitors, as well as a hindrance to additional innovation.

Let me give you an example of a real problem with patents. In the early 1970s, Xerox had received over 1,700 patents on various elements of the photocopying machine. What happened was, every time Xerox improved the photocopier by just a little bit, it would go get a patent on whatever that tiny little improvement was. So your standard photocopy machine had literally 1,700 patents. As the old patents ran out, Xerox was, of course, continually improving the machine, so they were continually getting new patents. Consequently, no one could enter the photocopy market, no other firms, because no one could get through this hedge of 1,700 patents. Even if you could figure out different ways to do a few things, it was very hard to think of a photocopier that wouldn't infringe on some of Xerox's patents. So in the early 1970s, the U.S. government, the antitrust folks, went to Xerox and said basically, "You're abusing the patent process. You're abusing the patent process by using this possibly everlasting stream of patents to block the entry of other firms into the photocopier market. You're essentially using the patent process not for a temporary gain, but to create a permanent monopoly."

Well, in 1975, Xerox, of course, didn't admit it had done anything wrong, but it did agree to allow all other companies to use its patents, and to drop all of its outstanding lawsuits against other companies for violating its patents, and to provide competitors with access to certain future patents. Perhaps not as a big surprise, a flood of new competition opened up in the photocopier market and Xerox's market share of the photocopier market—which had been 95 percent of the U.S. photocopier market in the early 1970s—fell to less than half of the photocopier market by 1980.

This problem of many interlocking patents is sometimes called a patent thicket and it can still be a real problem in lots of industries, particularly in some technical industries like pharmaceuticals, or in semiconductors and certain kinds of electronic products, where any given product may rely on a whole bunch of different patents. What often happens, in fact, is that established firms all get together in a room and trade access to their patents. They literally all go in—their patent lawyers, their businesspeople—and they all sit down and say, "Look, these are the patents we've got. What are the patents you've got? What are you willing to trade? You can use ours if we can use yours." But if you're a new firm trying to get into the market, that doesn't help you much, because you don't necessarily have any patents to trade. So it can be a real problem for preventing entry of new firms into those industries.

Copyright extensions can also be extended in a way which doesn't make a lot of sense from a standpoint of helping innovators. In 1998, something was passed called the Sonny Bono Copyright Term Extension Act. It increased the length of copyright terms, which used to be the life of the creator plus 50 years, and now it became the life of the creator plus 70 years. It's hard to believe that extending copyright for an extra 20 years after the death of the person who created it is really going to have a big impact on their incentives to innovate. But that 20-year extension mattered a lot to firms that were worried that certain longtime images that they owned might be about to go off of copyright and into the public domain. The scuttlebutt, that one big concern, was that Mickey Mouse was just about to go into the public domain, and Disney wanted to protect Mickey Mouse.

In the physical world, too, new innovations often build on old ones. If you give current inventors a lot of power to protect their inventions, the result can be that you block later inventions. This is especially a problem if groups of innovations all work together, and any one of the current patent holders can block the new invention.

Remember again, the ultimate goal here is not being nice to innovators; it's not just being sweet to people who invent stuff. The goal is to encourage a steady stream of new innovations that will increase the standard of living in the U.S. economy. Indeed, it's been common for a long time for people to say that one of the interesting things about the U.S. economy is that it was built so much on invention. One reason that the U.S. economy went from a small backwoods country in 1800, to being on the verge of being the richest country in the world in 1900, was the way in which there were all sorts of new inventions.

Now, some people said, "Well, look, it's a big empty country without a lot of labor, so people were forced to invent." Other people have said, "Well, it's a cultural thing." But a lot of economists would say it's because in the United States, the U.S. Constitution recognized the importance of property rights early on. By recognizing the importance of property rights early on, and rewarding inventors, we created a society where innovation and invention would be rewarded.

Lecture Fourteen
Public Goods

Scope:

Public goods are *nonrivalrous* and *nonexcludable*, which means that a potential seller cannot exclude people from using the good and that the good itself is not used up as more people use it. Examples might be national defense or basic scientific research. Because of these two key characteristics, markets often do a poor job of producing public goods; thus, there is a case for people to band together and agree to pay for such goods through government action.

Outline

I.   What is a *public good*?

    A. A public good has two characteristics: It is *nonrivalrous* and *nonexcludable*.

        1. *Nonrivalrous* means that the good itself is not diminished as more people use it.

        2. *Nonexcludable* means that a seller cannot exclude those who did not pay from using the good.

    B. Examples of public goods include national defense, education, public health, physical infrastructure, and basic research and science.

    C. A *free rider* problem emerges when some people can receive benefits from public goods without a need to pay their fair share of the costs. If there are many free riders, the public good will not be produced.

II. The pursuit of self-interest can, in some cases, bring undesired results to all parties.

    A. The Prisoners' Dilemma is a classic example in game theory of how the pursuit of rational self-interest can make all parties worse off.

        1. The starting point of the game is that two prisoners are arrested. They are then separated. Both prisoners are told that the other is going to confess and that if they don't confess, they will be worse off.

2. If the two prisoners cooperate and neither one confesses, they will be better off. But if both prisoners act in their own self-interest, they will both confess, because confessing can make them better off whether the other prisoner confesses or not.

3. The analytical structure of the Prisoners' Dilemma is that if the two prisoners can cooperate and remain silent, they will be better off. But given the structure of the game, each individual has an incentive not to cooperate and to confess, and if they both follow this incentive, they will both be worse off.

		PRISONER B	
		Remain silent (cooperate with other prisoner)	Confess (don't cooperate with other prisoner)
PRISONER A	Remain silent (cooperate with other prisoner)	A gets 2 years B gets 2 years	A gets 8 years B gets 1 year
	Confess (don't cooperate with other prisoner)	A gets 1 year B gets 8 years	A gets 5 years B gets 5 years

4. Players in the Prisoners' Dilemma may be able to use various mechanisms to ensure cooperation, such as threats for those who fail to cooperate or promises of cooperation in future plays of the game.

B. The free rider problem is a version of a Prisoners' Dilemma.

1. Imagine that there are two players, who are deciding whether to make an investment in a public good. Each player must decide whether to cooperate, which means making a contribution to the public good, or not to cooperate.

2. If the two players cooperate, and both make a contribution to the public good, they will both be better off. But if each player acts in his or her own self-interest, they will both decide not to contribute to the public good, because not contributing can make one player better off whether the other player contributes or not.

3. The free rider problem becomes greater if expanded to include many people.

C. The Prisoners' Dilemma game, in which both parties benefit from cooperation but have an individual incentive not to cooperate, arises in many different settings.

    1. In an oligopolistic cartel, every firm has an incentive to increase its own profits by expanding output, but all firms in the cartel will be better off if they cooperate to hold output low and act like a joint monopoly.

    2. An arms race can be a situation in which no country has an incentive to cut back on its own accumulation of weapons, but everyone would be better off if all countries cooperated in cutting back.

    3. Conspicuous consumption can be a situation in which no household dares to cut back on its own, but everyone would be better off if everyone cooperated in cutting back.

    4. Overuse of natural resources can also be a case in which no individual has an incentive to cut back, but everyone would be better off if everyone cooperated in cutting back.

D. The Prisoners' Dilemma is of great importance to economic analysis, because it illustrates a fundamental situation in which the pursuit of self-interest by each individual party leads to outcomes that no one would ultimately desire if all players could find a way to cooperate.

III. How can public goods be provided?

A. A variety of social mechanisms can help to solve the public good problem, including personal recognition and shaming.

B. Public goods can also be financed through the political system, by imposing taxes and using the proceeds to pay for the public good.

Essential Reading:

Peter Asch and Gary A. Gigliotti, "The Free Rider Paradox—Theory, Evidence, and Teaching," *Journal of Economic Education*, Winter 1991, pp. 33–38.

Russell Hardin, "The Free Rider Problem," in *The Stanford Encyclopedia of Philosophy*, plato.stanford.edu/archives/sum2003/entries/free-rider.

Supplementary Reading:

R. H. Coase, "The Lighthouse of Economics," *Journal of Law and Economics*, October 1974, pp. 357–376.

Questions to Consider:

1. Explain why a producer in a market will hesitate to enter production of public goods. Use some concrete examples of public goods in your explanation.

2. What is the Prisoners' Dilemma game and why is it important to economists?

Lecture Fourteen—Transcript
Public Goods

The discussion of negative externalities in Lecture 12 focused on what happens when there's a willing buyer of a good and a willing seller of a good, but the production of the good had negative effects on an external third party, like pollution. The discussion of positive externalities in Lecture 13 focused on what happens when there's a willing buyer of a good and a willing seller of a good, but production of the good had positive effects on an external third party, like the invention of new technology.

The subject of this lecture considers the case that economists call public goods, which can be thought of as an extreme example of a positive externality. In this situation, it becomes very difficult, or even impossible, for a seller to charge buyers for the cost of producing a good. Or to put it another way, a producer of a public good is likely to be giving away lots of positive externality benefits to lots of people who haven't paid for them. As a result, private markets are just not going to do a very good job of producing public goods.

As we'll see, the discussion of public goods then opens up a deeper issue. Are there categories where rationally self-interested behavior by all participants can end up having undesirable effects? Let's start off, here, by pinning down, in a more formal sense, exactly what a public good is. A public good has two characteristics: it is non-excludable and nonrivalrous. Now, of course, I'm afraid, this is the sort of definition that just creates the need for more definitions, but sometimes you can't quite help that.

When we think about what's meant by nonrivalrous, nonrivalrous means that the good itself is not diminished as more people use it. An example would be something like national defense. Now, let's think about a private good and a public good here. If you have a private good like pizza—if Max is eating pizza, then Michelle cannot also eat the pizza. The two people are rivals in consumption; one or the other of them gets it. But if you have a public good, like national defense, one person's—Max's—consumption of national defense does not reduce the amount left for Michelle. So, they are nonrivalrous in their consumption of that good. If new babies are born, you don't have to add more national defense to protect them.

Non-excludable means a seller cannot exclude those who did not pay from using the good. Again, think about a private good like a slice of pizza. If you don't use that private good, that slice of pizza, you don't pay for it. And if you don't pay for it, you can be stopped from getting that private good. But now consider a public good, like national defense. If someone doesn't wish to be protected by the armed forces, you can't really say, "Well, everyone else in the country is protected, but I don't have to be." It covers you whether you want to be covered or not. If an extra baby is born, we don't use up a greater extent of national defense services because there's an extra person there.

Now, let me give you some other examples of public goods. I talked about national defense already, but let's think about some other possibilities. I should emphasize, when I'm talking about public goods, some of these are not perfect public goods, in the sense that they are not perfectly nonrivalrous and perfectly non-excludable, but they still recognizably have these traits, in a way that would make it difficult for a private market to provide them.

For example, let's think about education. Many of the benefits of education aren't just to the person who gets the education; there are benefits to society as a whole. It's generally better to live in a society where people are educated, where workers are educated. Adding some population doesn't diminish the benefit of education. It's also nonrivalrous: you don't exclude people from enjoying the general benefit of living among educated workers and educated citizens.

The same thing can be said for public health, like the issue of whether people have infectious diseases. It's nonrivalrous because adding population doesn't diminish the benefit of reducing infectious disease. It's also non-excludable. If you reduce infectious diseases, you can't say, "We exclude you from enjoying not having any infectious diseases around."

Having a good system of transportation gives all kinds of benefits. My benefit from having roads typically doesn't come at your expense, except in the case of highway congestion. It's hard to exclude people from using the transportation system, although we do have some toll roads out there.

Scientific research and basic knowledge can be considered a public good as well. It's nonrivalrous in the sense that adding more population doesn't diminish the benefit of living in a society with good knowledge and good technology. You can't really exclude people from the benefits of new technology if they're living in the society.

Thomas Jefferson actually expressed in elegant language the notion that many ideas are nonrivalrous and, perhaps, non-excludable as well. Jefferson once said,

> If nature has made any one thing less susceptible than all others of exclusive property, it is the action of the thinking power called an idea. No one possesses the less because every other possesses the whole of it. He who receives an idea from me receives instruction himself without lessening mine, as he who lights his taper at mine receives light without darkening me.

A free-rider problem, as economists call it, emerges when some people can receive benefits from public goods without a need to pay their fair share of the costs. The useful metaphor, here, for thinking about why it's called a free rider comes up if you ask people to pay for roads. Imagine that you surveyed people individually and you said, "I'd like you to pay for your road, just like you pay for your pizza or your groceries." A lot of people would, at least implicitly, reason as follows: "Why should I offer to pay for a road? After all, whether I pay for the road or don't pay for the road won't make much difference to whether the road is actually built. No one can really stop me from using the road, at least if we're talking about local roads going here and there." So what most people would actually prefer, if they were guided by their own narrow self-interest, would be that everyone else should chip in and pay for the road while I act as a free rider; I ride on the road without paying for it. But, of course, if everyone reasons this way—"I won't pay; I'll just let everyone else pay for the road"—then eventually, the road won't be built at all; the public service won't be provided at all.

Because of this intertwined pattern of goods with nonrivalrous and non-excludable characteristics, and the possibility that goods with nonrivalrous, non-excludable characteristics will have lots of free riders, essentially, a public good is an extreme example of a positive externality. Remember that with a positive externality, an inventor got only part of the return from the invention. With a public good, however, an inventor really can't get anyone to pay, because they can't exclude people from using it. Moreover, in an economic sense, people could say, "Hey, when I use it, I'm not really imposing any cost on anyone else by consuming the good because it's a nonrivalrous good. So I'm not really taking from anyone else when I use the public good." So someone who's thinking about building a public good or inventing a public good has to fear that they could end up with a return of almost zero, kind of like when Thomas Edison was inventing that automatic voting machine that we talked about in the previous lecture.

How can we get public goods provided? Before talking about how societies might address this problem of getting people to pay for public goods, we need to take a little intellectual detour, because it turns out that public goods are a manifestation of a broader situation where people act in their own rational self-interest, like a free rider does, with the result that everyone ends up worse off. I want to illustrate the situation with a famous problem in game theory that's called the prisoner's dilemma. Now, at this point, you've probably noticed that economists like to take a complex situation, like a market, and break it down into pieces, like demand and supply, that can be analyzed one piece at a time. The prisoner's dilemma is a classic example in game theory of how, when all parties pursue their own rational self-interest, it can make all of them worse off rather than better off.

Most game theory problems have a story behind them, so let me tell you the story of the prisoner's dilemma. Two guys commit a crime together. They're taken to the police station and they're split up into separate rooms. The police come into the first guy's room and they say something like this: "You know, your buddy is confessing in the next room. He's only going to get one year because he's confessing and cooperating with us, helping us out. You're going to get eight years because you're stuck. So why don't you confess, too? If you confess, too, we'll just give you five years—and we've got you already."

Of course, at the same time, they're going over to the other guy's room and saying, "Oh, why don't you confess? Because the guy next door is confessing, and you're about to be on the hook for eight years. But we'll offer you a special deal: if you confess, we'll cut it down to five years." That kind of deal might be quite successful in pressuring both criminals to confess. But what if the criminal says, "How do I know you're telling the truth? How do I know the guy in the next room really is confessing?" Now, our criminal has to be presumed to be a little sophisticated here. Well, the police might answer in this way: "Okay. You can't really know whether we're telling the truth. But think of it this way: if your partner next door is confessing, you're going to get eight years if you don't confess and five years if you do. So, you ought to confess. You'll be better off if you confess. If we're lying to you, and the guy isn't confessing next door, then if you shut up, you might get only two years. But we'll make a deal with you. If he isn't confessing and you do, we'll give you a special break, and you only get one year in prison. So either way, you win. If he confesses, you're better off confessing so you don't get stuck with a big punishment. If he's not confessing, you're still better off confessing, because we'll give you some time off." Of course, they can say this to both prisoners at the same time.

This prisoner's dilemma game, as I've described it here with these particular examples and these particular numbers, has four possible outcomes. One outcome is that neither party confesses and they both end up with two years, and there's a total of four years of jail time for the two guys. The second and the third outcomes are that one prisoner confesses and the other one doesn't—it could be Prisoner A confesses and Prisoner B doesn't; or Prisoner B confesses and Prisoner A doesn't—in which case, the confessor gets one year and the non-confessor is stuck with eight years. So between the two of them, they serve a total of nine years of jail time. The fourth outcome is that they both confess, they both end up with 5 years, for a total of 10 years of jail time. Those are the four possible outcomes of the situation I described.

In effect, the threat of getting stuck with that outcome—where one guys confesses and the other doesn't, combined with the promise that if the first guy doesn't confess and the second guy does, guy number two will get light treatment—pushes both players to a situation where everyone confesses. But if everyone confesses, the result is the total jail time is 10 years, five for each person, and that's the worst outcome of all.

The analytical structure of the prisoner's dilemma is that, if the two of them could cooperate and remain silent, they'll both be better off. But given the structure of the game and how they're separated, each individual has an incentive not to cooperate, and to confess. If they both follow this incentive, they both end up worse off.

Now, there's an obvious objection to this prisoner's dilemma game, which perhaps can be phrased as, "Who the heck are you kidding?" If the prisoner confesses, he's going to get killed, perhaps in prison, so he's not going to confess. Now, this may be true, but it just opens up, in terms of the prisoner's dilemma game, a broader question: if the prisoners in the prisoner's dilemma game are separated from each other, how can they trust the other person? How can they believe that it's good for them to cooperate, no matter what? How can they get away from this situation where they're being pressured to confess?

The basic answer is that the players need to believe that the trade-offs of the prisoner's dilemma game are not all there is. For example, if they say, "Well, how ever many years in prison you're giving me, I know I'm going to get beat up or perhaps killed in prison. I'm going to face future retaliation," then that might pressure them to cooperate now and remain silent. Or they could say, "I'm going to be a criminal all my life. I'm going to be in this situation over, and over, and over again; so, if I'm going to be a criminal all my life, I know it's better for me just to shut up, because if I have a reputation for being someone who talks, I can't be a criminal anymore." So if the game is repeated, or if there are external penalties in the game, then the players may be able to get to a situation where they can cooperate.

The free-rider problem we talked about before, in terms of building a public good, is exactly like, in a mathematical sense, a prisoner's dilemma game. Let me try and describe why. Imagine that, in the public good game, there are two players and they're each deciding whether or not to invest in a public good. Each player has to decide whether to cooperate, which, in this case, means making a contribution to the public good; or not to cooperate, which would be not making the contribution. Mathematically, this situation is actually identical to a prisoner's dilemma game.

Instead of two prisoners, let's take people thinking about making this contribution to the public good. Let's say that the two people are called Rachael and Samuel, just to make this concrete. Let's say that when either of them contributes to a public good—call it the local fire department or something like that—the personal cost of their contribution is four, and the social benefit of the contribution is six. The investment is a good idea for society as a whole. If they each invest four in the public good, society will benefit six. But here's the problem: while Rachael and Samuel each pay the entire cost of their personal contribution to the public good, they only receive half of the benefit of their contribution to the public good, because the benefit of a public good is divided equally among all the members of society.

So, in this numerical example, Rachael says to herself, "Look, if I contribute four to the public good, there's a social benefit of six, but I only get three of that benefit. I only get half of the social benefit, and Samuel's the one who gets the other three." So if Rachael just looks at her own personal situation, she says, "Why should I contribute four to the public good if I'm only getting three benefit?" Samuel makes the same logic. Now, of course, if they both contribute, they both benefit the other person and receive benefits from the other person, and they're both better off. But from an individual point of view, it doesn't make sense for them individually, just looking at their private payments and private returns, to contribute.

Again, this game has four possible outcomes, just like the prisoner's dilemma game I said before. One possible outcome is that neither person contributes. They don't invest anything in the public good; they don't get anything; they both end up with zero. Another possibility is that they both contribute to the public good. They each put in their contribution of four—so they invest a total of eight—and they get a social benefit of 12. When they divide that up, they each get a benefit of six, and so they each come out ahead by two.

The last two options would be that one of them contributes and one of them doesn't. In that case, the person who contributed to the public good loses, because that contributor put in a cost of four, but only gets half of the benefit of six; they get three. The non-contributor, the free rider, didn't put in anything, but gets a benefit of three anyway.

So, the difficulty with the prisoner's dilemma arises because, as each person thinks through their personal strategic choices, they're not thinking about how things benefit society as a whole, or what would happen if everyone participated; they're just thinking about the outcome for themselves. Rachael reasons in this way: "If Samuel doesn't contribute to the public good, I'd be a fool to contribute, because I'll just suffer. But if Samuel does contribute to the public good, then I can come out ahead by not contributing. So either way, I should choose not to contribute, and just hope that I can be a free rider who uses the public good that's paid for by Samuel." Samuel reasons the same way about Rachael. When both people reason in that way, that public good never gets built. There's no movement toward the option where everyone is cooperating—the option that's best for all parties.

In fact, this free-rider problem becomes even more obvious if the concept of a public good is expanded to include many people, not just two people, as in this example. For example, say that 10,000 people are asked to pay $100 in taxes to finance a new road. Each person might reason as follows: "Look, this new road costs me personally $100, but the actual benefit from the $100 I pay is divided up by all 10,000 people using the road; so, my personal $100 only brings me one cent in benefits"—that is, $100 divided by the 10,000 users. "If I act as a free rider, and I refuse to contribute to the road, the road will still be built. My $100 isn't going to make any difference. I can still drive on the road because it's a public good—it's non-excludable and nonrivalrous—and I can save my $100 for something I want to buy for myself." But, if everyone reasons this way, if everyone tries to act as a free rider, then no money gets collected and the road never gets built in the first place, and the social benefits are lost.

This idea of a prisoner's dilemma game—where both parties benefit from cooperation, but everyone has an individual incentive not to cooperate—arises in many different settings. For example, in the oligopolistic cartels we were talking about in earlier lectures, every firm has an incentive to increase its own profits by expanding its output. But all firms in the cartel will be better off if they cooperate to hold their output down and act like a joint monopoly, so they can earn high profits.

The participants in a cartel are, in effect, just like the criminals in a prisoner's dilemma. If they can all act together and cooperate, they can act like a monopoly, and make high monopoly profits, and divide them up. But each member of the cartel can reason as follows: "If the other firms don't cooperate and start producing more then I'd be a fool to cooperate and hold down my own output. If the other firms do cooperate and hold down output, then I can make more money by expanding my own production. So in either case, I should expand my own production." If everyone follows that logic, however, the cartel collapses, and the oligopolistic firms start competing with each other.

An arms race is another situation in which no country has an incentive to cut back on its own, but all countries could be better off if all countries cooperated in cutting back. Again, the form of logic here is identical. Each country reasons, "If other countries don't cut back on their arms buildup, I'd be a fool to cut back because I'd fall way behind, so I better build more arms. On the other hand, if other countries do cut back, I can gain a military advantage by building more arms, so I better build more arms." If all countries do this, they're all fighting to stay ahead, and there's an arms race, where everyone would benefit from cooperating to avoid the arms race, but no individual nation can step aside.

A final example is that of conspicuous consumption: buying a bigger car, owning a bigger house, or owning the newest thing compared to everyone else. That can be a situation in which no household or individual quite dares to cut back on their own because of social pressure, but everyone would be better off if everyone could cooperate on cutting back.

Some social critics—some of them economists—have argued that many people have an arms-race mentality about conspicuous consumption. Again, the logic is just the same: "If other people don't cut back on their conspicuous consumption, I'll look ridiculous if I cut back, so I better continue on my conspicuous consumption. If other people do cut back on their conspicuous consumption, then I'll look really cool if I keep up with my own conspicuous consumption. So in either case, I should continue my conspicuous consumption," and everyone continues on.

One more example, just because I'm feeling on a roll: The overuse of natural resources can also be a case where no individual has an incentive to cut back on their own, but everyone might be better off if everyone cooperated in cutting back. One more time, everybody reasons: "If no one else cuts back on their use of natural resources, I'd be a fool to suffer the costs of cutting back. Me, individually, cutting back doesn't make any difference. If everyone else cuts back on their use of natural resources, they'll save the environment, and I'd be a fool to suffer the costs of cutting back myself; so I'll just free ride on their efforts."

Now, this list of applications of the prisoner's dilemma game theory isn't meant to be exhaustive. The point is to emphasize that this prisoner's dilemma is really of great importance to economic analysis, since it indicates that there's a fundamental situation in which the pursuit of self-interest by each individual party leads to outcomes that no one would ultimately desire, if only everyone could find a way to cooperate.

A standard argument in economics, which I've been emphasizing in these lectures, is that, if producers and consumers follow their own self-interest, the result can be highly beneficial for society. But in a prisoner's dilemma situation with free riders, if everyone follows their own self-interest, the result is actually worse for everyone. In the public good game, everyone choosing to be a free rider makes everyone worse off.

So, society faces the problem: how can public goods be provided? There are a variety of social mechanisms that can help solve the public good problem. Let's start off with what happens when non-government institutions want you to contribute to a public good. For example, public radio is a public good. It's nonrivalrous in a sense that if I listen to public radio, that doesn't stop you from listening to it. It's non-excludable in the sense that if somebody's got a radio, you can't stop them from picking up the signal. So how do you get people to pay for public radio? The answer is, of course, pledge drives; but in a more specific sense, it's offering certain kinds of incentives: the free album if you sign up; offering a bumper sticker;

encouraging you, haranguing you, using social pressure in that kind of a way. So some combination of social pressure, and little incentives, and belonging to a group can encourage folks to make contributions to a public good.

There are lots of volunteer efforts and contributions in everything. You think about, for example, fundraising for colleges and universities largely happens on that model. Discouraging littering often happens on a social pressure model. Giving to the United Way is also a kind of social pressure that often happens within the workforce. These have a broadly similar structure. You're trying to overcome the free-rider problem with a mixture of public recognition, and little gifts and incentives for those who do contribute, and maybe some form of shaming—at least in a mild way—for those who don't contribute. Moreover, when people are in a repeat play situation, where they know that they'll face the equivalent of this prisoner's dilemma game over and over again, they often pressure themselves to find a way to cooperate. But, of course, at a big level, government and taxes are one way for society to decide that certain goods are going to be provided and everyone is going to pay for them, whether they wish to purchase a particular amount of that particular good or not.

In passing, I should point out that just because the government decides to finance a particular public good, the government doesn't need to produce that public good directly. For example, the government might decide to finance the building of roads, but it could hire private companies to actually build the roads. The government could, in theory, decide to finance public education, but hire private teachers in order to provide that education. I don't want to argue that necessarily that's the way to reform education or anything like that. I just want to emphasize that when society comes together to do something through the government, I'm really talking about collecting the money to pay for it, and leaving open the question of whether that good would be provided by public workers or paid for by the private sector to provide.

In a way, of course, government collecting taxes and buying public goods overcomes the free-rider problem by brute force. If you don't pay your taxes for the public good, you go to jail. But a gentler way to put the same point, perhaps, is that people are not just individuals;

they are members of a society. When you're a member of society, you face certain benefits; you face certain costs. We can think of these benefits and costs of being a citizen as part of an implicit social contract. Part of the contract is that even when we disagree with the results of the democratic process, we attempt to change the outcome through political means. If I think not enough is being spent on police or not enough is being spent on schools, then I go and try and change that through the political process, not through defiance or revolution.

From an economics viewpoint, the key lesson, here, is that if people don't find a way to come together—either through political mechanisms or through social mechanisms—to provide public goods, you can end up in situations that few or none of us would actually prefer to be in. In this particular case, the extraordinary power of individuals and firms following their own interests in a market economy is not going to help us. It will not produce the things that people want to see produced. There's a reasonably strong case that positive externalities do exist in many areas involving the creation and dissemination of new information; research and development; scientific research; and K–12 education. Those are all areas where, if we don't find ways to come together as a society and pay for those public goods, we can all end up worse off than if we all follow our own self-interest.

Lecture Fifteen
Poverty and Welfare Programs

Scope:

A free market can create great wealth for some while leaving others in poverty. This lecture begins with how the government defines the poverty line and notes the strengths and weaknesses of that definition. Various policies are available to address poverty; not unexpectedly, economists have tended to favor cash subsidies and wage subsidies over trying to set prices low or wages high for the poor. However, the recent trend in welfare reform emphasizes another feature—a requirement that people on welfare take jobs as soon as possible.

Outline

I. Discussing poverty requires defining a poverty line and figuring out how to adjust that line both for families of different sizes and over time.

   A. The concept behind the U.S. poverty line was invented by Mollie Orshansky, who was assigned the task of defining an official poverty line in the mid-1960s.

   1. In the early 1960s, thinking about poverty was very much on the public agenda, but there was no official government definition of poverty or even any clear way to think about what *poverty* meant.

   2. Mollie Orshansky based her definition on two notions: how much it cost to buy a basic diet (which allowed an adjustment for different family sizes) and the notion that food was one-third of a family budget.

   3. That poverty line has remained basically the same, although it has been adjusted upward over time according to the inflation rate.

   B. Any measure of poverty, including this one, will be subject to a range of potential criticisms—but some line is better than none.

   1. The average family now spends much less than one-third of its income on food; thus, a key assumption behind the poverty line is incorrect.

2. The poverty line is adjusted upward for inflation but not for the economy becoming richer.
3. The standard of living can be very different in different areas.
4. In-kind government benefits, such as food stamps or Medicaid, aren't included in the measure of poverty.

C. The U.S. poverty rate has been projected back to the 1950s, then measured each year since then by the Census Bureau.
1. The poverty rate fell dramatically in the 1950s and early 1960s, rose a bit in the early 1970s, and has stayed at more or less the same level since then.

US Poverty Rates Over Time

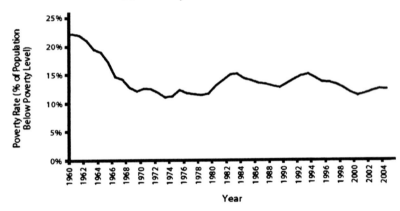

2. The composition of the group classified as poor has shifted. It used to be that the elderly were disproportionately poor; today, single mothers and children are disproportionately poor.

II. Any policy aimed at helping those with low incomes will also create incentive problems.

A. If you give a person a fish, do you discourage him from learning to fish? But if you don't give him a fish, he may starve to death while learning to fish.

B. To illustrate the problem, consider a proposal in which any families with less than poverty-level income will receive government assistance to reach the poverty level. The difficulty with this reasonable-sounding proposal is that a low-income family will not receive any net gain for any work it does up to the poverty level of income.

    C. A negative income tax arises when the government reduces welfare benefits as the recipient earns additional income. A negative income tax of 100%, or even more, creates a poverty trap in which the poor have a greatly reduced incentive to earn income.

III. Government has a range of policies available that seek to reduce the negative income tax and address the poverty trap.

    A. One choice is to reduce the rate at which welfare payments are reduced as income is earned.

    B. The earned income tax credit gives low-income families additional income when they earn money, which helps offset the withdrawal of other government benefits.

    C. Work requirements are an attempt to overcome any disincentives to work.

    D. In-kind benefits, such as Medicaid and food stamps, still create issues of a negative income tax, because such benefits are reduced as income increases.

    E. There are about 80 federal programs to help those with low incomes. Some prominent ones not already mentioned here include housing assistance, Supplemental Security Income for the elderly, and subsidized school lunches.

Essential Reading:

Sheldon Danziger and Rucker C. Johnson, "Trends: Welfare Reform Update," *Milken Institute Review*, 1st quarter 2005, pp. 9–15, www.milkeninstitute.org.

Deborah A. Stone, "Making the Poor Count," *The American Prospect*, Spring 1994, pp. 84–88.

U.S. Census Bureau. "Poverty." www.census.gov/hhes/www/poverty.html.

Supplementary Reading:

Constance F. Citro and Robert T. Michael, *Measuring Poverty: A New Approach*.

U.S. House of Representatives, Ways and Means Committee, *2004 Green Book: Background Material and Data on the Programs within the Jurisdiction of the Committee on Ways and Means*, www.gpoaccess.gov/wmprints/green/2004.html.

Questions to Consider:

1. Poverty can be measured in at least two ways. The current method uses an absolute standard, which is based on the amount needed to purchase a certain standard of living. An alternative would use a relative method; for example, the poverty line could be set at half the average-level income. Which approach do you prefer?

2. How would you like to see government assistance to those with low income structured so that it both helps those in need and provides incentives to work? How costly would your proposal be?

Lecture Fifteen—Transcript
Poverty and Welfare Programs

The last few lectures have been discussing things that could go wrong in markets for goods—problems of competition, antitrust, anticompetitive practices, pollution, technology, and public goods. With this lecture, we shift the focus a little bit, and begin to talk about problems that can arise in labor markets, specifically problems that can arise when some people end up poor and other people end up rich.

A market economy uses supply and demand to set prices, wages, and interest rates. It doesn't make any intrinsic judgments about the worth, or the fairness, or the justice of these outcomes. In such an economy in the labor market, there are always going to be some people who are unlucky, or disadvantaged, or disabled, or even just plain lazy, who end up with lower income. Conversely, there will be some people who are lucky, or advantaged, or talented, or just extremely hard workers who will end up with additional income or additional resources. A market can easily create great wealth for some while leaving others in poverty.

This lecture focuses on the issue of poverty and the government welfare problems that seek to address poverty. The next lecture then looks at the issue of inequality of incomes, which covers the entire range of the income distribution, not just those with low incomes.

The starting point for discussing poverty is that we have to define what we mean by being in poverty. What do we mean by the poverty line or the poverty rate? To get you in the mental spirit for this, I have to take you back to the early 1960s, when Michael Harrington has just published his famous good *The Other America*, which offers vivid portraits of what it really meant to be poor. The idea of poverty was very much on the public agenda in a way it really hadn't been before. But government didn't have any official definition of poverty and there was no clear sense, in policy terms, of what it would take to lift people out of poverty. The working definition of poverty in 1963 was that poverty was any household with less than $3,000 in income; but there were no adjustments for, say, the number of children, or whether it was a one-parent or two-parent family, and there was really no deep justification for that $3,000 figure except than it was sort of a nice round number.

A woman named Mollie Orshansky was working for the Social Security Administration, and she was transferred over to the department that was given the job of defining what poverty was going to be. She based her definition on two ideas. The first idea was: how much did it cost to buy a basic diet? Since that cost of buying a basic diet would vary according to the size of family, then there would be an automatically built-in adjustment for different family sizes. The second notion was that food was one-third of the family budget.

So Mollie Orshansky is working in the Social Security Administration—and remember, Social Security is responsible for survivors' benefits. Survivors' benefits get you into the issue of poverty, and what you're going to pay people who are surviving after a spouse has died. Orshansky had previously worked in the Department of Agriculture, where they put together food plans for how much it cost to feed families of different sizes. The Department of Agriculture had various plans for what it would cost to buy a basic diet, ranked by level of spending. They had a high-cost plan, a medium-cost plan, and a low-cost plan. What they called the economy plan was the cheapest plan for how much it would cost to give a family a nutritionally adequate diet.

Orshansky's idea was to link this concept of poverty she was being asked to define to something concrete, like food. She said in an interview later, when she was asked about this, "I wanted to show what it was like to not have enough money. It's not just that the poor had less money; they didn't have enough. I knew you couldn't spend for one necessity without taking away from another."

Orshansky looked at this economy food plan, and she figured out what the economy food plan would cost for 62 different family types, depending on age, number of children, and whether it was a single-parent or a two-parent family. She looked at the economy plan for feeding all 62 different groups. She also looked back at a 1955 study, which said that the average family spends about one-third of its income on food. She also did a separate set of calculations for farm families, to take into account that they could produce a certain amount of their own food.

She went to the Census Bureau with these numbers. She had what it would cost to buy an adequate diet for these 62 different groups, and then multiplying that by three—since one-third of what you were spending out of your income was food—she said, "That'll be my poverty line." She went to the Census Bureau and said, "Okay. Here are my income numbers. How many people are below the poverty line?"

To give you a sense of the state of play at this time, at that point, the Census Bureau had published breakdowns of income by family size, but they had never before broken down income taking number of parents, or gender of head-of-household, or age of the children into account. It actually cost them about $2,500, which is close to the poverty level income for a year, to find out how many people were below Orshansky's poverty line. They found out that in that year, by that poverty line, about 20 million children were living in households that were below the poverty line.

This general way of looking at what the poverty line meant spread very, very fast. It was being used in prominent government reports as early as 1964, and by 1969, it actually became the official definition of the poverty line. Ever since then, the poverty line has remained basically the same as what Orshansky defined back in the early 1960s. There have been some minor changes. The separate poverty lines for farm households and for female-headed households were abolished in 1981. And Orshansky's original poverty line went up to seven children; it's now been expanded up to nine children. Orshansky liked to emphasize, when she talked about the poverty line, that the actual amounts in the poverty line were really not a heck of a lot of money. She would do simple long-division to show that. Let me give you a modern example.

In 2003, the poverty line for a family of four with two parents and two kids is $18,660. Now, let's say that they spend one-third of that on food—Orshansky's assumption. So that's $6,220 a year for food. With 365 days in a year, that's about $17 per day. With three meals per day and four people at each meal, that's an average of $1.42 per meal for the entire year. That's not what you would call an exorbitant standard of living.

Now, any measure of poverty, including this one, will be subject to a range of potential criticisms. Let me give you some of the criticisms that have been raised about Orshansky's line. What's going on, for example, with this multiple, that households spend one-third of their income on food? That was a study from the mid-1950s. But later in the 1960s, the average household was spending something like one-fourth of income on food, and now it's more like one-fifth of income on food. The share of income being spent on food has gradually declined over time. But we haven't raised the multiple and taken the food expenses, and instead of multiplying by three, multiplied them by four or by five.

Why use the economy food plan? Actually, if you look in the documents of the time, the economy food plan was supposed to be for emergencies, like what you could really just barely scrape by with. Why not use the low-cost food plan, or the moderate food plan, that would be a little bit more reasonable in terms of what people actually spent on food?

The poverty line that Orshansky set is increased each year for inflation, so it does rise with inflation over time. But should it also be increased to reflect economic growth and the fact that we're living in a richer society? After all, some part of our idea of what poverty means is relative to the other people in society. So, just increasing for inflation, but not for economic growth, doesn't take into account that relative feeling.

Should the poverty line take modern technology into account? Should poor people have enough money to have access to cable TV, or cell phones, or broadband Internet access at home? What about geographic disparity? Shouldn't the poverty level be a higher number in a high-income state, like California or New York; and a lower number in a lower-income state, like Arkansas or South Dakota?

The poverty line is measured on before-tax income. Should it take other factors into account? For example, if you get government benefits like Medicaid or Food Stamps, should those be added to your income when you're thinking about whether you're poor or not? What about help provided through the tax code, through tax credits, like this earned income tax credit that we'll talk about later on in this lecture? That's not included because it's an after-tax benefit, not before tax.

Should a working poor family that doesn't have health insurance be viewed as having less income than a working poor family that does have health insurance, even if their income at the end of the year looks just the same?

There was a National Academy of Sciences panel in the mid-1990s that looked at how poverty is defined. Their suggestion was, that rather than basing it just on food, you should set the poverty line by looking at what the average household spends on a combination of food, clothing, and shelter, and then taking some percentage of that. So you would still link the idea of poverty to what it costs to buy basic necessities, but you would link it in a relative way; that is, what the average person is buying would pull up what the poverty line was.

Now, there are a lot of interesting philosophical things to think about regarding what alternate poverty lines might make sense. In fact, the Census Bureau publishes what the poverty rate would be if you used different kinds of definitions. But it's really, really, really useful to have a single poverty line over time, not to be changing the definition every year because, if you change the definition every year, you don't know whether the poverty rate changed because of the definitional change, or because of actual poverty changing. If you leave the definition alone—mostly alone—you can at least be pretty confident that changes in the poverty rate are telling you something about what happened in the economy.

So, U.S. poverty rate is the percentage of people in the U.S. population who are below Orshansky's poverty line. It's been projected back into the 1950s and measured each year by the Census Bureau. If you look at those numbers over time, the poverty rate in 1960 would have been about 22.2 percent. That's the share of the U.S. population that would have been below the poverty line. However, that drops dramatically during the rapid economic growth of the 1960s. By 1969, the poverty rate is down to only 12.1 percent. By 1973, it's down to 11.1 percent. So an enormous number of people move above Orshansky's poverty line over that time. But during the bad economy of the 1970s—big recessions, high inflation—by 1982, the poverty rate is back up to about 15 percent. In 1993, although it's fluctuated up and down a little bit, it's still about 15 percent. During the strong economic growth of the late

1990s, the poverty rate begins to sag down again, and by 2004, it's bounced up a little, but it's about 12.4 percent.

Another way to say that in broad terms is, there's a sharp decline in the poverty rate during the 1960s and perhaps into the early 1970s, but since then, the poverty rate really has not changed a heck of a lot. It's been in that range of 15 percent in bad years with recessions, maybe 12 percent in good years, when the economy's been growing for a while.

However, the composition of who is poor has shifted over recent decades. It used to be that if you looked at who the poor people are, back in about 1960 or 1970, you could say, in some ways, if you had to describe the poor in a word, you would say it's the elderly, because the elderly were disproportionately poor. But today, with help from Social Security, and Medicare, and other programs for the elderly, it's no longer true that the poverty rate for the elderly is higher than the poverty rate for the rest of the population. For a while now, it's been true that if you want the group that is disproportionately poor, it's single-mother families with children.

My immediate reaction to the existence of poverty in a country as rich as the United States is to support government programs to assist the poor. My second reaction is still to give assistance, but also to give some careful thought as to how that assistance is provided, and what incentives are involved. Sometimes when I'm thinking about this problem of incentives, I go back to this old statement: "Give a man a fish and he'll eat for a day, but teach him how to fish and he'll eat forever." I don't know who actually said that. Some websites say it's a Chinese proverb, but as far as I know, that might actually be from China or it might be from a fortune cookie.

But I would argue that when you're thinking about poverty, that statement contains both a great truth and a great dilemma. Now, here's the great truth: it's better if people can earn their living than if they just keep getting handouts. It's better to teach them to fish than just give them fish. Here's the great dilemma—or what my old philosophy professors used to call a tension. There's a tension between giving people immediate assistance and helping them learn how to help themselves. What is the man supposed to eat while you're teaching him to fish? It's nice to teach him how to fish, but it's going to take him a while to learn. You're going to need to give him fish for a while, while he's learning. But if you're giving him fish all the time, why is he going to bother to learn to fish? Why won't he just take the fish and not bother trying to learn?

Every method of trying to help those with low incomes runs into this fundamental tension, and there's really no way out of it. If you don't help the poor in a wealthy society, it seems cruel and immoral. But if you do help the poor, you will reduce, at least to some extent, their incentive to support themselves. The social safety net shouldn't be a hammock. It shouldn't be something that is hard to climb into and hard to climb out of. Instead, the social safety net should be like that kind of net that's used in circuses to catch trapeze artists. You fall into it and it's soft, but then you bounce up and out again, and go back into the real world, and into a regular life where you're supporting yourself. There's no way to avoid this problem altogether, of the tension between helping people and reducing their incentives to support themselves. But you can set up programs so this conflict is either relatively large or relatively small. That's where we get into these issues of incentives.

So, to consider the fundamental problem, let's consider a basic proposal: the U.S. government guarantees people will receive the poverty level of income. So a family of four in 2003, like we said before, will get $18,660. If you earn less than that amount, the government will give you enough money to bring you up to that level, up to that $18,660.

What could be wrong with this proposal, other than maybe not being generous enough? But in terms of incentives, what could be wrong with it? Well, let's think about the incentives for a moment. If the family works zero, total income is $18,660, all from the government. Now, imagine one parent gets a full-time job, but it's a low-wage job; they work 2,000 during the year—that would be 50 weeks of 40-hour weeks—and they earn $6 an hour. So, 2,000 hours, $6 an hour, they earn $12,000. Their reward for going out and earning those $12,000 is that total family income is—you got it—exactly the same: $18,660, because the government tops you up to the poverty line, no matter how much you earn.

Now, imagine the second parent gets a half-time job and earns an additional $6,000 a year. So now total family earnings are $18,000. Total family income is—you got it—$18,660. You're topped up to the poverty line if you're below it. If both parents worked full time and they each earned $12,000 a year, then total family income could be $24,000 a year, and they would be above the poverty line.

But think about this for a moment. Now they're working a total of 4,000 hours a year, and their total gain in income is only about $5,400 over not working at all, because not working at all, they would have gotten the $18,660. At an hourly rate, their gain from working is only about $1.30 an hour. And if they're both working full time, they probably have extra expenses for childcare and transportation; they're going to owe taxes. It's not clear they're going to come out ahead at all.

The fundamental problem here is called, by economists, a negative income tax. A negative income tax arises when the government reduces your welfare benefits as the recipient earns additional income. So let's think about how a negative income tax happens. A regular positive income tax, where you earn money and the government takes part of the money, is the tax most people are familiar with. With a negative income tax, when you earn money, the government reduces your benefits. But both kinds of taxes affect the incentive to work. A positive income tax can discourage you from working by reducing how much your take-home pay is. Removing benefits as you work also reduces the gain you get from working. The example I just gave a moment ago is a negative income tax, which is set at 100 percent. That is, every time that family earned $1, they lost $1 in government benefits. So the negative income tax was 100 percent; the offset was 100 percent.

When the negative income tax gets very high, especially 100 percent, there's what economists call a poverty trap. For that family, there is no incentive to take a low-paying job. There is no incentive to take that starting point on the employment ladder where maybe you could get promoted and get experience, because you literally get zero gain from working.

Now, you might at this point say something like the following: "Well, Tim, this is really interesting in a hypothetical sort of way, but no moron would ever set up a welfare system that offered no reward at all for working. That would be stupid beyond belief!" So how about a realistic view of what's happening in these government welfare programs? Here's the bad news: actually, that 100 percent negative income tax is a completely accurate description of how the main welfare program—called Aid to Families with Dependent Children—worked through the 1960s and '70s and into the 1980s in most states. That is, every time you earned a $1, the government took away $1 in welfare benefits.

In fact, it's even worse than that because there are other welfare programs—like Food Stamps and Medicaid. So when you worked or thought about earning $1 of income, you not only lost $1 of AFDC or welfare benefits, but you could also lose some Food Stamps and some eligibility for Medicaid. You don't get to keep the whole $1 you earned anyway, because of the positive taxes you owe on it. So if you think 100 percent negative income tax is crazy and a terrible poverty trap, well, the negative income tax of 120 percent or 140 percent is even crazier. If you understand that argument, you are giving a standard critique that economists gave of the U.S. system for helping those with low incomes, as it existed from at least the mid-1960s up into the early 1980s.

Now, government has a range of policies available that seek to reduce the negative income tax and address this poverty trap problem. One choice, for example, is phase out the welfare payments more slowly, reducing the rate at which the welfare payments are phased out as someone earns income.

In 1996, there was a big welfare reform act, and the old Aid to Families with Dependent Children was changed to a new program called TATNF, Temporary Assistance to Needy Families. Under that program—although this varies state by state—it's now common that there's a 50 percent reduction in TATNF benefits for each dollar earned. Now, again, it differs some state by state. Some states even have rules that you can earn a certain amount without having your benefits reduced at all, or you don't have your benefits reduced if you marry someone who is working. There are a lot of different state rules. But the point is, the 100 percent negative income tax has pretty much gone away. It's still 50 percent, which is pretty high, but it's not 100 percent.

Another option: the earned income tax credit is a provision of the tax code that gives low-income families additional income when they earn money, and that helps to offset the withdrawal of other government benefits. It works like this: this example is based on a family with two children in 2004. As you start off earning income—up to $10,510—you get an extra 40 percent back in a tax credit. So if you were earning $10,510, that 40 percent means you'd get $4,202 extra. Then, as you increase your earnings from $10,510 up to $13,710, you're earning more money, but there's no reduction in that $4,202 you were getting. Above that level, they start phasing out the money. So every additional dollar you earn loses 26 cents of the tax credit money. Now, the point is that work is subsidized for low-income workers. Now, of course, it does phase out; it does have a negative income tax part as it phases out, but you have to phase it out somehow. It's interesting that the amount of money that is paid out through this earned income tax credit in 2004 was about $34 billion a year, and that was actually worth more than the welfare payments for the country in that year, which were only about $24 billion.

For some programs, like Medicaid, which pays for medical care for poor families with children, various states have changed the rules, so that, as you get above the poverty line, you can keep getting Medicaid up to two times the poverty line. So, the incentive to work and get that job that gets you started in the labor market is not removed. The big trick here though—the big question is—don't force poor people to choose between working in a job with no health benefits and losing Medicaid and losing health insurance for their children.

Another way in which we've tried to get around the problem of these negative work incentives is through work requirements. Starting in the late 1980s and up into the mid-1990s, there were a series of welfare reforms passed by individual states that required welfare recipients to go back to work fairly quickly. In 1996, that big welfare reform bill I mentioned before said this is now federal law, that all the states had to have basic rules to get federal money. They needed to get a certain percentage of their welfare recipients back to work. I think it was 25 percent of welfare recipients had to be in a work-related activity in 1997; then that was going to raise five percent a year until 50 percent of the recipients were in a work-related activity by 2002.

Now, a work-related activity could be a job, either a public-sector or a private-sector job, or it could be on-the-job training. States had a lot of ability to define what it meant to be in a job-related activity.

And there was a two-year cutoff. You had to get that work started after no more than two years of welfare benefits. You had a lifetime limit of five years.

So there had been about 14 million recipients of the old AFDC welfare program back in 1994. Remember, the economy's doing pretty well in 1994. After the 2001 recession, when the economy wasn't doing so well, there were actually less than six million people receiving TATNF. So the number of welfare recipients was cut very substantially by the welfare reform bill.

Now, these work requirements are controversial. I think it's an open question—what society's going to do, if and when a large number of families with kids hit the wall, and they aren't eligible for government assistance. Some of the poor may need expensive services like daycare and transportation to make work possible, since their wages are not likely to be high. But it also seems like a culture of non-work had developed, at least among some welfare recipients. The work requirements helped to break up that culture.

Another way to get around the poverty trap is to provide in-kind help, meaning help not in the form of cash, but in the form of some service, like Medicaid, medical services for the poor, or food stamps that can be spent on groceries. But these still create issues of a negative income tax because they are phased out as income increases.

The big idea of Medicaid and Food Stamps is that with Medicaid—if you are a poor family with kids and if you're eligible—then your medical bills are almost entirely paid by the state and federal government. The way Food Stamps works is, you calculate what it would cost to buy the economy food budget. If it would be more than 30 percent of your income, you can get Food Stamps to pay for the rest. Food Stamps are not really stamps anymore; most of the time it's now a plastic card; but the name continues on.

Those approaches are often politically popular because they seem to promise that the poor won't use the assistance unwisely. They have to spend it on medical care or food. But economists have pointed out that they have incentive issues too. For example, Medicaid can create a problem of what's sometimes called job lock, where you're worried about moving to a different job because you're worried about losing your Medicaid benefits. Maybe the insurance from the new employer wouldn't be as good as the Medicaid you're getting. Food Stamps are also—for a lot of people—basically equal to income. After all, you can use the Food Stamps and that frees up money to spend on something else.

Now, I've mentioned welfare, the TATNF program, the earned income tax credit, Medicaid, and Food Stamps; but just to be clear, there something like 80 other programs from the federal government where benefits are tested by income level. So, those with lower income get the benefits and they phase out over time, or they phase out as your income goes up.

Some examples would be for supplemental security income. That's the part of the program that assures a basic minimum income for the elderly, but issues of whether you expect the elderly to work are a little tricky. There are housing programs like housing vouchers or what's called Section 8. There's a federal childcare program. There's the Head Start Program that some kids are eligible for. There are things in the tax code, like a tax credit for children that phases out. There are things in the Bush tax cuts, various kinds of tax changes that, for those of us with several kids, that child tax credit has really made a big difference. There are school lunch programs; there's something called Women, Infant, and Children, the WIC Program, which is food support for women who are pregnant, or have babies, or small kids. There's the low-income home energy assistance program to help with heating bills in the winter. All of these programs create potential trade-offs between assistance and incentives.

Now, with some of them, we don't worry too much about the trade-offs, because programs aimed at the elderly or at kids may not have a big incentive on whether they work or not. We're not expecting retired people to work; we're not expecting kids to work. But we need to address this tension. The issue isn't just how much money you give people with low incomes, although that's obviously a big and important question. It's not just how much money you give people, but it's how, as they earn more money, you phase out that assistance. Because the way in which you phase out that assistance is going to be critical to the work incentives that you're providing, and the incentives you're providing to help people get out of poverty and stay out of poverty.

The more we think about that incentive problem, the more we think about how assistance is phased out, the more it will be true that we aren't just helping the poor, but we would be helping the poor to help themselves.

Lecture Sixteen
Inequality

Scope:

Inequality refers to the gap between those with high incomes and those with low incomes. Starting in the late 1970s, inequality has increased in the U.S. economy. A variety of explanations have been proposed for this rise in inequality, but the most likely explanation is that changes in information and communications technology have favored high-skilled workers and raised their wages while substituting for low-skilled workers and thus not helping their wages. This lecture discusses other possible causes of inequality: government tax and spending policies, globalization, unionization, and the minimum wage. The rise in inequality raises the question of whether some government response is appropriate—and, if so, what kind of response.

Outline

I. Poverty and inequality aren't the same thing.

    A. *Poverty* refers to being below a certain line. *Inequality* describes the gap between the poor and the rich.

    B. If the rich get much richer while the poor get a little richer, then inequality can go up and the poverty rate can go down at the same time! Or if the poor do a little worse and the rich do much worse, poverty can increase at the same time that inequality is falling.

    C. The concern over poverty is based on a fear that people are not receiving basic necessities of life. Concern over inequality has more to do with fairness in how the rewards and disparities in society are justly distributed.

II. Measuring inequality requires capturing the overall distribution of income, including both poor and rich.

    A. A standard approach is to split the income distribution into parts, such as fifths or tenths or even single percents, and determine what share of income is being received by each part. For simplicity, this lecture will stick with dividing up the income distribution into *quintiles*, or fifths, with some mention of the top 5%.

B. The level of inequality in the U.S. income distribution can be measured by looking at the share of income received by different quintiles. For example, in 2000, the bottom fifth of the income distribution received 4.3% of total income; the second fifth received 9.8%; the middle fifth received 15.4%; the fourth fifth received 22.7%; and the top fifth received 47.7%. The top 5% received 21.1% of all income.

U.S. Income Distribution: Share of Total Income Received

	Lowest fifth	Second fifth	Middle fifth	Fourth fifth	Highest fifth	Top 5%
1970	5.4	12.2	17.6	23.8	40.9	15.6
1975	5.6	11.9	17.7	24.2	40.7	14.9
1980	5.3	11.6	17.6	24.4	41.1	14.6
1985	4.8	11.0	16.9	24.3	43.1	16.1
1990	4.6	10.8	16.6	23.8	44.3	17.4
1995	4.4	10.1	15.8	23.2	46.5	20.0
2000	4.3	9.8	15.4	22.7	47.7	21.1
2002	4.2	9.7	15.5	23.0	47.6	20.8

Source: U.S. Bureau of the Census

C. The shares received by the top fifth and the top 5% have risen over recent decades. In 1975, for example, the top fifth received 40.7% of all income; by 2002, the top fifth was receiving 47.6% of total income.

D. It's difficult to say whether this level of inequality is a bad thing. After all, there are many reasons for some degree of inequality: People tend to have lower incomes when they are young, higher incomes in middle age, and lower incomes when elderly. Even year to year, there are shifts between rich and poor; some people make earning money a top priority in their lives, while others do not.

E. Mobility across the income distribution has not been increasing in a way that would offset the increased level of inequality.

III. The most plausible reason for the rise in inequality is the change in information and communications technology, but other possible reasons include globalization and changes in labor market institutions, such as unions and the minimum wage.

  A. The single biggest reason for the rise in inequality appears to be the changes in information and communications technology, which have favored the productivity of high-skill workers.

  B. Globalization is often accused of contributing to the rise in inequality, but most analyses show that it has had a fairly minor role, because trade with low-wage countries is a fairly small share of overall trade.

  C. U.S. labor markets have seen some institutional changes that have tended to add to inequality, such as weaker unions and lower minimum wages.

  D. Household incomes have also become more unequal because of changes in family patterns: specifically, the rise of single-parent families and the rise of high-earners marrying each other.

IV. What public policies are available to reduce inequality?

  A. Higher taxes on the rich can be used to diminish inequality. The share of federal taxes paid by those with high incomes is fairly high by the standard of recent decades in the early 2000s.

Share of Total Federal Taxes Paid by Each Group

	1980	1985	1990	1995	2000	2002
Lowest quintile	2.0	2.3	1.9	1.3	1.1	0.9
Second quintile	7.0	7.2	6.8	5.8	4.8	4.8
Third quintile	13.3	13.2	12.6	11.4	9.8	10.2
Fourth quintile	21.3	21.3	20.7	19.3	17.4	19.1
Top quintile	56.3	55.8	57.9	61.9	66.7	64.8
Top 10%	40.0	39.5	41.7	46.6	52.2	49.0
Top 5%	28.7	28.4	30.6	35.4	41.4	37.3
Top 1%	14.2	14.8	16.2	20.1	25.6	21.1

Source: Congressional Budget Office, "Effective Federal Tax Rates: 1979–2002," March 2005

B. An alternative method of reducing inequality would be to increase government spending that especially benefits those with low and middle incomes.

    1. One approach is to expand direct payments to the working poor, such as the earned income tax credit.

    2. An alternative is to spend money on public goods and services that especially benefit those with low and middle incomes, such as schools, mass transit, libraries, and parks.

C. Taking actions to strengthen labor market institutions that lead to more equal wages, such as establishing stronger unions and a higher minimum wage, would reduce inequality somewhat—although such policies could also involve tradeoffs.

D. Part of the American dream is that everyone has a reasonable ladder of opportunity, so that those who complete their education and work full-time and do their best with the hand they are dealt have a good chance to achieve a satisfactory middle-class life.

Essential Reading:

Paul Krugman, "Technology's Revenge," *Wilson Quarterly*, Autumn 1994, pp. 56–64.

Rudolph G. Penner, Isabel V. Sawhill, and Timothy Taylor, "Chapter 3: Inequality and Opportunity: Winners and Losers in the New Economy," in *Updating America's Social Contract: Economic Growth and Opportunity in the New Century*, pp. 88–121.

Supplementary Reading:

Congressional Budget Office, *Historical Effective Federal Tax Rates: 1979 to 2002*, March 2005, www.cbo.gov.

U.S. Census Bureau, *Historical Income Inequality Tables*, www.census.gov/ hhes/income/histinc/ineqtoc.html.

Questions to Consider:

1. Does the existing level of inequality seem like a social problem to you? If it does seem like a problem, how much inequality seems reasonable? If it doesn't seem like a problem, how much more inequality would need to occur before you felt that it was a problem?

2. Of the available policies to reduce inequality, which ones (if any!) are most attractive to you?

Lecture Sixteen—Transcript

Inequality

The subjects of poverty and inequality are often scrambled together in public discussions, but they aren't at all the same thing. As discussed in the previous lecture, poverty refers to those who are below a certain level of income. Inequality, on the other hand, describes the gap between the poor and the rich. Imagine, for example, that the rich get much richer while the poor get a little richer. Then, inequality might go up because the spread between the poor and the rich is rising, but the poverty rate could be going down at the same time. Or imagine that the poor do a little bit worse and the rich do a lot worse. In that situation, poverty could increase—because the poor are doing worse—at the same time that inequality, the gap between rich and poor, is falling.

At a fundamental level, we care about poverty and inequality for somewhat different reasons. At a basic level, we care about poverty because some people are being deprived of basic necessities. I would say that we care about inequality for reasons that have more to do with a sense of fairness of opportunity, a sense that it would be a good thing to live in a society where the rewards and the disparities are not just distributed by birth, or by luck, or by family connections, but they have at least some connection to producing what the rest of society wants.

How do we measure inequality? We need some way of capturing the entire distribution of income, not just the low end of it. A standard approach is to split the income distribution into parts like fifths or tenths, or even single percents, and then say, "What share of income is being received by each share of the income distribution?" Now, for simplicity, in this lecture, I'll mainly stick with dividing up the income distribution into fifths, with some mention of the top five percent.

The level of inequality in the U.S. income distribution can be measured by looking at the share of income received by different quintiles, or different fifths. If each fifth of the U.S. income distribution got exactly 20 percent of total income, then income would be equally distributed. If the bottom 20 percent got 20 percent of the income; the middle, 20 percent; the next, 20 percent; the fourth, 20 percent; the top, 20 percent. But, in fact, of course, the bottom fifth gets a lot less than 20 percent of total income, and the top fifth gets a lot more.

In fact, starting in the 1970s, there's something of a trend toward those with high incomes having a larger proportion of all total income. Now, just to give you some perspective here, the top fifth of all families in the year 2000 started at about $95,000 in total income and went up from there. So today, it's probably some number above $100,000, but not necessarily a whole lot above.

Let me give you some actual numbers on the income distribution. In 2002, the bottom fifth of the income distribution got 4.2 percent of total income. The second fifth got 9.7 percent of total income. The middle fifth, the middle quintile of the income distribution, got 15.5 percent of total income. The fourth fifth got 23 percent of total income. The top fifth, the top 20 percent of the income distribution, got 47.6 percent of the income. If you look inside that top fifth a little bit, then you just look at the top five percent of the income distribution. In 2002, the top five percent of the income distribution for about 20.8 percent of the total income in the economy.

Over time, that distribution, the spread between the bottom fifth and the top fifth, has actually been rising somewhat over time. For example, if you go back to 1975, the top fifth of the income distribution, at that point, was getting 40.7 percent of total income. So it goes from 40.7 percent of total income, then by 1985, up to 43.1 percent of total income. By 1995, up to 46.5 percent of total income. By 2000, up to 47.7 percent of total income—right about where it was in 2002, after the recession. To put it a little bit differently, the top fifth of the income distribution was getting 40.7 percent of the income distribution back in 1975, and by 2002, it was getting seven percentage points more: it was getting 47.6 percent of total income by 2002. That's quite a large shift.

If you look at a more detailed breakdown and you particularly focus on that top five percent, almost all of that increase going to the top fifth of the income distribution was actually going to the top five percent of the income distribution. For perspective, the top five percent of all families in the U.S. in 2002 started at about $164,000 and went up from there. So now it's a few years later, I suspect it's some number that's less than $200,000, but maybe not a whole lot less than $200,000 a year.

So that's the level of inequality we've got, and we know that the level of inequality, as measured by these quintiles, has been going up. Is that a bad thing? Well, some degree of inequality is surely understandable. There's absolutely no reason to think that we ought to have an economy where everyone gets exactly the same income all through their life. For example, most people, when you first start out working in your 20s or in your teens, have a somewhat lower income. Then you build up your income over time in middle age, and have high-income years in your 40s and 50s; and then when you're elderly, and you start going to part-time work or retirement, you have lower income. There's no reason you should have the same income every year of your life.

Even year to year, there are shifts between rich and poor. People might have an especially good year or an especially bad year. In some industries, like construction or farming, or for people who write books or record music, there are good and bad years. There are also people who make earning money a top priority in their life and others do not.

There are friends of mine who worked for a time in investment banks in New York City—and I'm thinking particularly of the hot-hot go-go days of the late 1990s. But I remember at least one of them telling me that her standard schedule was that she worked straight through the night a couple times a week. She would show up in the morning, Monday morning, and she would go home Tuesday night, get a night's sleep, come back Thursday morning, and work through the night, and leave Friday night. Now, this person made an extremely high income level, much more than my income level, but obviously at some cost in terms of time. She's probably working the equivalent of two jobs in terms of hours. And there are people who work two jobs and there are other people who don't. There are some people who would prefer to have a job where they earn enough money to afford a house and so on, but they would rather stay home and read than buy an expensive vehicle or a boat. There are some people who like to travel cheap, and there are some people who like to travel and stay in luxury hotels. There are some people who want a huge house and car, and there are some people who don't. To some extent, inequality in incomes is just going to result from these kinds of preferences.

So we know that perfect equality just isn't going to be a sensible goal. There's going to be some inequality because people are different. With all this taken into account, is the level of inequality we have now reasonable or not? Perhaps not a big surprise—these are lectures about how to think about things—I'm going to sidestep that question a little bit.

A famous economist from the University of Chicago named Henry Simons was talking about inequality, and he wrote in 1938, "The case against inequality depends on the ethical or aesthetic judgment that the prevailing distribution of wealth and income reveals a degree and/or kind of inequality which is distinctly evil or unlovely." That phrase about "evil or unlovely," and whether it's an aesthetic judgment, is something that's echoed down among economists over time.

In fact, I find that there's almost an inability of people on both sides of inequality disputes to even understand the way the other people think. In some cases, some folks are just upset about the level of inequality they see. It just bugs them. It bugs them down to their toes. If you say, "It doesn't bother me that much," they think that you're not telling the truth somehow because it's obvious—isn't it obvious that it's a terrible thing? Isn't it obvious that it ought to bug you? On the other side, there are people who say, "It doesn't bother me all that much," and they just honestly can't understand why people on the other side get so excited about it. They think, "What makes you so excited about the level of inequality that's happening?" So, I think that we need to recognize that people just have different aesthetic judgments there.

What about the question of mobility across the income distribution? The income distribution at any given time is a snapshot. It tells you how people are located along the income distribution, but it doesn't tell you about how people are moving toward higher and lower levels. If there's a lot of movement from lower quintiles to higher quintiles, and higher quintiles to lower quintiles, then maybe you worry somewhat less about income distribution, because everyone gets their chance at the top; everyone gets their chance at the bottom.

Now, to know whether there is movement from people between the quintiles, you need to track the same people over a long period of time. Most government surveys don't do this—they just look at the population, but they don't tell you if that person went up or down, according to where they were last year. However, there is a survey project at the University of Michigan called the Panel Study of Income Dynamics. Starting in 1968, it started tracking a nationally represented group, and it's been tracking those people, and their children, and their relatives, and it tracks people after they split up after divorce. You can actually track people over time, and watch people move in and out of different quintiles, as they get older, as they move in and out of the workforce, as their life patterns change.

The patterns that you see looking at this PSID data from the University of Michigan are pretty much what you might expect. That is, there is a fair amount of movement, but it tends to be moving maybe one or two quintiles. People who are the very bottom of the income distribution move up a little bit, but they don't always move right to the top. Similarly, people at the very top of the income distribution might move down a little bit, but rarely do they fall all the way down to the bottom.

Here's my key point: the amount of mobility between quintiles doesn't seem to have changed much over time. It seems much the same in the 2000s and 1990s as it did in the 1980s and 1970s. So, although we know for sure that the level of inequality has been rising, and we know there's some mobility, we also know that the higher level of inequality is not being counterbalanced by a greater level of mobility. Mobility isn't making us worry less about the rise in inequality than it otherwise would.

Indeed, in a world where the skills of labor are especially and increasingly important, the pattern may be that high-income parents have the human and the financial resources to invest in their children in a way that helps their children to have higher incomes too. In that sense, it may be easier than it was in the past to pass a high income to the next generation, because of the importance of investing in children as they grow up.

There are international comparisons where they look at intergenerational mobility. That is, do children tend to follow the income pattern of their parents? The answer seems to be, in the last

30 years or so, that the U.S. does not have more intergenerational mobility than most countries of Western Europe. Indeed, there are several studies that suggest that the U.S. has less intergenerational mobility than either Canada or Sweden. So there's less of people moving back and forth across the income distribution than in those other countries.

The bottom line: inequality is up, mobility is not up, and if you're worried about inequality—if it's an aesthetic thing that bothers you—there's certainly some reason to be concerned. I'll dip my toe in the water there and just say that the rise in inequality does bother me. Having some inequality doesn't, but a continual rise does bother me.

What are the reasons for this rise in inequality? We need to look for reasons that have been more or less continuously happening over the last several decades, because the rise in inequality started in the 1970s and has continued for the last 30 years. It can't be something that just one president did or one law that passed. It has to be a continuous force over time. We also want to look for reasons that might apply internationally because, to some extent, we've seen an increase in inequality in most of the world's high-income economies, and so we want something that goes across international borders— and again, not something that's one law passed by the U.S. Congress, or something like that.

The single biggest reason for the rise in inequality appears to be the changes in information and communications technology that have been happening over recent decades. Essentially, those changes have complemented, or worked with, the productivity of high-skilled workers. The way I imagine this in my mind is, imagine that there's a level of demand for high-skilled workers and a level of supply for these high-skilled workers. The supply of skilled workers is expanding over time because today's students are more likely to complete high school and go on to at least some college than the older workers, who are retiring, were likely to go on and do some college 40 or 50 years ago. So, the supply of these skilled workers is going up. However, the changes in information and communications technology, including the phenomenal developments in computers and the Internet, have dramatically increased the demand for high-skilled labor. So the supply of skilled labor's gone up some, but the demand for skilled labor has been going up faster, and faster, and faster.

It used to be, for example, that in lots and lots of companies, there were middle-level managers who collected information from a sales force and they wrote reports, and then they essentially handed those reports up to the chain to other managers who read the reports. There were lots of people in organizations whose job was to file shipping invoices, and accounts receivable things, and deal with payroll checks, and inventory, and all the nuts and bolts. Those people had managers and departments, and there was a whole hierarchy of them.

But a manager who is skilled in the use of information and communications technology can now essentially compile that kind of information and oversee a lot of those processes without all those middle managers, without all those people. If you want to look over a sales force, for example, you don't have to have someone go and collect all the information from the people in the sales force and write you up a thick report. All you need to do is hit the computer and the good computer software will spit out for you a graph, trend lines, whatever you want to see about what happened for all those salesmen that you're overseeing. You don't need the middle managers to look at that stuff anymore.

So, the result of these changes in technology has been much higher productivity for this group of highly skilled, highly placed workers. Conversely, at the other end of the wage scale, many lower-skilled jobs, like being a file clerk, have largely disappeared. I worked my way through college in the late '70s and early '80s in the summers by working as someone in a company who put things in files and put the files in drawers. I somehow don't think they have four people doing that job anymore.

In short, the demand for high-skilled labor increased faster than the supply. The productivity of high-skilled workers was able to go way up, and it drove up the wages for that high-skilled labor. This theory also suggests that, in the future, inequality could swing back in the other direction, as more and more people get accustomed to computer and information technology, and as it becomes more widespread and widely used across the economy.

The main cause of the rise in inequality is technology, but there are some other causes, too. Another underlying cause often mentioned is the increase in foreign trade, which is sometimes called globalization. U.S. workers are having to compete more directly with workers for other countries like Mexico, and China, and India, where wages can be much lower.

Now, U.S. workers are far more productive than workers in those countries. They're more educated; they have more physical capital; they're working in an economy with better infrastructure and usually better management. So U.S. workers are worth much more pay, but still, competing with people in low-wage economies can have some impact. By some estimates, some economic studies, maybe one-fifth or so of the growth in inequality is due to the pressure of globalization on wages. But this is a little bit controversial because some people would say, "What is globalization?" Globalization is really new technology as well. It's reaching around the world with the Internet and with different connections to be able to manage all of those enterprises all around the world.

Yet another cause of inequality is institutions in the U.S. labor market. We've seen a number of changes in recent decades that have tended to add to inequality, two in particular. One is minimum wages. Minimum wages were higher in the 1960s and 1970s than they are today, adjusted for inflation. For example, if you look at the minimum wage in 1981, it was $3.35 an hour. But if you adjust for inflation since then, it would be about $7 an hour in 2005. The actual minimum wage in 2005 is $5.15 an hour. So the minimum wage hasn't grown relative to inflation to keep up with what's happened in the rest of the economy.

Now, again, I'm not saying here that the first thing we ought to do is raise the minimum wage to $7 an hour, or $10, or $12 an hour. As we talked about in earlier lectures, if you push a minimum wage too high, you can discourage hiring. But it is it true that historically, the minimum wage has had the effect of pushing up wages for workers at the bottom of the wage distribution.

Another important labor market institution, the second cause here, is unions. Back in the early 1950s, about one-third of the U.S. workforce belonged to a union. By the mid-2000s, about 13 percent of all U.S. workers are in a union. If you leave out public sector unions, the teachers' unions, only about eight percent of private sector workers are in a union. Now, again, I don't mean this to be an unconditional endorsement of more unions. Unions are complicated; as we talked about before, they can work for better or worse. But it is true that unions have historically tended to encourage a more equal distribution of income. So the weakness of unions tends to lead to a greater level of inequality.

It's also true that if you look at household incomes, those have become more unequal because of changes in family patterns, specifically, the rise in single-parent families and the rise of high-earner couples marrying each other. The proportion of families with a single parent and children has gone up over time. In 1968, about 10 percent of all children lived in a household with a mother and no father. By 1996, 23 percent of all children lived in a household with a mother and no father. It stayed at that level—dipped a little bit—into the mid-2000s.

It's now more common also to have two high-income earners marry each other—a man and woman, both doctors or both lawyers, marry and then they both continue to work. The pattern in the old gender-segregated workplace was that the high-earning spouse—usually the man—would marry a woman with a lower earning path. The lawyer would marry a secretary; the doctor would marry a nurse, and often, the woman would then drop out of the labor force. So, this process of high-income earners marrying each other has tended to push up the inequality that we observe among households.

What public policies are available to reduce inequality? Well, one obvious choice would be high taxes on the rich. If we tax the rich a lot, we can certainly reduce their incomes and diminish inequality in that way. But it's interesting: the share of federal taxes paid by those with high incomes is actually relatively high, by the standards of recent decades, in the early 2000s. Let me cite you some numbers from a Congressional Budget Office study. If you look at the top quintile of earners, back in 1980, those folks paid 56.3 percent of all federal taxes. Of all federal taxes, I mean to include not only income tax, but payroll taxes for Social Security and Medicare, excise taxes; even the corporate income tax is attributed back to people in the economy. In this calculation, we're looking at all the federal taxes and who pays them.

In 1980, the top quintile of income paid 56.3 percent of all the taxes. By 1990, that was up a little bit, to 57.9 percent of all taxes. By 1995, the top quintile was paying 61.9 percent of all federal taxes. By 2000, the top quintile was paying 66.7 percent of all federal taxes. Then it dropped off a little bit by 2002, after the tax cuts in 2001, and it was 64.8 percent of all taxes were paid by the top 20 percent at that point. If you look at just the top five percent, the top five percent of the income distribution was paying 37.3 percent of all federal taxes, as of 2002.

Now, I'm not against the rich paying more, but it's a fair point to say that, compared to, say, the 1980s in the Reagan years, they are paying more. They are paying a larger share of federal taxes. Again, one might argue, "Well, it should be still higher," and that's a fair enough argument, but it wouldn't be right to say that they're paying a historically low share of taxes. It's also worth remembering that not all of the rich folks in this top quintile are multi-millionaires. Remember, the top 20 percent kicks in with families with an income of about $100,000 a year. That's obviously good money, but it's not millionaire level.

So when we think about whether or not we should tax the rich more, what we really need to carry in our minds is that that might be a good idea, but compared to the standard of the last few decades, we actually are taxing those with high incomes at a relatively high level, in the sense that they're paying a fairly large share of the existing federal taxes.

The question of whether to push even harder, and have the rich pay an even larger share of federal taxes, essentially takes us back to Henry Simon's statement about whether you find the current proportions unlovely or not. Some people say, "I just can't believe that we don't have the rich pay more taxes." And some say, "Well, that percentage looks about right."

What if we get beyond taxes, and try and think about alternative methods for reducing inequality? If we got away from the tax side, we could look at the government spending side. For example, we could think about increasing government spending in a way that especially benefited those with low- and middle-level incomes. Distributing more money to the poor, in whatever form, will reduce inequality. But, as we talked about in the previous lecture, there are going to be some important issues here about the effect of such redistributions on incentives to work, and on whether such redistributions are a band-aid that really doesn't address the underlying social problems of, perhaps, bad education levels of families that are not passing along good skills to their kids.

One proposal has been to dramatically expand the earned income tax credit that we talked about in the previous lecture. Basically, the idea would be that, if someone is working full time then we should make sure they earn a decent wage. We won't force firms to pay more by raising the minimum wage a whole lot because we don't want to create a situation where we're discouraging firms from hiring these folks. But, for example, let's say that you've got a relatively low-wage job; you're making $8 an hour. So you're working 2,000 hours a year, which works out to $16,000 a year. Could we expand the earned income tax credit by enough so that you would make $24,000 a year, the equivalent of $12 an hour instead?

A really aggressive plan like that could be extremely costly. It might cost ten of billions of dollars, depending on how it was structured. But a plan like that could also be a powerful reward for working that might really pay large social dividends, in terms of family stability and reductions in certain kinds of social problems.

Also, government spending doesn't have to be a direct cash payment to families that are poor in order to have a disproportionate effect of helping folks with lower incomes. You can imagine, for example, expanded spending on public schools or on school lunches. In cities where geography favors it, you could think about expanding mass transit, which tends to be ridden more by families with lower incomes. You could imagine better public safety protection, more police in low-income areas. You could imagine more resources committed to public areas, spaces like libraries, parks, schools—maybe having schools open in the evenings—community centers, even things like making post offices into safe places, where you could have automatic teller machines. All those kinds of steps wouldn't distribute income directly to those with low and middle incomes, but they would expand the safeness and the security of public spaces and public resources, which those folks could then rely on.

Yet another way of reducing inequality would be to strengthen the labor market institutions that lead to more equal wages. For example, pass laws that would make it somewhat easier for workers to vote to join a union. Right now, there are these big disputes between management and labor. The laws could be changed in a way that would make it a little bit easier to join a union. Or you could raise the minimum wage, at least a little bit. Again, I'm not saying that these steps—more unions, higher minimum wage—are without trade-offs or costs. But if your specific goal is to reduce inequality—if that's the goal you have in mind—then those steps probably would help that goal. Of course, another thing that would probably help reduce inequality would be to aggressively fight against the remaining elements of racial, ethnic, and gender discrimination, wherever they're occurring in the economy.

The final step toward assuring inequality could be reduced, and that equality could be a greater value, is to think about the ladder of opportunity that people face in U.S. society. For example, if we could assure that each child born in the United States gets a fair start in life—and by a fair start, I mean things including, but not limited to, good education, decent healthcare, decent nutrition—then I think that much of the concern over inequality would be somewhat diminished. Of course, almost everyone, in theory, is in favor of good education, and good healthcare, and good nutrition for children, but there are difficult issues about how to do it, and what the cost might be, and what the potential interference would be with parents and families.

In this world we live in, the chances are that we aren't ever going to have exactly identical, equal opportunities for all people out there in the economy. For one thing, some children are just going to have better parents than others—better, more involved parents who read more stories and take them more places. And, at the end of the day, that's going to be a very tough difference for any social policy to overcome. But it's also true that part of the American Dream, part of the American ethos, is that everyone should have a good, solid chance of success, and that those who go through a public school education, and who work full time, and do their best with the hand they're dealt, that all of those people should have a good chance at a reasonable, successful middle-class kind of life. If we could work on the ladder of opportunity, and make sure it really existed for everyone, then, my guess is that concerns over inequality would be quite a bit diminished.

Lecture Seventeen
Imperfect Information and Insurance

Scope:

Imperfect information can raise havoc with markets. A simple example is when a firm misleads consumers. More subtle questions arise in figuring out how much to pay a worker when information about job performance is imperfect or how much to charge for auto insurance when information about the risks of auto accident is imperfect. Imperfect information typically raises two issues: the problem of *moral hazard*, in which those with better information try to take advantage of those with worse information, and the problem of *adverse selection*, which is that high risks will eagerly buy insurance while low risks may not buy it; this is a problem if the seller of insurance has imperfect information about who is a high and a low risk. The ongoing arguments over the provision of health insurance in the United States are fundamentally issues of moral hazard, adverse selection, and imperfect information.

Outline

I. The standard example of a market, with a willing buyer and willing seller, presumes that each party makes a voluntary trade because each knows what he or she is getting. However, the real world is full of situations of imperfect information, which can create real problems for markets.

   A. Would you buy a used car that was only about one-third of the price you would have expected it to be? Or would you reason that there must be something wrong with such a good deal and steer clear? The economic argument is to buy what's cheapest. But when you don't have complete information about the quality of the car, you may hesitate.

   B. Similar problems arise in labor and capital markets. For example, imagine a business trying to judge the quality of potential workers. A worker who is willing to work for much less may be a low-quality worker; thus, businesses may be unwilling to hire those who are willing to work for less pay.

   C. Markets have a variety of methods for attempting to reduce the problem of information.

1. Warrantees, guarantees, and service contracts can reduce the risk of imperfect information in the goods market.
2. Licenses and certificates can reduce the risk of imperfect information in the labor market.
3. In financial capital markets, requiring disclosure of financial records and history, along with collateral and cosigners, can reduce the risk of imperfect information.
4. Reputation can reduce the risk of imperfect information if economic interactions are repeated.

D. When government sets rules for disclosing information on the ingredients of products or the financial records of companies or when government requires that claims made in advertising be supported, it is seeking to ameliorate the problem of imperfect information.

II. Insurance markets rely on information: Sellers must estimate the risk that buyers will be involved in an event—such as an accident—that requires compensation. But information about who will suffer what events can be quite imperfect, and insurance markets often break down as a result.

A. An insurance market spreads risk over a group.
1. An undesirable event will happen to certain members of a group. The risk of the event happening is known, but exactly who will suffer is not known.
2. In this situation, everyone in the group can pay into a common pool of funds, which is then used to compensate those who suffer the negative event.
3. A fundamental rule of insurance markets is that what the average person pays into insurance over time must be very similar to what the average person gets out, with relatively minor variations caused by the investment income of the insurance company and the costs of running the system.

B. The payouts that insurance companies make are often concentrated on a relatively small share of large claims.

C. But now, consider what happens if the chance of a bad event happening is not randomly distributed. Instead, people's risk is determined to some extent by the actions that they take, and people know their own level of risk better than an insurance company ever can.

   1. *Moral hazard* is the problem that insurance markets face when the fact that people have insurance leads them to take fewer steps to avoid or prevent accidents in the first place.

   2. *Adverse selection* is the problem that insurance markets face when those who are especially likely to have an accident are more likely to buy insurance, while those who aren't likely won't find insurance a good deal—and the insurance company has only imperfect information about who is in which group.

D. Insurance plans try to address moral hazard and adverse selection in various ways: using copayments and deductibles and finding ways to pool many people of different risks together (such as through an employer).

   1. One method to reduce moral hazard is to require the injured party to pay a share of the costs, which is done through deductibles, copayments, and coinsurance.

   2. If insurance plans can draw upon a large pool of customers, then they can worry less about adverse selection, because a large pool is more likely to have a large number of low-risk participants to offset those who represent high risks.

E. Health insurance is a vivid example of an industry plagued by information problems of moral hazard and adverse selection. Other industrialized nations have addressed these problems with nationalized systems, but this has often brought problems of its own. The challenge is to build a system in which competitive forces push for better and cheaper health care, while minimizing the incentives to provide low-quality service to patients.

International Comparisons of Health-Care Spending in 2002

Country	Health-care spending per person	Health-care spending as a share of GDP
United States	$5,274	14.6%
Canada	$2,222	9.6%
France	$2,348	9.7%
Germany	$2,631	10.9%
Japan	$2,476	7.9%
United Kingdom	$2,031	7.7%

Source: World Health Organization, *World Health Report 2005*

Essential Reading:

Richard Zeckhauser, "Insurance," in *The Concise Encyclopedia of Economics*, www.econlib.org/library/Enc/Insurance.html.

"Health-Care Finance: The Health of Nations," *The Economist*, July 15, 2004.

Supplementary Reading:

Congressional Budget Office, *Federal Terrorism Reinsurance: An Update*, January 2005, www.cbo.gov.

Questions to Consider:

1. Can you think of a market transaction you would be willing to make—a good or service you would be willing to buy—if only you had better information about the quality you would receive of that good or service?

2. The federal government provides flood insurance in certain areas. Using the ideas of adverse selection and moral hazard, explain why private insurance markets may be unwilling to provide flood insurance to all.

Lecture Seventeen—Transcript
Imperfect Information and Insurance

With this lecture, we have one more shift in emphasis. The last two lectures have talked about difficulties that arise in labor markets, with poverty and inequality. The next two lectures are going to shift to difficulties markets face because of information problems, risk, and uncertainty. The standard example of a market, with a willing buyer and a willing seller, presumes that each party makes a voluntary trade because they know what they're getting. However, the real world is full of situations of imperfect information, where you don't quite know what you're getting, and that can create real problems for how markets function. To understand the problem, it may be useful to pose a series of economic situations and ask what you would do in each one.

First situation: imagine you're shopping for a used car, but you're basically clueless about what happens inside a car's engine. You have imperfect information. Now, sure, you do what you can, you read a magazine like *Consumer Reports*, you check some websites, maybe you even hire a mechanic to check out the car you're thinking about buying; but you still can't be sure. So you're out shopping. You find two used cars that are the make and model you wanted to get. These two cars look just about the same to you, and one costs just about what you expected to pay; the other one costs one-third as much. So which car do you buy? Do you buy the one that was what you were expecting it to cost, or do you buy the really, really cheap one? Think for a second about your choice.

Well, in a world of perfect information, your information says the two cars are equal. Buy the cheaper car; you're getting a great deal. In a world of imperfect information, you have to think to yourself, maybe that very, very low price is telling you something. Maybe that really, really low price means the low-priced car is a lemon the seller is trying to unload because it breaks down all the time, and no one wants to get it.

Now, my point here is that, because of imperfect information, your choice is not a simple one. You might decide to buy the higher-priced car, just saying, "Well, that's about what I was expecting; that makes sense to me." You might buy the cheap car and say, "Well, it's cheap and I'm just going to hope for the best." You might not buy a car at all. If you gripe and say, "Well, I'm not sure about buying this cheap car," the seller is likely to be really peeved. The seller will say, "Well, that's a great car. What do you mean? What, you think there's problems? What's the problem?" The difficulty is that imperfect information complicates the market, and it might even make the trade between buyer and seller impossible, if you can't be reassured about the quality of what you're getting or if you can't agree with the seller about the quality.

Now, similar problems arise in labor and capital markets. So here's a second situation. Imagine you're in charge of hiring at a certain company. Somebody applies for a job, and there's a line on the job application where it says "expected salary." That person names a salary that is half what you thought you might have to pay for that job, 50 percent less. Now, you can collect information about this worker. You can collect a résumé; you can collect references and all that sort of stuff. But at the end of the day, there's a certain degree of uncertainty. You have imperfect information about what sort of a worker that would really be.

So, if you're in that position, should you go ahead and hire that worker, who's offering to work for half of what you expected to pay? Well, you might. You might say, "Well, this is such a great deal, I just can't pass it up." You might also say, "There's a reason this person is offering to work for half pay. It either means they don't know what the heck is going on in this job, or it means that there's something really wrong with them, and they're a low-quality worker in one way or another. By offering to work for half pay, they're sort of saying to me, 'I'm not going to be a real reliable worker or a very high-quality worker.'" You just can't know for sure. Again, an element of risk and uncertainty has entered the picture because of imperfect information.

Third example: imagine you're in charge of making loans at a bank, and somebody applies for a loan and says, "I really, really want this loan. I want it so much I'll pay you 10 percent a year more interest than you usually charge. I really want the loan." Now, you can collect financial information and business information about this borrower, but at the end of the day, how would you feel about loaning to someone who offers to pay a really, really high interest rate? Maybe you'd say, "Well, that sounds like a good deal. Okay, here's the money." But you might also say, "Boy, it sounds to me like this person is kind of desperate. It sounds like they might be really high risk and they know it. It sounds like, maybe, they're the sort of person who's likely to not repay the loan at all, in which case, the high interest rate isn't going to do me any good." Again, risk and uncertainty has entered the picture because of imperfect information, thus complicating the idea of making a deal between buyer and seller.

Markets have a variety of methods for attempting to reduce this problem of imperfect information. Let me give you some of the examples. When you buy a good, for example, it might have a warranty that for a certain period of time, it will be fixed or repaired. There might be certain guarantees about how it won't break down. You might be able to buy a service contract, which says that if anything happens in the first 12 months, or 24 months, or 36 months, it would be fixed up somehow. All of those are ways of reassuring you that, even though you have imperfect information, you're not going to actually be taken advantage of.

Another thing is trademarks. We talked about intellectual property and trademarks in an earlier lecture. That helps to identify who made the product and whether or not you trust that company. There might be certain trademarks of clothing, or of electronics, or of cars that you think, "Well, if they made it, it's likely to be pretty good."

In the labor market, there are things like résumés and references to help reduce the problem of imperfect information. There are also licenses and certificates for a lot of different jobs. Some of the professional workers who have to hold a license are teachers, nurses, engineers, accountants, and lawyers. In fact, most states require a license to work in the following jobs: a barber, an embalmer, a dietician, a massage therapist, a hearing aide dealer, a counselor, an insurance agent, and a real estate broker. There are also some jobs that require only a license in one state. For example, in my own home state of Minnesota, there's a requirement for a state license if you're going to be a field archeologist. The neighboring state, North Dakota, has a state license for anyone who sells fishing bait for fishing bait retailers. In Louisiana, you need a state license to be a stress analyst—whatever that is. California requires a state license to be a furniture upholsterer. Now, you can laugh a little bit about some of those licenses, but they do give some assurance of quality, that the person has at least passed some sort of screening, and that could make you more comfortable about hiring that person or letting that person do a certain kind of work.

In the financial capital market, there are also ways of reducing imperfect information. For example, before you give a loan, you do a financial records check and a credit check on whoever's borrowing. You can require a cosigner—that is, someone else who promises to repay if the original borrower doesn't. You can require putting up collateral—that is, pledging something of value that will be sold to repay the loan if you don't. In a house loan, the collateral is your house. In a small business, maybe it's a piece of equipment that the business owns.

Another way of thinking about imperfect information being reduced is through reputation. If you're in a business where reputation matters, and repeat business or repeat interaction matters, your reputation can serve as a way of reducing the level of imperfect information. If a restaurant wants you back, that restaurant needs to build up a reputation. If you have a certain reputation in your industry or at your firm, that can help you get jobs other places.

In many markets—not all markets, but many markets—these kinds of mechanisms provide enough information so that the market can work fairly well. But in other cases, there's an argument for the government entering the picture, to set certain kinds of rules for what information will be available.

For example, the government sets rules for disclosing information, like on the side of packages, all the ingredient of products need to be listed in order of the quantity in which they're used. There are also rules about disclosing the financial records of companies and having them audited by independent auditors. Now, those sorts of rules may not always be followed; they may not always be perfect; but they do tell you that the government views it as important enough to have certain information out there, that it's going to be required that the information be out there.

In fact, the government also gets into questions about advertising. It requires that, if a firm makes a claim in advertising, that claim has to be supported. It has to actually be something of a true claim. That sort of regulation is, again, seeking to ameliorate the problem of imperfect information. Let me give you some classic cases of misleading advertising.

One classic case from the 1950s occurred when Colgate-Palmolive created a television ad that claimed to show Rapid Shave shaving cream being spread on sandpaper and then the sand was shaved off the sandpaper—shaving cream that was so good, you could take the sand off sandpaper. But what the TV ad actually showed was that they had some Plexiglas, they sprinkled sand on it—no glue, just sprinkled the sand on top—and then they scraped the sand off with the razor. So that ad had to be pulled.

In the 1960s, in magazine ads for Campbell's vegetable soup, the company was having problems getting a nice, pretty, appetizing picture of the soup because all the vegetables kept sinking to the bottom, so it just sort of looked like soup with no vegetables inside. So they filled up a bowl with marbles and poured the soup over the top, so the vegetables sat on top of the marbles, and it looked like the bowl was just crammed with vegetables. Again, prosecuted; not legal to do that.

In the late 1980s, Volvo filmed a TV ad, and it showed a monster truck driving over cars, and it was crunching their roofs—crunch, crunch—until it got to the Volvo, which did not crush. However, the Federal Trade Commission investigated this ad and they found that, in making the ad, the roof of the Volvo in the advertisement had been reinforced with an extra steel framework, while the roof supports on all the other car brands had actually been cut. It wasn't exactly a fair comparison.

Even in the last few years, the Wonder Bread company ran TV ads featuring some guy identified as Professor Wonder. He said that because Wonder Bread contained extra calcium, it would help children's minds work better and improve their memory. Now, that claim was disputed, the government objected, and in 2002, the company agreed to stop running those ads.

Of course, it's easy to point out cases where companies have been deceptive in their accounting records these last few years, with the frauds at Enron and many other large companies. I'll talk about those issues a little bit in the next lecture. My point here isn't that these rules are perfect or that they catch all the problems—they clearly don't catch all the problems. My point is that a decent level of information is necessary if markets are to work well. So thinking about how that information is provided is really crucial.

In many markets, but not all of them, some combination of this reputation, and guarantees, and licenses, and collateral, and all those kinds of things, reduces the risk of imperfect information by enough, so the market can work pretty well. But there is at least one set of really important markets in the economy, where imperfect information creates extraordinary problems that are really very difficult to resolve, and they deserve special attention in this lecture. I'm speaking of markets for insurance.

Insurance markets rely on information. The sellers of insurance have to estimate the risk that buyers will be involved in some event—like an accident—that requires compensation. But the information about who will suffer what events is really quite imperfect and, as a result, insurance markets can completely break down. When I talk about insurance markets, I'm explicitly talking about health insurance, auto insurance, property insurance, life insurance, as well as social insurance, like Social Security, unemployment insurance, workers' compensation, government-provided flood insurance. All these kinds of insurance markets face the same sort of difficulties because of the problem of imperfect information.

Let's start off here by talking about how insurance markets work, and then illustrate how the problems of imperfect information arise. At the basic level, how does insurance work? We know that an undesirable event is going to happen to certain members of a group. Let's say that the risk of the event happening is known, but what we don't know is exactly who is going to suffer from the event. We know, for example, what proportion of people in a certain age group are going to die, but we don't know exactly which ones. We know roughly how many people are going to have a car accident, but we don't know exactly which ones.

In this situation, everyone in the group can pay into a common pool of funds, and then the common pool of funds is used to compensate those who suffer whatever the negative event is. To make all this a little more concrete, let's use the example of a market for car insurance. Let's suppose that there's a group of 1,000 drivers—of course, it's more like 10,000 or 100,000, but let's keep the numbers simple—and you could divide that group of 1,000 statistically into four groups. Nine hundred of the 1,000 don't have any accidents in a year. Fifty of the people have only a few door dings or chipped paint, really tiny little accidents that cost $100 each. Thirty of the drivers have medium-sized accidents that cost an average of $1,000 each in damages. Twenty of the drivers have really big accidents that cost an average of $15,000 apiece in damages. Now, let's say that at the beginning of the year, there's some way of identifying which drivers are low risk, high risk, or medium risk. That assumption is obviously unrealistic because of imperfect information. We'll come back to it later. But for right now, let's assume that we don't know.

What's the total loss that the company is going to face in a year? What are the total damages incurred by the car accidents for this group of 1,000 drivers? If you multiply it all out, it will be $335,000, so that's the 50 drivers having $100 accidents, 30 drivers having $1,000 accidents, and 20 drivers having $15,000 accidents. Multiply it out, add it up, and you get $335,000. So, if each of the 1,000 drivers paid an insurance premium of $335 each year, then the insurance company would collect the $335,000 that it needs to cover the cost of all the accidents that are going to happen.

In reality, of course, insurance is more complicated than this in at least two key ways—probably more than two key ways. One way is that the insurance company has costs of running the company, so it can't just collect the money and hand it out. There are some additional costs there. Also, the insurance company can take the money it's received—the premium it's received—and invest them for a time before it needs to pay them out in damages. So the insurance company can get some extra revenue from the rate of return on investing that money before it needs to be paid out. However, in an average year, the costs of the company—the cost of running and administering the company—and the investment returns more or less balance each other out. So this basic example, that the money is paid into a pool and then it's paid out again, actually comes pretty close to capturing the intuition of what really goes on in insurance markets.

That description of insurance markets implies a fundamental rule, which is worth remembering whenever somebody talks about insurance. The fundamental rule is that, what an average person pays into insurance over time must be very similar to what the average person gets out of insurance over time. You're not going to have a situation where the average person pays in a little, but the average person gets out a lot. They have to match up with each other. Now, of course, there are going to be some variations caused by the investment income of the insurance company—because they can invest the premiums for a time—and the costs of running the system. But year in, year out, it has to be true that what goes in is very similar to what comes out.

It's also true that the payouts that insurance companies make are typically concentrated on a relatively small share of the people who have very large claims. In the example I just gave, it was going to be true that of the total of $335,000 in losses, $300,000 of that, almost all of it, occurred for the 20 people out of 1,000 who suffered major accidents. So at the end of a given year, those 20 people are protected, but a lot of other people are going to feel like they paid money into the system and didn't get very much back.

Similarly, for health insurance, in any given year, it's going to be true that a relatively small proportion of people who get very, very sick and need to be hospitalized for an extended period of time are going to account for a large share of costs. So year in, year out, most people are going to be paying into health insurance without getting very much back. It's when you get very, very sick that it makes a huge difference to you.

The same is true for property insurance. The U.S. government has something called The National Climactic Data Center, and it found that, over the 23 years from 1980 up to 2002, the U.S. experienced 54 weather-related disasters that caused at least $1 billion in damages. For example, tropical storm Allison caused $5 billion in damages in Texas, and Louisiana, and other states in June 2001. Major forest fires caused $2 billion in damage across 11 western states in the summer of 2002.

So again, if you're someone buying property insurance, most years, you're going to pay, and pay, and pay, and nothing all that terrible is going to happen to you. But every now and then, there will be a forest fire, there will be a hurricane, there will be a true disaster and, at that point, all the money flows toward that disaster.

Now, up until this point, our whole example has been based on the idea that, of those people getting insured, the chance of the bad event happening to those people was randomly distributed, so they could all just be pooled together. But what happens if the chance of people having that bad event is not randomly distributed? Indeed, people's risk of bad things happening to them is often determined, at least to some extent, by the actions that they take. Moreover, people know what actions they take. They know something about their own level of risk, and they know it better than an insurance company can ever know it, no matter how thorough the information the insurance company tries to collect. There's a problem of imperfect information here. The insurance company doesn't know what the information is that the people have about who is high risk and who is not. So several problems arise as a result.

The first big problem is called moral hazard. Moral hazard is the problem that insurance markets face because the fact that people have insurance leads people to take fewer steps to avoid or prevent the bad event from happening in the first place. For example, people who have fire insurance have something of a less incentive to prevent fires. People who have medical insurance have less incentive to care about the costs of the medical tests and procedures that they receive. They have a little bit less incentive to take steps that might change their diet or their exercise habits in a way that would result in lower medical costs. They even have less incentive to become very informed about what medical care is likely to be extremely helpful, or moderately helpful, or maybe only has a small chance of being helpful. Doctors in a health insurance system, have less incentive to hold down costs or not to order tests. If you have Social Security—a form of insurance—you have less incentive to save money for your own retirement because, after all, Social Security is out there. The result of people having less incentive to act in a way that would cause them to avoid bad events is that the size of the losses is bigger for everyone, the size of the costs is bigger for everyone, and insurance costs more, on average, than it otherwise would.

Now, this term moral hazard can be a little bit confusing. In some cases, like outright insurance fraud, it really is a moral issue. But more often, we're not really talking about a moral issue here. We're just talking about a change in incentives. If you're protected against a negative outcome, you have less incentive to try and avoid that outcome from happening. So things that are insured against tend to have bigger losses as a result because of moral hazard.

The other big issue with every insurance market is the problem of adverse selection. Adverse selection is the problem that insurance markets face because those who are especially likely to have the bad event, like those who are especially likely to have a car accident, are often more likely to end up with insurance, while those who are very low risks, and aren't likely to have an accident, won't think that insurance is a very good deal because, after all, they know they're a good risk, and they know they're not very likely to need the insurance.

The insurance company has only imperfect information about who's likely to be high risk and who's likely to be low risk. So it's going to be hard for the insurance company to figure out how to charge different prices to these different groups. If the insurance company just sets the price of the insurance at the average loss, then everyone who knows they're safer than average will tend to say, "Well, this really isn't worth it to me," or they'll take the minimum possible insurance coverage. Also, on the other side, those who have great risk are going to load up on insurance because they know it's going to be a really good deal for them. So the average insurance price will tend to attract people who have losses more than people with low losses. The insurance company will soon find that the average is losing all the low risks and they need to keep raising the price of the insurance higher, and higher, and higher. As they do that, low risks are going to keep dropping out because it's not worth it to them, and even high risks will drop out because the insurance ends up costing so much. Because of adverse selection, insurance turns into a game that isn't about spreading risk across a population; it's about the insurance company trying to select safe risks, and exclude all the unsafe risks, and make money from that selection process.

Insurance plans have a variety of ways of trying to address moral hazard and adverse selection. One way to address moral hazard, for example, is to require the injured party to pay a share of the costs. You can do this through deductibles, and co-payments, and co-insurance. A deductible is an amount that the insurance policyholder has to pay out of their own pocket before the insurance coverage kicks in. For example, with auto insurance, you might say the insurance company only pays if the loss is greater than $500.

Health insurance policies often have a co-payment in which the policyholder must pay a small amount. For example, in the health insurance policy I have, you need to pay $20 each time you have a doctor visit, and then the insurance company usually covers most of the rest.

Another method of cost sharing is co-insurance. Co-insurance means that the insurance company covers a certain percentage of the cost, like say, the insurance might pay for 80 percent of the costs of repairing a home after a fire, and the homeowner would pay for the other 20 percent.

One classic study of health insurance found that, when one group of patients had modest co-payments, like $20 for a doctor visit, and another group didn't, those who had the co-payments got one-third less healthcare. However, the health status of the two groups was actually exactly the same. So the co-payments were discouraging care, but they didn't seem to be affecting the health of the people involved.

This fits with some other estimates in the health economics literature that maybe one-third of all healthcare spending is largely precautionary in the sense that it doesn't provide any direct, measurable medical benefit. Now, of course, some precaution is good, and I wouldn't say we should get rid of precaution, but in a situation with moral hazard, where people have no reason to back off from any tests or anything that might possibly help them, the precautions can get a little bit crazy, too.

Another thing insurance plans can do: if they can draw upon a large pool of customers, then they don't have to worry as much about adverse selection because a really large pool of customers is more likely to have a large number of low-risk participants, which can offset the people with high risks. In health insurance, for example, the common way of getting a big pool of participants is using employers. If everyone in a certain employer is signed up, then the assumption is that will include some low and high risks, and the company doesn't have to worry as much about adverse selection. In car insurance, there are laws in almost every state that everyone has to get car insurance. So low risk can't drop out of the car insurance market; they're required by law to get car insurance. That helps reduce the problem of adverse selection and those people selecting out.

In many countries, you get a large pool for health insurance by nationalizing the industry. Absolutely everyone is inside the health insurance industry in those countries. In fact, health insurance is a vivid, vivid example of an industry that is just plagued by the information problems of moral hazard and adverse selection. All the other industrialized nations of the world, other than the United States, have said essentially, "The problems of imperfect information in healthcare are so severe that a private market in health insurance just isn't going to work." So, those nations have essentially said, "We're going to get rid of the moral hazard problem in which people demand more and more care by having some sort of government controls over what can be provided, how much is going to be spent, how soon people are going to get certain kinds of care. We'll get rid of the adverse selection problem by having the whole country in the insurance pool."

How does that work out if you've got the whole country in the insurance pool? Well, as you perhaps well know, the United States spends a lot more on healthcare than other countries do. Here's some data from the World Health Organization: as of 2002, U.S. healthcare spending was about $5,274 per person, which includes all government health care programs and all private health care spending. If you look at other countries like Canada, France, Germany, Japan, and the United Kingdom, healthcare spending in those countries was between $2,000–$2,600 a person. So it was half or less of the U.S. level on a per-person basis. If you look at healthcare spending as a share of GDP, healthcare spending in the U.S. was 14.6 percent of GDP. If you look at Canada, France, and Germany, healthcare spending was nine to 11 percent of GDP. If you look at Japan and the United Kingdom, healthcare spending in those two countries was roughly eight percent of GDP.

So the United States is spending extraordinarily more on healthcare. Now, of course, we're getting something for that healthcare spending. If you are an insured person in the United States, you get extremely good healthcare. Many of the healthcare innovations come out of the United States, whether it's pharmaceuticals or whether it's equipment because, after all, those are things which are rewarded by the U.S. health insurance system. They're not rewarded by the systems in other countries. But still, at the end of the day, you have to ask yourself: is spending literally double worth it? Is the U.S. really getting enough of a payoff from that, especially given that 40 million people in the country don't have any health insurance at all?

In other countries, they've decided that the problems of adverse selection and moral hazard are so great that they need to nationalize health insurance. I'm not sure if that's quite the right answer—and many of those countries are moving toward more incentives—but it shows you how powerful the problems of imperfect information can be.

Lecture Eighteen
Corporate and Political Governance

Scope:

Large corporations are typically headed by a chief executive officer, who reports to a board of directors, who are elected by shareholders. Economists call this situation a *separation of ownership* (the shareholders) *and control* (the chief executive officer). Democratic governments are headed by an elected official, who reports to a group of voters. For similar reasons, shareholders may have a hard time constraining the actions of top managers and voters may have a hard time constraining the actions of politicians. Thus, some skepticism is warranted about whether firms will seek profits and efficient production and whether politicians will act in the best interests of society.

Outline

I. Issues of political and corporate governance can be analyzed with the analytical structure of what economists call a *principal-agent problem*. In a political context, citizens are the principals and politicians are their agents. In the corporate context, shareholders are the principals and top executives are their agents.

   A. In a principal-agent problem, one party, the *principal*, wants another party, the *agent*, to do something. The relationship between an employer and an employee is a common example of a principal-agent problem.

   B. Principal-agent problems typically involve imperfect information. The principal often has a hard time knowing whether the agent is working hard or efficiently or producing a high quality of output.

   C. The principal-agent problem in corporate and political governance involves many principals—either voters or shareholders—and few agents. In this situation, the principals face a free rider problem: Their individual efforts to monitor the agent is likely to make little difference, and they would all prefer that someone else take on the time and costs of monitoring the agent. As a result, the agent—that is, the politician or corporate manager—may end up not being monitored very much at all.

II. Large firms have a separation of ownership and control; that is, they are owned by shareholders but controlled by their top managers. What or who will monitor and constrain the managers?

    A. In a classic 1932 book, *The Modern Corporation and Private Property*, Adolf Berle and Gardiner Means identified an immense gap between ownership and control.

    B. Executives at top companies do have a variety of parties watching them.

        1. Shareholders elect a board of directors, who hire and fire top executives. However, the top executives often decide who will be running for the available slots on the board of directors.

        2. Publicly owned firms are required to be audited and to report public financial statements. However, in recent years, some auditors haven't been as aggressive in questioning financial arrangements as shareholders might have liked.

        3. Large outside investors, such as those who invest large mutual funds or pension funds, have some incentive to monitor top executives because they have a large enough ownership share to give them some power.

        4. The financial community, including stock market analysts who give advice to financial investors, banks that make loans to firms, and even journalists who write for the business press, all have some power to monitor top executives.

    C. Corporate takeovers and mergers can be a way for financial markets to discipline top management. But sometimes, they also provide a way for existing management to build their own empires.

    D. Stock options for top executives are touted as a way of aligning the incentives of top executives and their shareholders.

        1. Stock options succeeded in getting top executives to hold a lot of stock.

2. Stock options also cost quite a lot and provide some incentives for imprudent management.

E. The Sarbanes-Oxley Act of 2002 imposes a number of new rules on the institutions of corporate governance, including boards of directors, auditors, and stock market analysts, along with a new government accounting oversight board. But it remains uncertain how much difference the new rules will actually make.

III. Many of the difficulties in markets identified in the preceding lectures, including monopoly; negative externalities of pollution, poverty, and welfare; imperfect information; and others, have suggested a possible role for government to act in a way that might improve social welfare. But government is a complex organization of elected and appointed officials, and such organizations may not always be focused on the greatest good for the greatest number.

A. In the simple theory of democracy, voters monitor elected officials. But many people don't vote, and a strictly rational person may decide that his or her vote doesn't much matter.

B. *Special-interest groups* are groups that are numerically small but quite well organized. A focused special-interest group can pressure legislators to enact public policies that benefit the group at the expense of the broader population.

C. When legislators are negotiating over whether to support a piece of legislation, a common request is to include *pork-barrel spending*, which is defined as legislation that benefits mainly a single political district. *Log-rolling* occurs when two or more politicians agree to each support provisions that are especially important to the other, with the result that many bills important to individual legislators but perhaps not important to the broad social welfare become law.

D. When multiple choices exist, the majority vote can have a hard time choosing the best outcome, and the eventual choice may depend on the order in which the choices are presented.

E. In the private sector, a firm that fails to satisfy customers will go out of business. But government has no equivalent mechanism to provide incentives for good performance.

IV. Economic wisdom requires understanding several seemingly contradictory factors at the same time. Markets are useful but imperfect—and so is government.

   A. Markets are extraordinarily useful institutions through which society can allocate its scarce resources.

   B. Markets may sometimes produce unwanted results: monopoly, negative externalities, inequality, and more.

   C. Governments can sometimes act to reduce the problems of markets, but government failures can also sometimes make matters worse.

Essential Reading:

Lucien Bebchuk and Jesse Fried, "Pay Without Performance: The Unfulfilled Promise of Executive Compensation," *Milken Institute Review*, 2nd quarter 2005, pp. 75–89, www.milkeninstitute.org.

Jane W. Shaw, "Public Choice Theory," in *The Concise Encyclopedia of Economics*, www/econlib.org/library/Enc/PublicChoiceTheory.html.

Supplementary Reading:

Robert Gibbons, "Incentives in Organizations," *Journal of Economic Perspectives*, Fall 1998, pp. 115–132.

Questions to Consider:

1. Explain in your own words what checks and balances can limit the discretion of corporate managers to enrich themselves and, instead, to act in the best interests of their shareholders. How might these checks and balances break down?

2. Explain in your own words how checks and balances might encourage politicians to focus on the broad public good, rather than just on their own reelection. How might these checks and balances break down?

Lecture Eighteen—Transcript
Corporate and Political Governance

Some people trust corporate leaders in the private sector, but distrust the government. Some people trust political leaders in the government, but they distrust firms in the private sector. Economists say that everyone responds to incentives, or the lack of them, and economists don't trust anyone.

After all, we all know that sometimes, business leaders are instrumental in creating companies that provide high-quality goods and services at a great price and great jobs for employees, and sometimes politicians really do look to the public interest with far-sighted legislation. But other times, business leaders run their companies into the ground while they personally get rich. Sometimes, political leaders may seek to extend their own term in office, or raise their own salaries, or respond to the loudest special interest group.

These observations raise the issue of governance. How are organizations governed? What set of incentives are leaders of organizations responding to? The issues of political and corporate governance can be analyzed with the analytical structure of what economists call a principal-agent problem. In a political context, citizens are the principals and politicians are the agents, or in theory, at least, acting in the interest of the citizens. In a corporate context, the shareholders in the company are the principals and the top executives are the agents, who are supposed to be acting on behalf of the shareholders.

In general terms, in any principal-agent problem, one party—the principal—wants another party—the agent—to do something. The relationship between an employer and an employee is a common example of a principal-agent problem as well. What makes principal-agent problems interesting is that they all typically involve imperfect information. The principal has a hard time knowing whether the agent is working hard, or efficiently, or acting in their best interest; or if they're really doing the best they could to produce the right kind of output and a high quality of output. Thus, a common problem for principal-agent problems in the employment context is how to set pay.

For example, if all the output that someone makes is perfectly observable by both principal and agent, then you can just agree that you'll just pay for what's produced. But most of the time, output is not perfectly observable. Think of jobs like being one research scientist in a laboratory or one cash register operator in a McDonald's restaurant. What's your personal output? Was the output of high quality or not? What happens if certain circumstances let one worker produce a lot of output by blind luck, and maybe someone else worked just as hard, but they didn't produce as much just because of bad luck? How do you determine what rate of pay is appropriate for those different cases?

Well, typically, you try and put together some sort of a pay package, where the worker gets a certain amount; the worker could get more if everything went really well, but there's some subjectivity about whether things have gone well that needs to be hammered out.

Another problem arises for principal-agent problems in political governance and in corporate governance. In both cases, there are a lot of principals. There are either a lot of voters, who are the principals for the politicians, or a lot of shareholders, who are the principals for the corporate executives. In that situation, the principals face a free-rider problem, in the sense we talked about before. For any individual, their effort to monitor the agent is not likely to make a heck of a lot of difference. All the principals would prefer that someone else take the time, and cost, and energy of monitoring their agent, monitoring the politician, or monitoring the corporate executive. As a result, the agent—the politician or the corporate manager—may end up not being monitored very much at all. Principal-agent problems are never perfectly solved. You just need to find ways to try and reduce the conflict between principal and agent to some sort of manageable level.

Now, holding that principal-agent concept in mind, let's now talk about issues of governance. We'll first talk about problems of corporate governance, where shareholders are trying to get corporate executives to act in their interest. Then we'll talk about political governance, where voters are trying to get politicians to look after their interests.

Large firms have what economists call a separation of ownership and control. That is, a large firm is owned by a shareholder, but controlled by the top managers. So in that situation, what or who is going to monitor and constrain the managers, and force them to act? This problem has been around for a long time. It first came up, I think, in a classic 1932 book, called *The Modern Corporation and Private Property*, by two economists named Adolf Berle and Gardiner Means. They talked about this gap between ownership and control.

When megacompanies first came into real prominence in the U.S. economy in the late 19th century, they were often more or less run by individuals, like Andrew Carnegie, or John Rockefeller, or J. P. Morgan. But the early decades of the 20th century began to see more and more companies that were publicly owned. By publicly owned, I mean they were owned by thousands or millions of somewhat anonymous shareholders.

How are those who own the company in that way—those anonymous shareholders—to manage those who ran it day to day? How were the principals supposed to give incentives to the agents? In a way, if the principals lack power to control the agents, the agents lack any incentive to act in a way that will benefit the principals.

Now, let's flash-forward to the present. Perhaps the classic case in recent years is what happened at Enron. On December 31, 2000, stock in Enron—a company that bought and sold natural gas and electricity, among other goods—was selling for $83 a share. That stock price had risen 87 percent in 2000; 56 percent in 1999; and 37 percent in 1998. It was on a roll. Enron was rated the most innovative large company in America by *Fortune* magazine's survey of the most admired companies, for all of its Internet-based markets and all these strategies with long-term contracts. But by December 2, 2001, less than one year later, Enron had filed for bankruptcy, and a bunch of legal investigations had been started into the accusations that some of the firm's financial records were highly misleading, or even fraudulent.

So how does a company go from being a role model—most admired in the country—to having its top executives threatened with jail in less than a year? What safeguards were supposed to be in place, but failed to happen? Well, executives at top companies are supposed to have a variety of parties watching them. One, of course, is the individual shareholders, but I argued a moment ago that most individual shareholders are a very small scale. They really lack the power and the incentive to spend a lot of time and energy trying to monitor top executives.

So who is going to monitor those top executives? Well, shareholders elect a board of directors, and the board of directors are the ones who directly hire and fire the top executives. The problem is that often, the top executives are the ones who decide who will be running for the available slots on the board of directors. So the top executives are hired and fired by the directors, who are elected by the shareholders, but often those who are on the board of directors are handpicked by the top executives in the first place. So the independence of the board of directors can be questioned. Often, there's this fear that there's a case among top executives from different companies of, "Well, you be on my board; I'll be on your board. Wash my back, I'll wash your back." While there have been more independent board members in recent years than there used to be, those interpersonal relationships can still be fairly cushy in a way that it's not clear who is monitoring whom.

It's also true that being a board member is a part-time job. It consists of a few big meetings a year, where information for those meetings and the agenda for those meetings are often provided by the top executives of the company in the first place. So an aggressive board of directors can provide some oversight, but there are limits on what it can do. It's not a second level of management.

Publicly owned firms are also required to be audited and to report public financial statements. However, in recent years, it seems clear that some auditors have not been as aggressive in questioning financial arrangements as the shareholders might have liked. Auditors are a firm that's hired to go over the financial records of a company and certify that everything looks reasonable. But the auditor works for the firm, is paid by the firm, and can make suggestions about financial and business strategies to the firm. At the same time, it's supposed to be monitoring the firm. It's not clear exactly how this is supposed to work.

Clearly, a number of accountants got what I think of as the tax lawyer mentality. Tax lawyers think up ways to beat the tax code. In fact, some people say tax lawyers are the only lawyers who really make their money by figuring out how to avoid the law. It seems to me that a lot of accountants got a view that they needed to deliver certain profit numbers, regardless of the underlying reality. The auditors for Enron were the Arthur Andersen company. In 2000, Andersen earned $52 million in fees from Enron, which might have created a certain incentive not to risk offending top management at the company.

Another possible monitor for top executives would be large outside inventors, like those who invest in large mutual funds or pension funds. They have a larger ownership share so, unlike the person who owns 100 shares of stock, they actually have some incentive to watch the owners more carefully, and to monitor them, and spend time and energy in looking after them.

But in the Enron case, the large investors didn't seem to do much either. About 60 percent of total Enron stock was owned by large investors late in 2000. If you look at October 2001, it was still true that about 60 percent of Enron's stock was owned by these large investors, many months after it had become clear that something was deeply wrong with this firm. The large investors did not react quickly, and they didn't seem to monitor very aggressively.

Who else could monitor the executives? Well, the broad financial community: the stock market analysts who give advice to financial investors; the banks that make loans to firms; the journalists who write for the business press. They all have some power to monitor top executives. For example, *Fortune* magazine ran a prominent story in March 2001, questioning what was going on at Enron. None of these watchdogs really barked in the case of Enron.

After all, the pay of stock market analysts, and to some extent, their access to information, is determined by whether they are viewed as good team players. The same is true of business journalists and bankers. You have to always ask these folks, "How ready are you to be the skunk at the garden party?" Remember, skunks don't get invited to many more garden parties.

This was particularly a problem in the late 1990s, when the stock market and Enron's stock is going way, way up. A serious act of group seduction went on at that time, and when it was all over, everyone looked up and said something like, "Well, I thought you were to be the sensible one. I thought you were doing the monitoring." In fact, nobody really seemed to be. So these other methods of monitoring executives don't seem to be all that effective.

Corporate takeovers and mergers could be another way for financial markets to discipline top management. In theory, a poorly run company that, say, is funneling a really large share of its money to top executives, could be bought out and taken over by a better-run company—and it does happen that way sometimes.

In the 1980s, there was a lot of talk about how leveraged buyouts were used as a way of buying firms—companies that borrowed a lot of money and bought up a firm. A hot new trend in corporate finance in the mid-2000s is the rise of what are called private equity firms that buy companies and run them, or perhaps break them up or restructure them before selling them. So it's certainly possible that poorly run companies could be bought and reformed.

But the reverse is also true. A poorly run company that's temporarily attracted a lot of money might also take over a smaller, well-run firm. And the well-run firm will say, "Hey, if you're going to give me that much money, I might as well take the offer." The overall record of corporate takeovers and mergers is that, on average, they're a good deal for the firm being bought, but they are an average deal, at best, for the firm that is actually doing the taking over.

Stock options for top executives were touted as another way of getting top executives to act in the interests of their shareholders. The idea was that if top executives owned a lot of stock, then they would want to act in a way that would raise the stock price. Certainly, the growth of stock options meant that top executives had a lot more stock than they did before. If you look at the top few executives and the members of the company boards, and the top 1,500 publicly traded companies in the U.S., the top executives and the boards owned, on average, about 13 percent of the total stock of those companies in 1985. But by 1995, they owned 21 percent of a comparable sample of companies.

This business, though, of expanding the use of stock options was very costly. It succeeded in getting top executives to hold a lot of stock, but it also cost a lot, and it provided some incentives for imprudent management. For example, by one count, during five years, from 1998 to 2002, the total pay to the top five executives at the top 1,500 large firms totaled $100 billion, just to those 7,500 people.

The incentives of stock options are also not altogether clear. You want to have good management. You don't just want to pay because the stock market is going up. You don't want to just have the executives do whatever will pump up the short-term stock price, possibly including something that might skate on the edge of fraud. So it's not clear that rewarding every increase in the stock price is exactly the right thing you're looking for in giving incentives to managers either.

In 2002, in the aftermath of the Enron disaster and some other companies, a law was passed called the Sarbanes-Oxley Act. It imposed a number of new rules on the institutions of corporate governance, including new rules about how to choose boards of directors; about auditors; about stock market analysts; and a new government accounting oversight board. It probably wasn't a bad idea to alter these rules, but maybe the big problem is that all of these rules need to be interpreted and enforced; and bottom line, we've got a principal-agent problem here.

It remains true that top executives of firms have strong incentives to report high profits and to take high salaries for themselves. There is still a separation of ownership and control. Many of the people who are supposed to be monitoring the top executives have strong incentives not to upset or anger the people who ultimately are supporting their career, in one way or another. Given that basic reality, it remains uncertain whether Sarbanes-Oxley is really going to make a huge difference.

As noted before, principal-agent problems are never fully resolved. The best hope, I guess, is that we're in the course toward working out some new understandings for how shareholders will monitor the executives who, in theory, are working on their behalf.

Let's now shift over to the problem of governance in government. Many of the people who are most skeptical of the inability to monitor and constrain top management actually think, "Well, let the government take over some of this stuff. Let the government set rules instead of having these top executives run wild and free." But you can't really monitor the government either.

Many of the difficulties in the market identified in the preceding lectures—like monopoly, and pollution, and poverty, and welfare, and imperfect information—have all suggested a possible role for government, to act in a way that might improve social welfare. But government is a complex organization of elected and appointed officials, and such organizations might not always be focused on the greatest good of the greatest number.

Democratic governments are supposed to be—as President Abraham Lincoln famously said in the Gettysburg Address—"of the people, by the people, and for the people." In the simple theory of democracy, voters choose and monitor elected officials; but, in fact, many people don't vote at all. In recent U.S. presidential elections, only about half of voting-age citizens actually vote. In local elections, the turnout is typically even lower.

Why don't people vote? In most elections of any size, the margin of victory is measured in hundreds, or thousands, or even millions of votes. A rational voter will recognize that one vote is not likely to make a difference. In his 1957 work called *An Economic Theory of Democracy*, economist Anthony Downs put the problem this way. He said, "It seems probable that for a great many citizens in a democracy, rational behavior excludes any investment whatever in political information per se. No matter how significant a difference between parties is revealed to the rational citizen by free information, or how uncertain he is about which party to support, he realizes his vote has almost no chance of influencing the outcome."

Or, in his classic 1948 novel, *Walden II*, psychologist B. F. Skinner put the issue even more succinctly. One of the characters in the novel says, "The chance that one man's vote will decide the issue in a national election is less than the chance that he will be killed on his way to the polls." Rational people don't risk death in order to vote. Now, you can say, "Well, what about all these close elections? I remember this state was close in this election." It still wasn't one vote. One vote wasn't making the difference.

How do we get people to vote more? There are lots of proposals: keep the polls open for more hours; move election day to a weekend, when people don't have to worry about their jobs or their school commitments. And in general, we've been moving in that direction for a long time now, for decades, making it easier and easier to vote;

and at the same time, the voting rate has been falling, and falling, and falling. Casting an informed vote is always going to impose some costs of time and energy, and it's just not clear that rational people in a fairly stable country are going to do that.

If the majority isn't always going to make its wishes felt, who will? What's going to happen in the political process? Well, special interest groups are groups that are numerically small, but quite well organized. A focused special interest group could pressure legislators to enact public policies that benefit the group at the expense of the broader population.

For example, imagine an environmental rule to reduce some kind of air pollution. Let's say that it will cost 10 large companies $8 million each to comply with this rule; so the total cost is $80 million. Let's say the social benefits from this rule would benefit each person in the United States by $10. So, the benefits are $10 times a population of 280 million Americans equals be $2.8 trillion. The benefits are far, far higher than the costs, but who's going to lobby for this law? The 10 companies that have to pay the $8 million are likely to lobby much more fiercely than the other person is to argue for $10 worth of benefits.

Special interests don't just block things, like environmental legislation; they also get things passed that aren't such a good idea either. Special interests are often the ones who call for price controls, or subsidies, or tax breaks, or shutting out competing imports, or setting up regulations that especially favor them. When legislators are negotiating over whether to support a piece of legislation, a common request is for them to include pork-barrel spending. Pork-barrel spending is defined as legislation that benefits mainly a single political district. Pork-barrel spending can be thought of as yet another case where democracy is challenged by the problem where benefits are concentrated and costs are widely dispersed. The benefits of pork-barrel spending are obvious and direct to local voters; the costs are spread out over the country.

For example, U.S. Senator Robert C. Byrd of West Virginia—who was originally elected to the Senate back in 1958, and was still serving into the 2000s—is regarded as one of the great modern masters of pork-barrel politics. Here's a list of structures in West Virginia, at least partly funded by the government and named after

Byrd: the Robert C. Byrd Highway; the Robert C. Byrd Lock & Dam; the Robert C. Byrd Institute; the Robert C. Byrd Lifelong Learning Center; the Robert C. Byrd Honors Scholarship Program; the Robert C. Byrd Green Bank Telescope; the Robert C. Byrd Institute for Advanced Flexible Manufacturing; the Robert C. Byrd Federal Courthouse; the Robert C. Byrd Health Sciences Center; the Robert C. Byrd Academic and Technology Center; the Robert C. Byrd United Technical Center; the Robert C. Byrd Federal Building; the Robert C. Byrd Drive; the Robert C. Byrd Hilltop Office Complex; the Robert C. Byrd Library; the Robert C. Byrd Learning Resource Center; the Robert C. Byrd Rural Health Center.

Now, maybe every single one of those is completely well justified, but at least some of them smell like pork. Pork-barrel spending can also be encouraged by what's called log-rolling on the part of politicians. Log-rolling happens when two politicians agree to each support the provisions that are important to the other one, with the result that many bills that are important to individual legislators, but perhaps not important to broad social welfare, become law. Rather than just one legislator using government funds to build a new bridge or hospital, if 51 percent of the legislators come together, they can pass a bill that includes a pork-barrel project for every one of their districts. Some research has suggested that support for the U.S. government's defense budget is encouraged by spreading out military bases and spending on weapons programs to congressional districts across the country.

Another problem that is faced in monitoring politicians is that when multiple choices exist, majority vote can have a hard time choosing the best outcome, and the eventual choice might depend on the order in which the choices are presented. Consider this situation: there's a state where 60 percent of the population is liberal and 40 percent is conservative. So if there's two candidates, one liberal, one conservative, the liberal's going to win. But what if it's a three-way race, with two liberal candidates and only one conservative candidate? Maybe the liberal vote will split and victory will go to the minority party, in which case the outcome does not reflect the majority's preferences.

Think about the French national elections of 2002, for an interesting example. Before the election, the two leading candidates were expected to be Jacques Chirac and Lionel Jospin. But the French elections happen in two rounds. There's a preliminary round, which reduces the list of candidates to the top two, and then a runoff between those top two. In the preliminary round, the votes splintered. Chirac got 19 percent of the vote and Jospin got 16 percent. However, a candidate named Jean-Marie Le Pen received 17 percent of the vote, and snuck into second place; the other 48 percent of the vote was split between 13 other candidates. Jean-Marie Le Pen has been frequently criticized for extreme nationalist views that have sometimes crossed the line into intolerance and even racism. In the run-off, all of the other candidates united behind Chirac, who beat Le Pen by 82 percent to 18 percent. Now, it's possible that Jospin would have beaten Chirac in the run-off, but the voting was so splintered in the preliminary round that he never got the chance.

This is a general problem whenever support is splintered. Will the best two options make it to the final round; or did an option that was everybody's second-best choice and no one's first-best choice get eliminated too early?

A final difficultly for government is that there's no exit for government. When a firm produces a product nobody wants to buy, or produces at a higher cost than its competitors, the firm will suffer losses. If it can't change its ways, the firm goes out of business. This might be hard for workers or local economies for that firm, but it also puts a lot of pressure on firms for good governance.

But what if a government program isn't working? Who puts the government program out of business? What if a government agency provides bad service? Who competes it away? If you're upset, for example, that the Internal Revenue Service is slow in sending you a tax refund or isn't able to answer your questions, you can't say, "Well, I'll pay my income taxes through some different organization." There's no mechanism within government to allow exit and entry of better producers.

Now, where does all this take us? What I've been arguing is that there's a long list of reasons why what happens politically may not reflect the will of the majority, and may not reflect the broader self-interest. I don't want to take this overboard; I don't want to say that this means we should get rid of democracy. A classic line from the British statesman Sir Winston Churchill is: "No one pretends democracy is perfect or all wise. Indeed, it has been said that democracy is the worst form of government except for all of the other forms, which have been tried from time to time."

In that spirit, the theme of my discussion is certainly not that democratic government should be abandoned. My point is: a practical student of public policy needs to realize that democratic government is not ruled by all-wise economists. Hot breaking news here: government is political. It's a set of agents with voters and citizens trying somehow to exercise direction and control, but not always succeeding. So when we talk about the problems of markets and the possibility of government action, you need to take into account the problem of political governance. You need to realize that even well-intended government actions could make problems worse, rather than better.

We're drawing to the end of our microeconomics lectures, here, and I want to try and pull together a few big things. Economic wisdom really requires understanding several seemingly contradictory things at the same time. The American author, F. Scott Fitzgerald once wrote, "The trust test of a first-rate mind is the ability to hold two contradictory ideas at the same time." Well, at this point in your study of microeconomics, I want you to go one better than Fitzgerald and I want you to hold three somewhat contradictory ideas about the characteristics of markets in your mind, all at the same time.

The first idea: markets are extraordinarily useful institutions, through which society can allocate its scarce resources. They provide incentives for efficient production, for innovation, for the wise use of resources, for providing products that consumers want, and for increasing the standard of living over time. Markets are extraordinarily powerful and useful.

The second idea: markets may sometimes produce unwanted results. Unwanted results that we've talked about in these lectures include: monopoly; issues of imperfect competition; negative externalities like pollution; positive externalities in public goods, like research and development issues; problems with poverty; inequality of income; discrimination; failures to provide insurance; and all sorts of problems of runaway top executives. So markets are not, in any way, perfect.

The third idea: government can sometimes act to reduce the problems of markets, and government failure can also sometimes make matters worse. Governments can have a useful role to play in addressing the problems of markets; but government action is also imperfect.

The challenge here is to stay pragmatic. Be specific about the problem that the market is having. Be specific about the solution. Be realistic about what government is actually doing. Face the trade-offs and the risks openly. When you act like that, when you think like that, you're thinking like an economist.

Lecture Nineteen
Macroeconomics and GDP

Scope:

With this lecture, the focus shifts from microeconomics to macroeconomics; that is, instead of discussing issues involving market behavior of consumers, workers, and investors, the emphasis will turn to overall aspects of the economy. It is useful to think of macroeconomics as involving four policy goals and two main tools. The four goals are economic growth, low unemployment, low inflation, and sustainable trade deficits. The tools are federal budget policy and the monetary policies conducted by the Federal Reserve. Several different ways of measuring GDP are explained; these are useful not only in their own right, but also because they represent alternative ways of thinking about the economy.

Outline

I. The study of introductory economics is typically divided into microeconomics and macroeconomics, and this section inaugurates the macroeconomics section of this course.

   A. Macroeconomics is the aggregated top-down view of the economy, focused on such issues as unemployment, inflation, economic growth, and the balance of trade.

   B. A macroeconomic perspective isn't just a bigger version of microeconomics.

   1. Microeconomics discusses what happens in individual markets, but it has no language for talking about overall problems of the economy, such as growth, inflation, unemployment, and trade deficits.

   2. Behavior that is rational for individuals leads to unexpected conclusions when everyone in a group acts in that way, so that the logic of individual behavior in microeconomics can lead to unexpected outcomes at the macroeconomic level.

II. Gross domestic product (GDP) is the standard measure for the size of a nation's macroeconomy.

A. *Gross domestic product* is defined as the total value of final goods and services produced in an economy in a year.

B. GDP can be measured in different ways, either according to the value of what is produced or according to the value of what is demanded. Because the quantity supplied in an economy must equal the quantity demanded, these measures must be equal.

1. One way to measure GDP is to count up what is produced in the economy, which is typically divided into durable goods, nondurable goods, services, and structures.

Measuring GDP by What Is Produced (2004 data)

	In trillions of dollars	Share of total GDP
Durable goods	$ 1.7 trillion	14.5%
Nondurable goods	$ 2.1 trillion	17.9%
Services	$ 6.7 trillion	57.3%
Structures	$ 1.2 trillion	10.3%
TOTAL GDP	$ 11.7 trillion	100%

Source: U.S. Bureau of Economic Analysis

2. GDP can also be measured from the demand side and divided up into what is demanded for consumption, investment, and trade.

$$C + I + G + X - M = GDP$$

Measuring GDP by Sources of Demand

	In dollars	Share of GDP
Consumption	$8.2 trillion	70.1%
Investment	$1.9 trillion	16.2%
Government	$2.2 trillion	18.8%
Exports	$1.2 trillion	10.2%
Imports	$1.8 trillion	15.4%
TOTAL GDP	$11.7 trillion	100%

Source: U.S. Bureau of Economic Analysis

3. U.S. GDP statistics are measured by a branch of the U.S. Department of Commerce called the Bureau of Economic Analysis.

C. Per capita GDP refers to dividing GDP by the population. Looking at real GDP per capita is a simple, rough way of comparing standards of living across times and places.

D. To economists, the word *real* means "adjusted for inflation." Thus, a change in real GDP between two years is adjusted for inflation so that only the underlying change in the actual size of the economy is captured.

III. GDP has its share of conceptual imperfections, like all economic statistics, but it remains a useful measure of macroeconomic activity.

A. Many factors that affect human well-being are not directly included in GDP: "home production," leisure, the environment, health, and the presence of poverty or inequality.

B. GDP measures *final product*, which includes the production of intermediate products and avoids a risk of double-counting.

C. Transfers of ownership do not show up in GDP, unless they involve new production. When an existing item, such as a house or a used car, is bought or sold or when a share of stock is bought and sold, the transaction does not show up in GDP.

D. Even with these concerns, GDP remains a useful measure, in part because societies with higher per capita GDP do tend to be better off in a number of dimensions, including personal consumption, clean air and water, and personal security.

IV. The historical pattern of GDP shows a long-term upward trend over time, but with occasional short-term dips for recessions.

A. From a long-term perspective, GDP increases substantially over time. After adjusting for inflation, GDP in the mid-2000s was 5.5 times as large as in 1950.

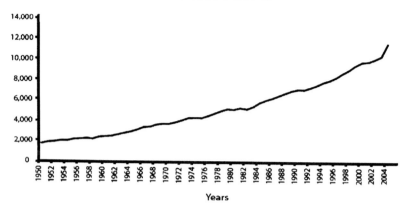

Real GDP (1950-2004)

Years

GDP in billions (chained 2000 dollars)

B. GDP also shows short-term fluctuations when recessions happen.

C. The starting and ending points of recessions are defined by a committee of academic economists at a nonprofit research institution called the National Bureau of Economic Research.

V. Macroeconomic policy can be summarized with four goals and two main sets of tools for accomplishing those goals.

   A. Four goals for macroeconomic analysis are economic growth, low unemployment, low inflation, and a sustainable balance of trade.

   B. The two main sets of tools for macroeconomic policy are fiscal policy and monetary policy.

   C. The basic macroeconomic model for describing the relationships and tradeoffs among the four goals and how the two main sets of policies can affect those goals is the *aggregate supply-aggregate demand model*.

Essential Reading:

Joseph A. Ritter, "Feeding the National Accounts," in *Review: Federal Reserve Bank of St. Louis*, 2000, pp. 11–20.

U.S. Department of Commerce, Bureau of Economic Analysis, *National Economic Accounts: Gross Domestic Product*, bea.gov/bea/dn/home/gdp.htm.

Supplementary Reading:

Katharine Abraham and Christopher Mackie, eds., *Beyond the Market: Designing Non-Market Accounts for the United States*, www.nap.edu.

National Bureau of Economic Research, *Information on Recessions and Recoveries, the NBER Business Cycle Dating Committee, and Related Topics*, nber.org/cycles/main.html.

Questions to Consider:

1. Make a list of considerations that might be important to public well-being but are not directly included in GDP.

2. In your own idea of what makes society better off, how much weight would you give to growth of the GDP?

Lecture Nineteen—Transcript
Macroeconomics and GDP

The study of introductory economics is typically divided into microeconomics and macroeconomics. This lecture inaugurates the macroeconomics section of this course.

What is macroeconomics? Well, we talked about it way back in Lecture 1, but maybe it's worth repeating. Macroeconomics is the aggregated top-down view of the economy, focused on issues like unemployment, inflation, economic growth, and the balance of trade. It may help to think of it in contrast to the microeconomic view presented earlier. Instead of thinking about how individuals react, and the incentives for firms, and competition, we're instead going to think about the whole economy as one large organism.

A macroeconomics perspective is not just a scaled-up version of microeconomics. Remember, microeconomics discusses what happens in individual markets; but microeconomics has no real language for talking about overall problems of the economy, like growth, and inflation, and unemployment, and trade deficits. For example, microeconomics can say, "Why does the equilibrium quantity grow for a certain good or service?" in terms of shifts in demand and supply. But it can't say, "Why does equilibrium quantity grow for the entire economy?" Microeconomics can say why the price rises or falls for a certain good, but it doesn't explain why all prices might rise together in a process of inflation.

Microeconomics can explain why the export of a certain good or the import of a certain good, rises or falls, but not why an overall imbalance in trade exists. Moreover, microeconomics has no structure for really talking about macroeconomic policies. What about the federal budget and budget deficits? What about the Federal Reserve and how it manipulates interest rates in the U.S. economy? What about national boundaries and issues involving international trade? All of those are topics we need to talk about as we work through macroeconomics.

In fact, behavior which is rational for individuals at the microeconomic level can sometimes lead to unexpected conclusions when everyone in a group acts that way. So you have to be really careful before taking the logic of individual behavior in microeconomics and using it to try and explain outcomes at the macroeconomic level. Let me give you a couple of examples of what I mean.

First, a non-economic example: imagine you're in a stadium and you're watching a concert or something where you're in a big crowd. You feel like you can't see well, so one person stands up for a better view, then others stand up, and eventually everyone is standing up. Now, everyone acted rationally from a microeconomic—an individual—point of view; that is, everyone stood up to see better. But the end macroeconomic result was that no one saw any better than they had before, if they'd all been sitting down. There's a possibility that the microeconomic behavior that made sense combined to produce an unexpected and undesired macroeconomic outcome.

Or imagine that you're a farmer and you want to make more money, so you decide to plant a lot more crops. That's a sensible, microeconomic approach. But what if all farmers want to make more money, and they all plant more crops? Supply of that crop expands dramatically; the price declines as a result, so that even when all the farmers are selling more output, everyone ends up making less money than they did before. Again, this raises the possibility that microeconomic behavior could combine to produce unexpected and undesired macroeconomic results.

What's our starting point for thinking about macroeconomics? Let's start with the basic idea of gross domestic product, which is the standard measure for the size of a nation's macroeconomy. Specifically, gross domestic product is defined as the total value of final goods and services produced in an economy in a year, usually. A lot of other economic issues and terms start off from this idea of gross domestic product—or GDP, as it's often called—as a basic concept.

I should mention in passing that there are some other ways of measuring the size of an economy too, like gross national product, GNP, or net national product, NNP. For practical purposes, it actually doesn't matter a heck of a lot which one you choose, as long as you don't jump back and forth between different definitions. But GDP is the standard, and it's the one I'll stick to.

GDP can be measured in different ways. It can be measured either according to the value of what is produced or according to the value of what is demanded and bought. Since the quantity supplied in the whole economy must equal the quantity demanded in the whole economy, these measures have to be equal to each other. One way to measure GDP is to count up what's produced in the economy. At a broad level, this is typically divided into the production of durable goods, the production of non-durable goods, the production of services, and the production of structures. The specific numbers here are going to change year to year and, personally, I always need to look up the specific data, but let me give you numbers for an illustrative year.

For 2004, the total GDP of the United States was $11.7 trillion. Divided up into the categories I just mentioned, 14.5 percent of that was durable goods, stuff like refrigerators and cars; 17.9 percent of it was non-durable goods, stuff like food and clothing; 57.3 percent of it was services; and 10.3 percent of it was structures.

What's interesting about this pattern is that many people, when they think about the economy, the first thing that leaps to mind is durable goods, stuff like cars and refrigerators, hard stuff that comes out of factories. But the non-durable goods, like food and clothing, are actually a bigger share of the economy than durable goods, and services—like healthcare, education, financial, legal, haircuts, car repair, lawn or home-cleaning services, childcare—are well over half of all U.S. output. You hear people say sometimes that we live in a service economy and this is literally true. The share of services in the U.S. economy has been expanding over decades. Well over half of GDP is now services, and it's probably heading higher still in the future.

You can also measure GDP from the demand side. Instead of measuring what's produced, you measure what is demanded for different purposes: what's demand by consumers; what's demand by business for investment; what's demanded by government; what's demanded for purposes of international trade. Let me give you the breakdown in those dimensions. Of course, it still has to be the same size of GDP. So GDP in 2004 was $11.7 trillion—just the same as if you measured it in terms of what was actually produced.

If you break that down into categories, first is going to be consumption. Consumption is the biggest demand category of GDP. It accounts for about 70 percent of the total.

Investment spending by business is much smaller. Investment spending is about 16 percent of GDP, but it tends to be much more volatile. Consumption spending tends to be about 70 percent of GDP, year in, year out. But when firms think it's a good time to invest or not a good time to invest, they tend to move in bunches: they all invest together or they all decide not to invest. So, even though investment spending is smaller, it tends to lead the fluctuations of the economy.

Government spending, government demand for goods and services, is about 19 percent of GDP. That may seem a little bit low if you recognize that federal, state, and local governments together collect about one-third of GDP in taxes in the United States. But remember here, we're just talking about government actually buying stuff directly—government demand for final goods and services. So all the government programs that take money and pass it along to citizens—like Social Security or welfare programs—show up as part of consumption. They don't show up in government spending.

The final categories of spending are exports and imports. Exports are demand from other countries for what is produced in the United States. That's a demand for something produced in the United States. We add that to total demand for the U.S. goods and services, but we need to subtract off imports. After all, imports are U.S. demand going to products made abroad. In recent years, imports have been a lot bigger than exports. That means the U.S. has a trade deficit, a subject we'll take up in depth a few lectures further down the road.

So quick shorthand here: if you ask an economist what GDP is, sometimes they'll say it's C plus I plus G plus X minus M. That is, consumption, plus investment, plus government spending, plus exports, minus imports. That's a working definition of gross domestic product.

Who actually measures this stuff? Who measures all these goods and services, and what's produced and what's demanded. All across the U.S. economy, it takes 14 digits to measure it in dollars? In the U.S., the statistical agency is a branch of the U.S. Department of

Commerce, called the Bureau of Economic Analysis. The BEA collects data from all sorts of surveys and sources—some of them are monthly; some of them are quarterly; some of them are annual. Often, the government statisticians need to extrapolate and make sure everything comes together somehow. What they do each quarter is an advanced estimate, right after the quarter has ended, of what they think GDP is during that quarter; then what's called a preliminary estimate; then a final estimate. If you look in the newspapers, you'll see sometimes that there could be large changes from the final estimate back to the preliminary estimate.

Also, every five years, the BEA goes back and reviews all the numbers and changes that it's made over that time, and sometimes, changes them quite substantially. So in some cases, our view of the economy and how it has proceeded is altered quite a lot, five years after the fact.

There's an old joke that there are two things that are hard to swallow after you've watched them being made: sausages and economic estimates. But still, I think the folks at the BEA do a creditable, professional job. Perhaps most important of all, there's a certain discipline of time. If they make a mistake, they tend to figure it out as time goes on; then over time, it gets adjusted.

I should also mention that the BEA has a really nice website. It answers lots of basic questions about GDP; it gives up-to-date data and historical data broken down in lots of different ways. If you want to learn more, that's a good place to start.

So we've got GDP. What do we look at next? Usually the next adjustment to make is per-capita GDP. That refers to dividing GDP by the population. Per-capita GDP is a nice simple, rough way of comparing the standard of living at different places and times. If we divide the U.S. economy in 2004 with the GDP of $11.7 trillion, and we divide that by the population of 294 million that will equal approximately $40,000 per person. So U.S. per-capita GDP in 2004 was about $40,000 a person.

Per-capita GDP is especially useful in comparing situations where population is really, really different. That could be two countries or two different time periods in one country. For example, the U.S., in 1900, had a population of 76 million, which is about one-quarter of the population early in the 21st century. So if you're comparing economic output a century ago and now, you really need to adjust for population, and look at per-capita GDP.

Per-capita GDP can also be really useful in comparing countries with large population to countries with less population. Let me give you an extreme example. China's economy has a GDP of about $1.3 trillion early in the 21st century. Belgium, on the other hand, has a GDP of about $250 billion, which is about one-fifth as large. Now, China also has a population of about 1.3 billion, while Belgium has a population of 10 million. Belgium has less than one percent as many people as China does. If you look at this on a per-capita basis, according to per-capita GDP, China is a $1.3 trillion economy divided by 1.3 billion people; so the per-capita GDP is about $1,000. Belgium has a GDP of $250 billion divided by a population of 10 million, for a per-capita GDP of about $25,000. So, by size of GDP, China is five times larger; by per-capita GDP, Belgium is 25 times larger than China.

The next important adjustment to make is to think about real GDP. To economists, the word "real" just means adjusted for inflation. You may remember this usage of the term when we were talking about real interest rates. The nominal interest rate was the interest rate that was announced; then you had to subtract off the inflation rate to get the real interest rate. Essentially the same issue arises here. Say that in 2004, GDP increased 4.4 percent, nominal GDP did. Now, some of that increase is due to an actual increase in production of goods and services; some of it is just due to inflation, the price of all goods being higher. As it turns out, in 2004, 2.2 percent of the overall 4.4 percent rise in GDP was just due to prices being higher; it was just due to inflation. The other 2.2 percent was the real increase in goods and services being produced.

When you're looking back over periods of time, it's always important to look at real GDP, adjusted for inflation. For example, if you look at the 1970s, when inflation is high in the United States, it looks like GDP is growing really, really fast; but if you adjust for inflation, then the record of growth doesn't look so amazing in that decade anymore. In the inflation lecture, a couple lectures down the road, we'll discuss how to adjust and how to measure real GDP in more detail.

GDP has its share of conceptual imperfections. In fact, one of the things I'll emphasize over and over in the next few lectures is that all economic statistics have a lot of conceptual imperfections. GDP is a measure of what is bought and sold. Thus, things that affect the quality of life but aren't bought or sold won't be directly included in GDP.

The classic example is what economists call home production. Around the late 1960s and the early 1970s, there was an enormous surge of women into the paid workforce. As a result, many goods and services that had been produced at home before—and I'm thinking here of meals, house-cleaning, and childcare—were now more likely to be bought and sold in the market. When those things were produced at home, they weren't being bought and sold, so they weren't counted in GDP. When they're produced in the market, then they were counted; but clearly, that's a change that is not a real change in what happened in the economy.

There are a lot of other things that affect people's standard of living, affect their happiness, but aren't something that's measured directly as something that's bought and sold. For example, leisure. Your time off is not valued by the market in any direct way. If everyone could have 10 hours a week off or an extra two weeks of vacation every year, but output remained the same, GDP would not show any overall gain. The environment is not directly included in GDP because it's not bought and sold. Greater or lesser pollution doesn't show up in GDP measures. Stuff like traffic congestion, or the time it takes to commute, doesn't show up as something that's bought and sold, except in an indirect way like the amount of gasoline that was needed. Certain bad things, like crime or natural disaster, can lead to more economic activity. If there's a disaster and then you have to rebuild a large part of a city, that might make GDP look great, but it's a lower standard of living to have suffered through a disaster like that. Health is not directly included in GDP. The fact that people have longer life expectancies and are living healthier longer doesn't show up in any direct way; only the healthcare services show up.

Even within GDP, you might ask—if you were in a skeptical frame of mind—if everyone bought and sold really deserves the same value, even if some things might seem to have different values in your mind. For example, is a bag of potato chips the same value as an organic fresh apple? Does *Newsweek* have the same value as a pornographic magazine? Is a ticket for admission to a violent movie exactly the same value as a ticket for admission to an art museum?

GDP is just about adding everything up. It's not about value judgments. Now, I don't want to minimize these issues about the linkage between GDP and standard of living. They matter, and in some cases, they can matter a lot. I certainly don't recommend that we pursue GDP at all costs. I don't think everyone should work 60-hour weeks just so GDP could be higher, or that we should pollute the environment just so GDP should be higher; and I don't know any economists who would believe that. But it just shows you that GDP is something of a limited measure.

When I was giving you the definition of GDP, I mentioned that it was the final product. What exactly does that word "final" mean? Well, GDP includes all the production of intermediate products. One question you can ask about GDP is on this list that I gave you—durable goods, non-durable goods, services, structures. Doesn't that leave out a lot of stuff? What about the inputs? What about the steel that goes into the car, or the lumber that goes into the furniture, or the oil that goes into the gasoline? Where does that fit in somehow?

All production includes a combination of inputs that are turned into outputs. Making a car includes steel, and petrochemicals, and computer chips—all sorts of different materials—but all of these inputs are included in the final value of the car when it's sold. If I was going to add up the iron ore industry, and the steel industry, and the car industry, I would, in effect, be counting the iron multiple times: when it was first produced, then when it was in the steel, then when it was in the car. I would be double-counting or triple-counting, depending on how many stages of production it went through.

The Bureau of Economic Analysis does create some very detailed tables that show all the inputs coming in and their value, and the outputs going out; but for calculating overall what an economy produces, you only need to add up the final product, because the value of the final product includes the earlier things that were produced.

It's also true that transfers of ownership do not show up in GDP, unless they involve new production. For example, say you sell a house and I buy it. Ownership has changed of the house, but nothing new was produced, so there's no addition to GDP. Only new construction of houses or physically fixing up the old ones adds to GDP.

Or, say that you sell some shares of stock in a company and I buy some shares of stock in a company. Ownership of the stock changed, but nothing new is produced. The stockbroker's fee is included in GDP, but not the value of the stock that was bought and sold. So when the stock market rises or falls substantially, it literally has no direct effect on GDP at all. People are placing different values on shares of stock, but they're just buying and selling, and for every buyer, there's also a seller.

With all these limits, with all these concerns, and with all these worries, at the same time, I don't want to lose what's worthwhile and measurable in GDP. Societies with higher per-capita GDP tend to be better off in lots of dimensions. They have more personal consumption, and we shouldn't be snooty about personal consumption. That includes healthcare, and education, and all sorts of things that most of us value. Societies with high per-capita GDP also tend to have cleaner air and water. They tend to have a greater degree of personal security.

A wise Nobel laureate from MIT named Robert Solow, once said, "If you have to be obsessed by something, maximizing real national income is not a bad choice." Maybe it's best not to be obsessed by any one statistic, but GDP really does matter. It makes a big difference over time, and it's unwise to take these kinds of criticisms and run with them, and pretend GDP just doesn't matter.

The historical pattern of GDP shows a long-term upward trend over time with occasional short-term dips for recessions. Imagine that you looked back at the pattern of GDP over time, going back a half century or so. Let's specify that we're looking at real GDP—that is, GDP that is adjusted for inflation—so you're seeing the actual patterns of economic production. What does it look like?

From a long-term perspective, GDP increases substantially over time. After adjusting for inflation, GDP in the mid-2000s was 5.5 times as large as it was in 1950. You can see it sloping up over time. If you take a long-term perspective, that average growth rate of real GDP, from 1950 through 2004, was about 3.2 percent per year.

However, this pattern of growth in GDP is not a straight line—just 3.2 percent gained every single year. Instead, when you look at the pattern of GDP over time, you see fluctuations around this long-term trend. Sometimes, the economy is below the average trend; sometimes it's a little above. In the 20th century, for example, the biggest dip in GDP was the Great Depression, especially the period from 1931 to 1933, when the economy contracted by about one-third. Those dips are called recessions.

A recession is technically defined as a significant and lasting downturn in GDP. You sometimes hear people say, "A recession needs to be a downturn in GDP that lasts six months or more, or two quarters," but there's nothing official about that. The upward movements between recessions are sometimes called recoveries or upswings. From a long-term perspective, the upward trend in standard of living is the most obvious thing that happens with GDP. But if you're living in the middle of a recession, it's pretty obvious that that's happening too. So there's a difference there between the long-run and the short-run perspective.

The starting and ending points of recessions are not defined by any U.S. government agency, but instead, they're defined by a committee of academic economists at a non-profit research institution called the National Bureau of Economic Research. NBER, as economists call it, is affiliated with lots of researchers who hold faculty positions at colleges and universities. It helps, to some extent, to fund their research, and it organizes conferences so they can meet with others working in their area, and share ideas, and criticize each other.

The U.S. economy, according to the NBER data, had 22 recessions from 1900 up through the recession of 2001. So it had a recession, on average, about every five years. However, more recently, recessions have been somewhat more rare. There's one in the early 1980s, one in 1990–1991, and one in 2001. So it seems like they have been more like 10 years apart recently. It also seems like the recent recessions have gotten somewhat shorter. From the start of the recession to the end—what economists call the peak to the trough—in 2001's recession was eight months. It was also eight months during the recession from 1990 into 1991. But the average length of the decline in the economy—if you look at the recessions since World War II—was more like 10 months. If you look at the inter-war years—that is, that time from World War I to World War II, which, of course, includes the Great Depression—the length of recessions then was 18 months. So it seems as if the recessions are getting somewhat shorter over time, although that's not a certain conclusion.

With this idea of GDP firmly in mind, I want to give you some guidance as to how the discussion of macroeconomics is going to proceed from here. Macroeconomic policy can be summarized with four goals, a framework, and then two main sets of tools for accomplishing those goals. As you look ahead through these lectures on macroeconomics, it's probably useful to have the structure of the discussion—the roadmap—in mind.

So let's first talk about the four goals of macroeconomic analysis. The first goal is economic growth. In the long term, is the economy increasing per-capita GDP? The next goal is low unemployment. How can the economy keep unemployment low on average, year in and year out; and during recessions, how can it help unemployment from rising too high or for too long? The third goal is low inflation. How can government act in such a way as to keep inflation under control? The fourth goal is a sustainable balance of trade. Now that word "sustainable" you may recognize as a bit of a fudge word; but what exactly does the balance of trade mean and why does it matter that the U.S. is running enormous trade deficits in the mid-2000s?

With those four goals—and those will be the next four lectures—we'll then introduce a framework for macroeconomic analysis. This framework is usually called the aggregate supply/aggregate demand model. What that framework will do is, it will help to organize macroeconomic analysis in some of the same ways that basic supply and demand help to organize microeconomic analysis. But aggregate supply and aggregate demand are not just microeconomics. What they'll help us think about is: what are the trade-offs between growth, and unemployment, and inflation, and the balance of trade?

With our four goals in mind, and our framework for thinking about how these are going to trade off against each other, we'll then able to move to the two main tools of economic policy. There are two main sets of tools for macroeconomic policy. They're broadly called fiscal policy and monetary policy. Fiscal policy is defined as government tax and spending policy—the federal budget, budget deficits, and taxes, and spending. Fiscal policy is, of course, decided by Congress, but needs to be signed by the president, as well. So that will give us a chance to discuss the issue of budget deficits and what happens when spending is larger than taxes.

The other big area is monetary policy. Monetary policy refers to the policies of the Federal Reserve—we'll need to talk about what that is, of course—that affect interest rates, and credit, and how much money is being loaned and borrowed in the economy. The Federal Reserve decisions and monetary policy are decided by a central bank of political appointees, and so that will raise questions about when they should raise or lower interest rates.

Finally, with all of this in mind, we'll then expand the scope of the discussion to international issues and consider global trade: why trade can benefit economies; what the arguments are for restricting trade; issues of exchange rates; international movements of financial capital; and the evolving shape of the world economy.

Lecture Twenty
Economic Growth

Scope:

Although economic growth happens at a seemingly slow rate of a few percent a year, over periods of a generation or more, different growth rates accumulate into extremely large differences in a nation's standard of living. In the long run, the rate of economic growth is by far the most important factor in determining the average standard of living. The most straightforward way to think about economic growth is as the percentage change in the real per capita GDP. The key factors behind economic growth are increases in physical capital, human capital, and technology, taking place within a supportive market environment; these all require investing resources now for a return in the future.

Outline

I. Would you prefer to be a rich person in 1925, with access only to the technologies and lifestyle available in 1925, or to be a person with an average standard of living today, with access to all the modern technologies?

   A. The case for living as a rich person in 1925 would be that you have the best of everything at that time: house, servants, and status.

   B. The case for choosing the present is that 1925 lacked many modern technologies, from antibiotics to consumer electronics, which many people value highly in their lives.

   C. This question has no right or wrong answer, but it tends to draw out some of the reasons why people value economic growth and how much they value it.

II. The economic growth of nations compounds over time, so that small differences in annual growth rates work out to enormous differences over a generation or two.

   A. The formula is PV $(1 + g)^t$ = FV, where PV is the present value of the economy, g is the percentage growth rate, t is the number of years the growth occurs, and FV is the future size of the economy.

B. Seemingly small differences in annual growth rates make an enormous difference in a nation's standard of living over several decades.

III. How do differences in growth rates matter?

A. GDP starts at 100.

B. Given growth rate g (shown in the rows) and time t (shown in the columns), the future size of the economy F can be calculated as:

$$100(1+g)^t = F.$$

How Large Will an Economy Starting at 100 Grow Over Time?

Annual growth rate of per capita GDP	10 years	25 years	40 years
1%	110	128	149
3%	134	209	326
5%	163	339	704
8%	216	685	2172

C. The big lesson is that seemingly small differences in growth rates of a few percent per year, sustained over time, make a *huge* difference in the standard of living

D. Countries that start out at lower levels of productivity may be able to take advantage of a period of catch-up growth—which implies that over time, lower-income nations should be able to close the gap in per capita income with higher-income nations.

    1. The world economy has seen divergence between the richest and poorest economies of the world over the last century or so, not convergence.

    2. However, this divergence is largely due to the fact that the lowest-income economies have barely budged in the last century or so. Once economies do start growing, they tend to make progress more rapidly for a time.

    3. The wealth of high-income countries hasn't been built on keeping Africa poor or India poor or western China poor. Those places aren't poor because of trade or globalization; instead, their lack of trade is a sign of their lack of development.

4. If the 20th century was a time of divergence among the high-income and low-income countries, might the 21st century be a time of convergence?

E. If a nation falls far behind in per capita GDP, it can take many decades to catch up. There are no quick fixes for economic development.

F. In the long run, internally generated growth is by far the single most important factor in a nation's standard of living, far outstripping the impact of redistribution from those with high incomes to those with low incomes.

IV. What are the sources of economic growth?

A. Productivity growth, measured as real output per hour worked, is a useful measure of economic growth.

B. Productivity growth is rooted in growth in physical capital, human capital, and especially new technology, which for economists, includes all methods of reorganizing and changing production, as well as new ways of applying scientific discoveries to production.

V. The U.S. economy experienced a great productivity slowdown through the 1970s and 1980s, but it may be on the verge of a long-term productivity upswing in the late 1990s and early 2000s.

A. U.S. productivity growth often hovered near 3% per year in the 1950s and 1960s. But from the 1970s into the early 1990s, it was more often in the range of 1.5–2.0% per year.

B. Starting in the late 1990s, the U.S. economy began to see a boost in productivity, amid a lot of talk about the "new economy," built on dramatic advances in information and communications technology. But many economists wondered at the time if the change was sustainable.

C. By the mid-2000s, the productivity boost of the new economy appears to be a real phenomenon, in which new information and communications technology are boosting productivity in a wide array of jobs.

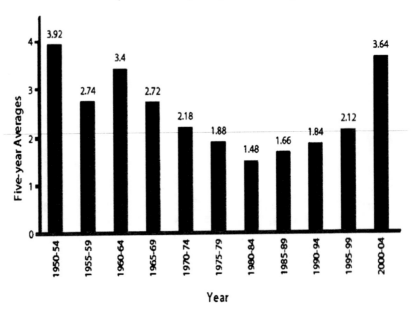

Productivity Growth in the Business Sector (Measured by Output Per Hour)

Essential Reading:

Timothy Taylor, "Thinking about a New Economy," *The Public Interest*, Spring 2001, pp. 3–19.

"American Productivity: The New 'New Economy,'" *The Economist*, September 11, 2003.

Supplementary Reading:

Council of Economic Advisers, "Chapter 6: A Pro-Growth Agenda for the Global Economy," in *Economic Report of the President*, February 2003, www.gpoaccess.gov/eop.

Questions to Consider:

1. Do you prefer the standard of living of a salary of $30,000 salary in 1925 or today? Remember, an annual salary of $30,000 would have made you a very rich person in the 1920s, but you have to live with the technology of the 1920s.

2. What are some examples of how the technological developments in information and communications technology in the last 10–15 years have changed how you live and work? Have they improved your productivity? What about the productivity of firms that you deal with in a business or personal context? Can you imagine how these technologies might produce further productivity improvements, or do you think they have already provided a large share of the benefits they will provide?

Lecture Twenty—Transcript
Economic Growth

Let's start by thinking about a choice, and listen up because you're going to need to make a decision here. I'm going to ask you about what you prefer. When asking about preferences, there's no right or wrong answer, but it can be instructive to think about why you prefer what you prefer.

So here's the choice: on one side, you could be a person with an average standard of living in the modern U.S. economy, say a member of a typical family—defined as two or more people living together—who would be earning about $55,000 per year in the mid-2000s. That's one choice. On the other side, you could have that same income, $55,000 per year living in, say, 1925. So you need to choose which standard of living you would prefer.

Before you choose too quickly, let me give you two things to take into account. Remember first of all, there's been a lot of inflation since 1925, so having an annual income of $55,000 a year in 1925 would have made you extremely rich by the standards of the time, probably far into the upper one percent of the income distribution. So in 1925, this income level means a big house, servants, and the best of everything that's available.

But here's the other kicker: if you choose 1925, you also need to live with all the technologies of 1925. That is, you need to live with the household technologies, the transportation technologies, the medical technologies, and the entertainment technologies—all the technologies of 1925.

So let me summarize your choice here: either you can be, relatively speaking, a very rich person in 1925, with access only to the technologies available in 1925; or you can be a person with an average standard of living today, with access to all the modern technologies. So, which do you prefer? Mull it over for just a moment.

When I've asked this question to various groups, it tends to be a choice of about 2-to-1 for the present. People prefer having an average standard of living in the present to being rich in 1925. Older groups, I've found, are a little more willing to choose the past; but even there, a majority tend to choose the present.

This question has no right or wrong answer, as I said at the beginning, but it tends to draw out some of the reasons that people value economic growth, and to show how much they value it. Think about the trade-offs that are involved in this choice. When I ask students this question— why they chose what they chose—they tend to focus on things like, there were no computers; there was hardly any access to recorded music. After all, in 1925, there were just a few radios, which were relatively expensive at the time. In 1925, there were no antibiotics. Travel is slow. If you want to go across the ocean to visit Europe, you're pretty much limited to a boat. You might rather have a modern dishwasher, and clothes washer, and microwave, and freezer than needing to manage a group of servants to deal with all your clothes.

Now, of course, each person will draw the line in their own way. Maybe you would be happy being a rich person in 1925, but not so happy being a rich person in 1870 or 1800. But the bottom line here is that, even when your income could be, in a relative sense, 10 times higher or more, even when you're comparing some of the richest people at certain times in our history—in our history not that long ago—the advantages of economic growth really do make a huge difference. They're really worth your consideration. They're really worthy as the first goal of macroeconomic analysis that we're going to discuss.

Let's talk about economic growth. The key thing about economic growth of nations is that it compounds over time. Small differences in annual growth rates work out to enormous differences in standard of living over a generation or two. The formula for taking the present value of an economy—looking at the growth rate, and the period of time, and figuring out the future value—is to take the present value, multiply it times one plus the growth rate of the economy, raised to the power of the number of years that you're waiting for this to happen, and that will give you the future value. That formula's just a little messy, but it's essentially the same formula we used before, when we were talking about economic growth, and we talked about rates of return. Mathematically, the process of compounding economic growth rates is exactly the same as the process of compounding growth in interest rates, which we discussed back in Lecture 7. The big lesson here is that small differences in growth can make a huge difference over time.

Let me give you some numerical examples. Let's first of all imagine that you've got an economy that is growing at one percent a year. It starts off—just to keep the calculation simple—where the GDP is 100. So GDP is 100, it's growing one percent a year. After 10 years, it would be 110—a little bit more, but not much; the compounding doesn't do much over those 10 years. Then after 25 years, one percent growth a year would be 128. After 40 years, it would be 149.

What if it were growing at three percent a year, which is more or less the average for the U.S. economy over a sustained period of the last few decades? Well, after 10 years, an economy growing at three percent a year would go from 100 to 134; after 25 years, to 209; after 40 years, to 326. In other words, over 40 years, growing at three percent a year, an economy would triple in size. So you can see the power of compounding beginning to kick in, the growth building on growth of previous years.

What if you had a growth rate of five percent a year? That's the rate the U.S. economy might have in a really good year, but many countries, like Brazil or Mexico, have rates like that on an ongoing basis for relatively long periods of time. Well, at five percent a year, our economy that starts out at 100 reaches 163 after 10 years; it reaches 339 after 25 years—so it more than triples after 25 years; and if you could sustain that for 40 years, the economy would be 704—it would increase more than sevenfold over 40 years.

Finally, let's think about an eight percent rate of economic growth. Now, eight percent is, frankly, a little bit crazy. When we talk eight percent, we're talking about the fastest periods of Japanese economic growth, back in the 1960s and '70s; we're talking China in more recent years. But let's think about it. With an eight percent rate of economic growth, in just 10 years, the economy would go from 100 to 216. So it would more than double in size in a decade. After 25 years, the economy would go from 100 to 685—it would increase almost sevenfold in 25 years, which is well within the lifespan of a person. It's even within the working life of a person. Someone who starts off working at 25, by the time they're 50, the economy's increased sevenfold. If you could sustain that eight percent rate of growth for 40 years—which no country has done, but just for the sake of the illustration—then the economy would grow from 100—at the beginning of that time—say when a person was 25—to 2,172 at the end of that period. In other words, over the course of a person's working life, from age 25 to 65, they could see the economy expand by a multiple of 22. That's an extraordinary change in standard of living.

My basic lesson here, by giving these numerical examples, is that seemingly small differences in the annual rate of growth—the difference between one percent and three percent; three percent and five percent; five percent and eight percent—it only looks like a percent or two. You might say, "Well, what's one or two percent? What difference can that make? But remember that it builds, and builds, and builds. It's one percent, or two percent, or three percent every single year; and over time, over several decades, it makes a huge difference in the standard of living. It makes all the difference. In the long run, you can argue that economic growth is literally the only thing that matters to the standard of living.

What are some examples of fast and slow growth rates over time? Well, just to give you some historical feel for what these numbers mean, if you go back to the start of the 20th century, the United Kingdom and Argentina were two of the countries with the highest per-capita GDP in the world. A century later, by the start of the 21st century, the United Kingdom was barely at average for Europe as a whole. And Argentina, if you ranked the countries of the world, ranked 80^{th,} or something like that. It wasn't even in the group of what we think of as high-income or highly developed economies.

What happened to the U.K. and Argentina? Well, it wasn't that they had one or two bad years, or even that they had a bad decade—the U.S. economy had a terrible decade in the 1930s. But what really happened was that the rate of growth for those economies was at a lower pace, and it was a sustained lower pace over a period of decades. As they more or less walked in place, or made gradual slow growth, the rest of the world surged ahead.

Japan and South Korea are another useful example. Those two countries have largely caught up to many western European nations in per-capita GDP. Japan is roughly the equivalent of some of the richer nations in western Europe. South Korea is the equivalent of some of the poorer nations in western Europe.

How did they do that? Well, it wasn't that they just woke up and over one three-year period or five-year period—Boom!—they caught up all at once. Instead, it was sustaining those 8 percent rates of growth, five, six, seven, or eight percent rates of growth for several decades, while basically healthy economies, like the United States, were growing at about a two to three percent annual rate. So that gap of five percent a year or four percent a year, makes an enormous difference when it's sustained over time.

When countries start off behind—like, say, Japan and South Korea did a century ago—can they catch up? What would it take to catch up? Well, there's an argument that countries that start off at lower levels of productivity might be able to take advantage of a period of catch-up growth. The idea of catch-up growth, as one economist famously said some years ago: there are certain advantages of backwardness, in an economic sense. One advantage of backwardness is that you can copy and use technologies that have been invented other places. You don't have to invent it all yourself. When you can do that, you can sprint ahead by relying on technologies that have been developed elsewhere. If there's catch-up growth, this implies that over time, the lower-income nations of the world should be able to close the gap in per-capita GDP with higher-income nations, gradually over time. However, this hasn't been happening in the last century or so. The world economy, since about 1870 up to the mid to early 2000s, has actually seen a divergence between the richest and poorest economies of the world, not a convergence.

Why is it that this gap has gotten bigger? What's going on with this gap? A standard historical starting point is usually about 1870, for various historical reasons in the U.S. and Germany, and for different kinds of comparisons. But here's a rough-and-ready comparison based on 1870: in 1870, if you took the richest countries in the world and you took their average per-capita GDP—countries with the highest incomes—and you looked at the poorest countries, with the lowest per-capita GDP, the ratio of the highest countries to the lowest countries was about nine to one, about nine times as high in per-capita GDP.

Now, project forward to 1960 and do the same exercise. Take the richest countries in the world—those with the highest incomes measured by per-capita GDP—those with the lowest incomes, lowest per-capita GDP. The ratio by 1960, instead of nine to one, is about thirty-eight to one. If you look at 1990, same exercise—per-capita income of the high-income countries versus per-capita income of the low-income countries—the ratio is about forty-five to one. So there seems to be divergence between high-income countries and low-income countries, rather than convergence.

Why is this? Why has this happened? In an arithmetic sense, if you look at the actual standards of living, what's going on here, is that the poorest countries in the world, in 1990 or in 2000, are essentially living at subsistence. They're living at the lowest possible level, where people are just barely getting enough to eat. If you go back to 1870, the poorest countries in the world are still living at subsistence, about the lowest possible standard of living. If you look just at the lowest countries in the world, there's been very little gain from 1870 up until the late 1990s. But if you look at the high-income countries of the world—say the United States, much of western Europe, Japan, and the like,—they've obviously grown extraordinarily since 1870. There seems to be some sort of a lesson here, that the problem is that some countries are stuck not growing at all. There is catch-up growth for countries like Japan, and South Korea, and China, once they start growing; but some countries are just stuck, and they haven't even gotten out of the starting gate yet.

In fact, at the start of the 21st century, Nobel laureate economist Robert E. Lucas of the University of Chicago wrote an article in which he described the process of long-run economic growth in this way. He says we can imagine economic growth between the countries of the world as a horserace; each country is a horse, and all the horses start off in their gates, around about 1800. Around about 1800, some countries start the process of economic growth, for example, the United Kingdom and the United States. So the gates go up, and those two horses, the United Kingdom and the United States, start running down the course, but all the other horses remain stuck in their gates. As you proceed through the 19th century, other horses leaves the gates, other countries start the process of economic growth. So Germany starts, France starts, the countries of Scandinavia start. In the 20th century, we see the starting gates go up for Japan, for east Asia; now for China; perhaps, for India. I'm not meaning for this to be an inclusive list, but to give you a sense. Now, as these latecomers start off, Lucas argued, they can experience catch-up growth by piggybacking on some of the lessons, and technology, and markets that already exist. But some countries have yet to get started at all.

The wealth of the high-income countries, that growth of the high-income countries, is really not built on keeping Africa poor, or India poor, or western China poor. Those places are not poor because they're helping make the United States rich; they're poor because they are completely detached from the world economy, and underdeveloped, and not involved in trade or globalization.

It's just hard to blame the international economy for the persistence of poverty. Globalization and the international economy have been extraordinarily helpful in lifting countries like east Asia, and Japan, and China, out of global poverty. Saying that globalization creates poverty is kind of like saying—and this doesn't make a lot of sense—exercise makes me overweight because I don't do it. If you're not participating then what you're not participating in is probably not the problem either.

But there's an interesting possibility here, as the gates have gone up for country after country, region after region. If the 20th century was a time of divergence between the high-income and the low-income countries, might the 21st century be a time of convergence? For example, the World Bank classifies all countries of the world into high income, middle income, and low income. If you look at the period from 1990 up until the early 2000s, a little bit more than a decade, real GDP in the high-income countries rose 2.5 percent a year over that time. The middle-income countries rose 3.2 percent a year, a little faster. And the low-income countries, led by China and India, rose about 4.3 percent per year. Thus, the economic gap between countries was reduced a little bit over this time.

In the process of economic growth though, it's worth remembering that those who started earlier have gotten off to a really, really big lead. As a result, the inequality between rich and poor countries, the highest and the lowest, has been growing, because the rich have been moving ahead while those with low incomes, the poor, have been standing still. As more catch-up occurs, however, the result could be less economic growth in the last half century or century. This prediction is controversial.

There are some who argue that continued divergence will occur. It's not clear whether, say, Africa will experience a productivity takeoff; there are countries of the world that have taken a few steps forward and then seem to also have taken some steps back. For example, in Latin America, there have been times when Argentina, and Peru, and Venezuela seem to be really zooming forward during the 20th century, and there have been times when they seem to have taken three or four steps backward. There are some people who argue that certain parts of coastal Africa showed signs of convergence in the first half of the 20th century, but since then, they've clearly experienced divergence, and haven't been able to keep up with the richer countries of the world.

When a country does fall behind in per-capita GDP, it can take a long time to catch up. Let's think about the problem, for a moment, of some desperately poor countries in the world, like those in Africa. Their per-capita GDP might be, say, $500. A high-income country like the United States might have per-capita GDP of $30,000. Let's imagine that the low-income country grows at a remarkably fast rate—let's call it eight percent per year—and it keeps that up for 40 years. Meanwhile, the high-income country grows at two percent a year. Now, you can do the multiplication here yourself, but bottom line: 40 years later, this low-income country that started off at $500 a year is now up to $10,862 a year; that multiple of 22 kicks in.

However, the high-income country, which started off at $30,000 a year, with two percent growth, after 40 years, it'll be up to $66,000 and change per person. Now, it's true that it's no longer a multiple of sixty to one, like it was at the beginning of the time period, but it's only a multiple of six or seven to one. That is an insanely optimistic growth forecast for the poorest countries of the world, and even with that insanely optimistic forecast, that they sustain eight percent growth for 40 consecutive years, those poorest countries will still be far, far, far behind in standard of living 40 years from now. There's just no plausible way to fix that. That's the most optimistic forecast for those countries I can really give you, in good conscience.

In the long run, internally generated growth is by far the single most important factor in a nation's standard of living. It's going to be far more important than trying to redistribute from rich to poor. Countries have to grow from within and grow across the board. Remember, if you redistribute a per-capita GDP of $500 a person, it's still $500 a person; that's the average.

Again, Robert Lucas, of the University of Chicago, described the importance of growth in this way:

> In this very minute, a child is being born to an American family and another child, equally valued by God, is being born to a family in India. The resources of all kinds that will be at the disposal of this new American will be on the order of 15 times the resources available to his Indian brother. This seems to us a terrible wrong, justifying direct corrective action—and perhaps some actions of this kind can and should be taken. But of the vast increase in the well-being of hundreds of millions of people that has occurred in the two-hundred-year course of the industrial revolution to date, virtually none of it can be attributed to direct redistribution of resources from rich to poor. The potential for improving the lives of poor people by finding different ways of distributing current production is nothing compared to the apparently limitless potential of increasing future production.

What are the sources of economic growth? How can we increase future production? Since I'm focused here on real economic growth, I'm going to leave out inflation and how it could drive up nominal GDP. Since I'm focused on per-capita growth, I'm going to leave out the issue of a larger population. I'm also going to leave out the issue of people working more hours. We're not trying to increase the GDP by having everyone work more hours; we're trying to get higher per-person output. My real focus is on the underlying causes of productivity growth. We can call that higher output per hour worked, or sometimes it's output per number of workers, in international comparisons.

Why might productivity grow, the increase in output per hour worked? Well, there are three big reasons. One would be an increase in physical capital, that is, more capital equipment for workers to use on the job. The second reason would be more human capital. Human capital refers to workers who have more experience or better education. The third big reason is better technology, that is, better ways of producing things, of using your physical capital and of using your time.

In practice, all of these work together. More skilled workers, with investment in new plant and equipment, which embodies better technology and production methods, all fit together to increase production. But you can do a calculation where you consider how much education per worker has increased, how much equipment per worker has increased, how much skill per worker has increased. Then, economists tend to find that those factors don't explain nearly all of economic growth, and so they say the rest must be a development in technology.

When you do the breakdown of the determinants of economic growth for an economy like the U.S., you find that about one-fourth of economic growth can be explained by growth in human capital: more education, more experience. Another one-fourth of economic growth can be explained by physical capital, that is, more machinery to work with, more plant and equipment. But about one-half of all growth is new technology. In other words, it's not using the same old capital or the same old skills as before, but actually new technology. Notice that these things that produce more productivity don't necessarily depend on a heavier use of the world's resources. Maybe they will; maybe they won't. But new ideas, new skills aren't necessarily a greater use of resources.

For low-income countries, if you do a similar breakdown of their reasons for growth, you tend to see that more of their productivity growth is coming from gains in physical and human capital, and not as much of their productivity growth is from new technology, although all three continue to play a role. So, part of the goal for low-income countries is to start the process of catch-up growth, which means tapping into the new technology that's available in a better way.

Let's talk a little bit about U.S. productivity experience in recent decades. If you look through the 1950s and 1960s, U.S. productivity growth—that's increase in output per hour—often hovered near three percent a year. But from the 1970s into the early 1990s, productivity growth sank. It was more often in the range of something like 1.5 percent or maybe two percent per year. It stayed at that lower level for approximately 25 years, and then began to move back up again in the late 1990s.

This period of the 1970s and into the 1980s had lots of economic issues. There were high oil prices, there was the OPEC situation; there was high inflation in the 1970s; there was a big defense spending drop and then build-up; there were tax cut issues and budget deficits. But of all those issues, the productivity slowdown is unarguably the worst issue of all.

Let's get a sense of the problem here. Let's say for the sake of argument, for purposes of illustration, that the economy lost 1.5 percent per year of productivity growth for 30 years. In rough terms, not worrying about compound growth rates, that means real per-capita GDP was 45 percent smaller at the end of the time than it would otherwise have been. So, imagine if real per-capita GDP was 45 percent larger in the mid-2000s. For example, in 2005, instead of having a GDP of roughly $12 trillion, GDP would have been $17.4 trillion. In that alternative universe, the government would have had plenty of money to pay for the Bush tax cuts of the early 2000s, and wipe out the budget deficit, and still raise spending on lots of programs. People would have had an average of 45 percent more in their paychecks. No matter what your issue or your problem is— whether it's tax cuts or spending increases—having per-capita GDP be 45 percent larger would make your problem a lot easier to fix.

Starting in the late 1990s, the U.S. economy began to see a boost in productivity amid a lot of talk about a new economy, built on the dramatic advances in information and communications technology. Productivity bounces back for a couple years in the late 1990s, up at about 2.5 percent a year. But a lot of economists at that time were skeptical of whether anything has changed. The worry was that the late 1990s also looked like a bit of an economic bubble of sorts, with rapid but perhaps unsustainable growth. There was this concern: maybe productivity was just high for a couple years, but would it last through the next recession?

Well, the U.S. economy had a recession in 2001. Usually, productivity slows down a lot in recessions, at least temporarily, because output it down, and productivity is output per hour. One of the remarkable things about the 2001 recession that productivity did not slow down much. In 2002, 2003, and 2004, productivity growth was near or above four percent each year, which made these three of the best years for productivity growth in the last 50 years.

It's always, of course, very hazardous to say, "We're seeing the start of a long-term trend," and maybe I'll look like an idiot for saying it. I can't imagine that productivity growth is going to stay above four percent per year for the long term. But maybe the U.S. economy has finally shucked off that time of 1.5 percent or two percent growth per year and is back to sustained, solid productivity growth in the range of about three percent per year. At least by the mid-2000s, the productivity boost of the new economy appears to be a real phenomenon in which new information and communications technology are boosting productivity in a wide array of jobs.

A professor of mine, when I was back in graduate school in the early 1980s, used to like to say that the standard job in the U.S. economy involved picking up a piece of paper, looking at it, doing something with it, and then picking up another piece of paper. A lot of jobs were in that category at that time. Sales records, billing, accounts receivable, shipping invoices, overseeing sales forces—all that kind of stuff. There were a lot of middle managers who spent all their time on those kinds of jobs. The new economy technologies, the new computer and information technology, wreaked havoc on those kinds of jobs.

One common example now is, you think of a hospital supply room, where everyone goes in, gets their supplies, swipes with a barcode, and walks out. The room automatically keeps track of what's needed, automatically orders more, automatically schedules delivery, automatically pays and acknowledges payment. It's just so much easier. Across the U.S. economy, examples like that are multiplying and multiplying. I may look like a fool for saying it a few years from now, but it does seem like we're seeing a great transforming surge of productivity growth in the U.S. economy.

Lecture Twenty-One
Unemployment

Scope:

Unemployment harms both the individuals who are out of work and the rest of society because of the lost potential output and lower government social spending if a greater share of the unemployed had been working. The official unemployment rates come from a government survey, which focuses on whether a person has a job and, if not, if that person is looking for one. The economist's view of unemployment is a little different; it focuses on the question of why supply and demand in the labor market are producing unemployment. The underlying causes of unemployment can be split into two broad categories. Cyclical unemployment rises during a recession or depression. The structural or natural rate of unemployment arises because of the incentives for hiring and working embedded in the labor market, even when the economy is not in recession.

Outline

I. What is unemployment? The answer may seem obvious, but those who are not working voluntarily, such as a spouse who is staying home with children, are surely in a different category than someone who is looking for a job to pay the rent.

   A. The official unemployment rate is based on a government survey.

   1. To be counted as unemployed, you must respond to the survey by saying that you don't have work but are looking for work.

   2. Those not looking for work are counted as "out of the labor force," not as unemployed.

   3. Defining unemployment in this way is at least consistent over time, but it can also be controversial. What about part-timers and discouraged workers, for example?

   B. Economists see unemployment in terms of the labor market.

   1. In a labor market, quantity demanded must equal quantity supplied at equilibrium. Thus, the only way that someone can be willing to supply labor at the going market wage and not find a willing employer is if the wage is stuck above the equilibrium level.

2. Wages might be stuck above the equilibrium level for a time for a number of reasons: minimum wages, explicit and implicit labor contracts, and fear of effects on morale—especially the morale of better workers.

II. A question only an economist could ask is: Why is unemployment bad?

    A. Unemployment harms the individuals who are unemployed.

    B. Unemployment also reduces the size of the economy, because the economy loses the potential output of the unemployed workers, and raises the need for government spending on welfare and social services.

III. Unemployment can be divided into two broad categories: the natural rate of unemployment and cyclical unemployment.

    A. The natural rate of unemployment describes the unemployment that occurs in an economy as a result of the dynamic ebb and flow of workers and industries, which occurs in the context of the laws and regulations that affect the incentives of employers to hire or affect the incentives of the unemployed to take jobs.

        1. Examples of laws that affect incentives to hire might be rules preventing businesses from forming or expanding in certain areas, taxes on employment, and rules prohibiting layoffs.

        2. Examples of the laws that affect incentives to work might be generous welfare or unemployment benefits with no particularly imminent cutoff date.

        3. The natural rate of unemployment isn't a "natural" law like the freezing point of water but, rather, an expected outcome given social institutions.

        4. The way to reduce the natural rate of unemployment is to think about ways to provide the desired social protections but to retain incentives to work and hire.

    B. Cyclical unemployment results from recessions, when many businesses all at once just don't see enough demand for their services to justify hiring.

1. In a recession, firms are not able to sell as much as they had expected; thus, they reduce their workforce or cut back on hiring.
2. The policy solution for cyclical unemployment is for government to pump up demand with temporary spending increases or tax cuts or with reductions in interest rates. These tools will be discussed in more detail in later lectures on fiscal and monetary policy.

IV. Unemployment rates in the United States and Europe in recent decades have reflected different natural rates of unemployment, as well as patterns of cyclical unemployment.

A. U.S. unemployment rates were relatively low from the 1950s and 1960s, then rose in the 1970s, and peaked at almost 10% in 1982; they have since dropped back to the earlier range, around 5%.

U.S. Annual Unemployment Rate

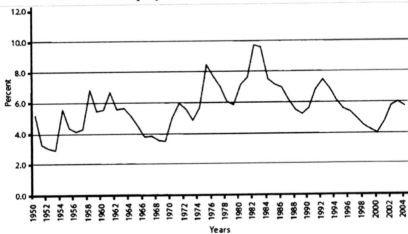

B. European unemployment rates rose dramatically in the 1970s and early 1980s, as did rates in the United States, but in Europe, the rates never came back down. Most economists think that some combination of structural factors, rather than cyclical or frictional ones, is at the heart of Europe's higher unemployment rate.

V. Society may face some tension between attempts to increase the number of jobs and efforts to increase wages.

    A. Since the 1980s, the United States has had relatively low unemployment compared to Europe but also relatively low wage growth. There may be a tradeoff here: a greater supply of labor (low unemployment) leading to a lower price (in the labor market, lower wages).

    B. Ultimately, wages are based on productivity of workers. Thus, the best long-term policy for high wages is to improve productivity.

Essential Reading:

Timothy Taylor, "Department of Misunderstandings," *Milken Institute Review*, 3rd quarter 2004, pp. 82–87, www.milkeninstitute.org.

U.S. Department of Labor, Bureau of Labor Statistics, *Labor Force Statistics from the Current Population Survey*, bls.gov/cps/home.htm.

Supplementary Reading:

"Counting the Jobless," *The Economist*, July 22, 1995, p. 74.

U.S. Department of Labor, Bureau of Labor Statistics, *How the Government Measures Unemployment*, www.bls.gov/cps_htgm.htm.

Questions to Consider:

1. Make a list of the costs of unemployment. Your list should include personal costs (thinking about your own experience or the experience of unemployed friends may be useful here), budgetary costs to the government, and costs for society.

2. Discuss what the concept of *unemployment* means and why not every adult without a job should be classified as part of the official unemployment rate.

Lecture Twenty-One—Transcript

Unemployment

Our first main goal of macroeconomics was rapid economic growth. Our second goal is reducing unemployment. What precisely is unemployment? That question may seem too obvious to need an answer. Unemployment—duh—is when people don't have jobs, right? But when you think about it, the question becomes a little more complex. Should a spouse who is at home and not looking for work be counted as unemployed? What about a worker who has an unrealistic idea of how much pay he's going to receive and he's waiting for a job offer that is never going to come? Defining unemployment is a way of clarifying these sorts of lines and definitional issues.

Let's first talk about the official government unemployment rate, which is calculated by the U.S. Bureau of Labor Statistics. They do a monthly survey, and to be counted as unemployed in the survey, you have to respond to the survey by saying you don't have work, but you are looking for work. Both of those—that you don't have work and that you're looking for work—have to be answered "yes" for you to be counted as unemployed. If you say, "I don't have work, but I'm not looking," then you're not counted as unemployed. You're counted as out of the labor force.

The official unemployment rate, which is announced about the first Friday of each month, is based on this government survey that's carried out by the U.S. Bureau of Labor Statistics. They have to think about whether you don't have work and whether you're not looking for work. The key thing about the survey is to remember that, when you divide up the U.S. population, it's not a matter of saying, "Do you have work or not have work?" It's actually a three-way division.

About one-third of all U.S. adults of working age don't have jobs at all, but they're considered out of the labor force. So that one-third is out of the labor force, and then the remaining two-thirds is divided up into those who are employed and unemployed. Unemployment is just counted relative to the group that is in the labor force.

When you define unemployment in this way, it has the usual advantage. You are at least using a consistent definition over time, so you can measure rises and falls. But the underlying meaning of it can also be somewhat controversial.

For example, what if we're thinking about a worker who's a discouraged worker? They were looking for work for a long time, they couldn't find any, and eventually, they gave up looking. They really would like to have a job, but they looked and looked, and there just didn't seem to be one available. Well, if they answered the survey as, "I'm not looking," they're not counted as unemployed.

What about if you've got someone who's working part time and so when you say, "Are you working?" they say, "Yes," but actually, the person would like full-time work. They're not counted as unemployed.

What if the government statisticians call you up and say, "Are you out of a job? Are you looking for work?" and you answer, "Oh, yes, I sure am. Yes, golly-gee, I'm out there pounding the pavement eight hours a day looking for jobs," but the truth is that you're not actually looking at all. You just don't want to say that to the government statistician who's on the other end of the phone line. In that case, you're counted as unemployed, even though in some sense, you may be out of the labor force altogether.

The basic bottom line here is—we talked about it with GDP; it'll come up over and over again—economic statistics are not like measuring temperature. They aren't like talking about freezing and boiling points. They are concepts that are a little bit looser and a little bit fuzzier than that.

Economists, when we look at unemployment, we see it a little bit differently from the government statisticians. When economists look at unemployment, economists see it in terms of the labor market and how that market works. In fact, economists define unemployment in terms of a supply-and-demand framework for labor.

To economists, unemployment occurs when someone is willing to work at the going wage that's appropriate to them, given their skill and experience level, but they can't find a job. Now, how can that happen? How can that happen that someone has a certain level of skill and experience, and they're willing to work, but no one's ready to hire them?

From a supply-and-demand point of view, what must be going on here is that wages are, for some reason, stuck above the equilibrium rate for that market, as what happened in the example of a price floor, which we talked about in Lecture 4. Remember that, if the wage is above the equilibrium level, then that's going to encourage people to want to work so there will be a large quantity of labor supplied at that wage. But because the wage is above the equilibrium level, that's going to discourage some hiring. So, the quantity demanded of labor at that wage is going to be somewhat less.

If the wage is, for some reason stuck, at least for a period of time, above the equilibrium wage, then there's going to be a situation where there's people who want to work at that wage, given their skill and experience levels, and they can see that other people, given the same skill and experience, are working at that wage, but there aren't going to be people ready to hire them.

Now, this, of course, just moves the whole question of unemployment back one level. If the problem is that wages are stuck above the equilibrium level, then why are they stuck above the equilibrium level? Economists have devoted considerable effort these last few decades to questions of why wages might not be flexible downwards; why wages might be sticky; why they might be slow to decrease; and also to the policy implications of this idea.

Let me give you some examples of why wages might be stuck above the equilibrium level for a time, at least for a time. One would be minimum wage laws. A minimum wage law, after all, is a price floor. It says the wage can't go down below that level. So for certain kinds of workers, maybe it would be worth hiring them at some wage below the minimum wage, but it's not worth it at the minimum wage.

There is also an issue of explicit labor contracts, like unions. If you have a union wage or a union contract and it's three years long, maybe something happens in that market—like demand for the product that's being produced could drop dramatically. But that doesn't matter. The union contract is what the union contract is, and it's going to be very hard for the union to go back and renegotiate a wage decrease in the middle of a contract or in the future.

There's also an issue of what are called implicit contracts. The idea here is that many workers who aren't members of unions, nonetheless, have an implicit contract with their employer. The implicit contract works like this: the business of the firm is, in any given month, or week, or even year, going up and down, and up and down, to some extent. They might make more money or less money. But you don't want your wage to be leaping up and down, a high wage when they're making money and then no wage at all when the firm is losing money. The implicit contract is that the firm will pay you a relatively steady wage over time, perhaps rising some with your experience or if you acquire more skills. In exchange for getting this steady wage over time, you won't get all excited if the firm makes higher profits one year—because you know it could be temporary—and then make lower profits another year. The implicit contract is, that the firm will pay smooth wages over time, rather than wages that directly affect the business conditions of the firm.

The implicit contract is enforced by the fact that, if you felt like the firm was really taking advantage of you, you would either quit or your morale would go way down. It's an implicit contract, not an explicit one, and it would make a firm reluctant to cut wages because workers would view that as a violation of the implicit contract that they thought they had with their employer.

More broadly, there's this question of a fear of what cutting wages would do to morale of workers, perhaps especially the morale of the better workers in a firm. In any firm, there's going to be a spread of workers, from higher quality to middle quality to lower quality. You can't have everybody being above-average here. In that situation where some workers are going to be quite good, if you reduce wages for everyone, those best workers are going to be the ones who find it easiest to go get jobs somewhere else. Any firm that cuts it wages has to worry about decreasing everyone's morale, but in particular, maybe losing its best workers altogether. So for all those kinds of reasons, economists have argued that wages are not likely to be sharply flexible downwards.

A final reason could be that people might wait to take a job that's a good fit. So, if wages aren't flexible downwards, and we're thinking about why wages don't go down, it could be that wages don't go down because when workers are looking for a job, they're just sitting and waiting for a period of time; and they look, and look, and look; and there's a natural process of searching. Employers are just going to wait for people to sort themselves out. They aren't going to push wages up and down to try and get someone and fire someone. They're going to set the wage and then they're going to assume that people are gradually sorting themselves out over time.

We've walked through a lot of possible reasons why wages might not fall. Now we need to think a little bit about what the implications of this would be. All firms are at least somewhat reluctant to cut wages and, as a result, wages could get stuck above the equilibrium level if they're stuck above the equilibrium level, then you're in a situation where the quantity supplied of labor can exceed the quantity demanded of labor, and unemployment will result.

Given that there's some unemployment out there, we now come to one of these questions that only an economist could ask: why is unemployment bad? Or if you prefer, how costly is unemployment?

Well, you can think about the costs of unemployment along two dimensions. One is, unemployment harms the individuals who are unemployed; they lack income. Beyond the lack of income, there are issues of social pathology. There are social problems like difficulties between parents and kids, or between spouses. There are issues like crime. They seem to be linked to whether or not someone is unemployed.

If you've had a family member be unemployed, as I have, or a relative, you know that it can be enormously stressful in that person's life. So the costs go beyond the loss of income and they include the costs, the deeper costs, that affect someone's life when they feel like they don't know what they're doing; they don't know how they're going to pay their bills; they don't know what's going to happen next.

From a big social point of view, unemployment also has costs. Unemployment reduces the size of the economy. After all, when a lot of people are unemployed, the economy loses the potential output of those unemployed workers. In very round numbers, let's say the U.S. economy is $12 trillion—a roughly accurate number for 2005. If you had one percent more employment—in very rough numbers—and you could produce one percent more output, that's worth $120 billion.

Now, it may be that, on average, people who are unemployed have slightly lower skills, so that projection isn't exactly right. But it's also true that those people who are unemployed raise the need for government spending on welfare and social services, so it's not just a cost in terms of lost output of what they could have produced. It's not just that opportunity cost of lost output. It's also a cost to taxpayers and to government, in terms of higher social and welfare benefits. So that combination of costs is real and important to society, both on the individual level and on the social level.

Let's think about the types of unemployment. Economists commonly divide unemployment into two broad categories. They're called the natural rate of unemployment and cyclical unemployment. Let me talk about each of those in turn.

The natural rate of unemployment describes the unemployment that occurs in an economy as a result of the dynamic ebb and flow of workers and industries. That occurs in the context of the laws and the regulations that affect the incentives of employers to hire, or they might affect the incentives of the unemployed to take jobs.

The idea of this natural rate of unemployment that exists within the economy was popularized among economists in a famous lecture given by Nobel laureate economist Milton Friedman, back in 1967. In effect in this lecture, Friedman pointed out that unemployment is never zero percent. In an economy, some workers are always moving between jobs, or they're entering the labor force out of college, or they're retiring, or there's some family reason why they're going to be in or out of the labor force for a few years.

The period of time that workers remain unemployed is also going to be affected by all the laws and regulations that affect the incentives of employers and of workers. Let me give you a couple examples.

For example, incentives that affect employers might be rules that prevent businesses from forming or make it hard to form a business; or prevent a business from expanding, or building a new factory or a new facility in certain areas. There are also various kinds of taxes on employment. Really, we often call them benefits, but anything where you say to the firm, "If you hire someone, you need to spend money on X, Y, and Z," to the firm, that looks like you're taxing employment.

There are also rules that make layoffs difficult. If you've got a layoff where you say, firms are not allowed to lay people off without 90 days notice, or 120 days notice, or there's some other rule about large severance benefits, firms are going to be reluctant to hire in the first place because, after all, they know that, if they need to fire someone, they're going to incur high costs.

Some examples of things that might affect incentives for unemployed workers would be if unemployment benefits or welfare benefits were relatively generous, and had no particularly soon cut-off date. In that case, people might be tempted—at least some people—to remain on those benefits for a while, and not to go ahead and change to something else—not going out and looking for a job in the best way that they could, and really trying to get a job as soon as possible.

So you take those kinds of factors, those incentives—the dynamic economy; people moving in and out; incentives for employers to hire; incentives for employees to work—and you're going to get some natural rate of unemployment that comes out of those different factors.

This natural rate of unemployment isn't a natural law, like the freezing point of water. It's an expected outcome, given the existing social institutions. It's important to think of natural unemployment not as something that's a constant, that can't change, that's fixed; but instead, you want to think of the natural rate of unemployment as saying there's a certain unemployment rate that you should expect year in and year out, given the rules, and regulations, and incentives that govern workers and employers in the labor force. You're going to get that natural rate of unemployment, even when the economy is going well.

If you want to change that natural rate of unemployment through public policy, you need to change some of the rules that set the incentives for hiring and firing. The key question, here then, becomes, how can society provide the protections it wants to provide, while still keeping incentives to work strong and keeping incentives to hire strong? Let's think about some of those possible programs. I should say I don't want to endorse all of these programs, necessarily, but I think they're the kinds of things that you would want to talk about if you were thinking about how you should reduce the natural rate of unemployment.

One example would be, when we think about the unemployment benefits that people receive, one thing that happens now is that unemployment benefits are commonly received for six months. One of the facts one observes is that there are an awful lot of people who, if they don't find a job right away after the first month or two, they spend the whole six months on unemployment and then they find a job just about when their benefits are running out.

So, instead of having a situation where the unemployment benefits are flat and then they cut off at some point, how about a situation where unemployment benefits are higher at the start—when you really need some help—but then they start tapering down over time, to provide a continuing incentive to go out and find work.

Another policy recommendation: be very careful before you pass a government policy that prevents or discourages firms from firing workers. Because if you prevent firms from firing, they'll be discouraged from hiring also.

Be careful before you advocate a government policy that raises the costs of hiring a worker, like by requiring that firms also pay for all kinds of additional benefits. Firms don't want to pay more than they need to, and that will tend to discourage them from hiring.

Be careful before you pass rules that limit the hours businesses can be open or the days businesses can be open, because when you pass rules like that, firms are not going to be hiring workers at those times. Of course, you can also think about expanding government programs that provide job search assistance or retraining that might help people find that next job more quickly.

That's the natural rate of unemployment. The other main kind of unemployment is called cyclical unemployment. In cyclical unemployment, the cyclical part refers to the business cycle. It refers to the economy moving in and out of recessions.

In a recession, firms are not able to sell as much as they had expected, and so firms will reduce their workforce or cut back on hiring. Sometimes economists say, "Labor is a derived demand." What they mean by that is: firms think about how much they're going to produce, and then they think about how many people they need to hire. So, labor is a derived demand from how much firms want to produce. In a recession, lots and lots of businesses, all at once, don't see a lot of demand for their goods and services. So, in terms of derived demand, they don't see why they should be hiring people. A recent example of this: in 2000, the year before the U.S. recession of 2001, the unemployment rate was 4.0 percent. In 2002, the year after the recession, the unemployment rate was 5.8 percent. A lot of that jump is probably a movement in cyclical unemployment.

What's the policy solution for cyclical unemployment? Well, the policy solution would be for the government to fight the recession, to fight the lack of demand for goods and services. How can government encourage people to buy more stuff? Well, we'll talk more about these sorts of policies and tools later on in these lectures, but the quick overview is that they can use fiscal policy. Fiscal policy, remember, involves taxes and government spending. If you give people tax cuts, then they're likely to spend more. Or the government could spend more directly. Either of those would have more demand in the economy, and more demand for goods and services should be a bigger derived demand for labor.

In terms of monetary policy in the Federal Reserve, you can have lower interest rates. Lower interest rates will encourage borrowing for things like cars and houses, and that, then, will encourage firms producing those kinds of things to hire more people. Again, we'll come back to these tools of fiscal and monetary policy in more detail in later lectures. We'll devote several lectures to each.

Let's talk about how unemployment rates have actually evolved in the United States and in Europe in recent decades. This evolution has reflected both different natural rates of unemployment, as well as the patterns of cyclical unemployment. If you look at a graph of U.S. unemployment rates over time, you'll see those unemployment rates were relatively low, from the 1950s, up to the early 1970s—and by relatively low, I mean they were typically between four and six percent. Really, really good years were a little bit under four percent unemployment; really, really bad years were a little bit over six percent unemployment.

But then, as you look at the 1970s and into the 1980s, you see unemployment rates getting systematically higher across the board. The good years are coming in at about six percent unemployment, or maybe a little bit less, and the bad years are often something like eight percent unemployment. Indeed, in 1982, for the year as a whole, there's nearly 10 percent unemployment for the entire year.

In the 1990s, then unemployment rates come back down, more in the range of the 1950s and 1960s. That is, again, good years are in the range of maybe 4 or 5 percent and bad years, like right after the 2001 recession, get up close to six percent.

The broad storyline here is, if you're tying to summarize all this: you can certainly see cyclical unemployment. Unemployment is rising and falling when recessions hit, like 2001, like the 1990–91 recession, like back in the early 1980s. But despite these fluctuations in cyclical unemployment, you can see that there's an underlying natural rate of unemployment, which doesn't seem to change a whole lot over time. And very roughly—very roughly, I'll emphasize—you might think that natural rate of unemployment for the U.S. economy is roughly in the range of five or six percent. However, there's some reason to believe that maybe the natural rate of unemployment was a little bit lower in the '50s and '60s, a little bit higher in the '70s and '80s, and then maybe has come down a little bit since then.

Why might that be? Why would the natural rate have moved over those decades? Well, one possibility is that the 1970s were a time of dramatic economic dislocation—there's the productivity drop-off we talked about in the previous lecture; there's high inflation; there's deep recessions—and that means there's a lot of uncertainty in the economy. So the incentives of firms to hire in that time were somewhat reduced. They had to worry about whether they were going to survive.

Another thing that was going on was that high inflation was eating away at the wages people were earning. So, people might have been uncertain about whether to work, whether it was really worth it, given the high inflation that was eating away what they earned.

Also, the Baby Boom generation—the generation born right after World War II—is beginning to age at about that time. As the Boomers go through the 1960s, a lot of them are entering the workforce and getting ready. By the 1970s and '80s, it's not clear if those folks are working as much or if they're beginning to move toward retirement, at least some of them. So that would also change the patterns of how many people are likely to work.

European unemployment rates rose dramatically in the 1970s and early 1980s, like unemployment rates in the United States. But the difference is that, across Europe, the unemployment rates, in a way, never came back down. In many countries of Europe, unemployment rates have hovered at 10 percent or higher for most of the last few decades.

Why is that? Why have they hovered at that higher rate? Most economists think the natural rate of unemployment is higher in Europe, and there's a bunch of reasons: if you look at European labor markets, why you might expect that to be true. Minimum wages are often much higher in a lot of European countries. Unions, as we talked about in an earlier lecture, are much, much stronger. The prohibitions against firing workers are much stronger as well. There are often limits on when businesses can open, whether they can be open on weekends or evenings. And there are often requirements from the government that there be lots and lots of benefits for employees. All of those things are going to tend to make the incentives to hire and to work somewhat less. So, all of those things are going to tend to generate a higher natural rate of unemployment.

Some evidence in favor of this hypothesis is that European countries that have made an effort to reform these kinds of policies—like the United Kingdom and the Netherlands—have seen a dramatic fall in their unemployment rates, more toward United States levels. They have managed to still keep their protections for workers and the unemployed at higher levels than those that generally exist in the U.S. economy.

Overall, society might face some tension as it tries to increase the number of jobs. This is a little bit disconcerting because more jobs and favoring job growth are practically a political mantra, even when the unemployment rate looks, in some ways, fairly good.

In 2004, for example, the unemployment rate for the year was 5.4 percent. Now, that wasn't great, compared with the boom years of the late 1990s, but those boom years may well not have been sustainable in the long run. A 5.4 percent rate of unemployment actually stacks up very well with unemployment rates going back through the '70s and '80s, and even back a little bit earlier. But during the political campaign of 2004, sometimes when politicians talked about unemployment, it sounded as if we were practically back in the Great Depression all over again.

Creating jobs is possible, but the difficult question is how to have good jobs and also jobs that pay decent wages. This is where we begin to really run into some hard trade-offs. Since the 1980s, the United States has had relatively low unemployment rates compared to Europe, but the United States has also had relatively low growth in average wages.

For example, if you look just at the category of production, non-supervisory workers—so not management—the weekly pay for that kind of worker, after adjusting for inflation, was essentially the same in 2004 as it was in 1980, after adjusting for inflation. It was actually a little bit lower for that kind of worker than it was in the 1970s. There may be a trade-off here, that the greater supply of labor and the low unemployment in the U.S. labor force is leading to a lower price in the labor market and helping to hold down wages.

Now, European countries, on the other hand, discourage work in a variety of ways, through all the rules we talked about: the longer vacations, the shorter workweeks, and all those sorts of things. But if you do have a job in Europe, you are well paid. So there may be some trade-off here, between low unemployment and lower wages, and high unemployment but high wages, for those with jobs.

Ultimately over time, the labor market will tend to push wages close to productivity. After all, if a worker is receiving more than he or she produces, then the business will fire them, or maybe just not give them much of a raise for a few years until matters level out. If a worker is worth more than their wage, then a competitive alternative employer should be willing to come along and offer them a job above their current wage because they're such a good producer. Over time, the question of average wages and how they increase over time really relates back to the question of the previous lecture, about productivity and economic growth.

From my own point of view, I think it can be frustrating or exasperating to watch top business executives rake in enormous multi-million-dollar bonuses—and I don't intend what I'm saying here as a big defense of those bonuses. But I do mean to say that, in the long run, achieving higher wages, on average, for 130 million workers in the U.S. economy is not going to happen by redistributing a few million dollars from top executives.

The only way for a sustained basis for strong wage growth over time is to have workers that are more productive, on average. That means investing in better education for those workers, better equipment, and being flexible about developments and new technology.

The best policies for job creation are to reduce the barriers to hiring and firing—that helps bring down the natural rate of unemployment—and in recession, to help stimulate demand in the economy. The best long-term policy for high wages is to improve productivity. If you can have an environment where all of those come together, then the mantra of good jobs at good wages becomes achievable.

Lecture Twenty-Two
Inflation

Scope:

Inflation refers to an overall sustained increase in the level of prices, not to the increase in any particular price. The inflation rate is obtained by defining a basket of goods that represents typical consumption levels, then tracking how the overall cost of that basket changes over time. The original source of inflation can be higher costs in the economy being passed on in prices or a high level of demand in the economy. Mild inflation is not a great policy concern, but a higher level of inflation can cause problems: It imposes an arbitrary pattern of gains and losses across the economy; it creates a lack of clarity about what prices really are, which makes it hard for markets to work well; and people and firms must spend their time worrying about inflation, rather than about real economic factors.

Outline

I.   Inflation represents an overall increase in price level, measured over a combination of all goods and services. But how is such an average to be calculated?

 A. Measuring inflation is done by defining a basket of goods, with the quantity of each good in the basket chosen to represent typical consumption levels, then tracking how the overall price of the basket changes with time.

 B. Instead of referring to the cost of the basket of goods by the actual dollar amount, the typical approach is to choose a "base year" and define the price level in that year as equal to an index number of 100. Then, all other years are expressed in relation to that base year, using the costs of buying the basket of goods in different years.

 C. There are a variety of measures of inflation, depending on what basket of goods is used. The two most common are the consumer price index and the GDP deflator.

 D. There is a longstanding concern that calculating the inflation rate using a basket of goods overstates the true rate of inflation.

1. One fear is that if you start with a basket of goods and the prices of some of those goods rise, people will substitute other goods, but the price index will not capture this substitution and, thus, can overstate the true rise in the costs of living.
2. Another concern is that a basket of goods chosen at some time in the past will not take the benefits of quality improvements and new goods into account and, thus, will overstate the rise in the true cost of living.
3. U.S. government statisticians have taken steps to reduce the impact of these concerns.

II. From 1900 to 1965 or so, U.S. inflation rates were typically between 1–3% per year. The exceptions were just after wars, when the high level of demand in the economy made the price level shoot up, and in the Great Depression, when the low level of demand in the economy created deflation. However, in the 1970s, inflation began to climb, hitting double-digit rates. In the early 1980s, annual inflation came back down and has typically been in the range of 2–4% since then.

III. A question only an economist could ask is: Why is inflation bad?

A. Inflation isn't necessarily bad, at least in theory.
1. Imagine that one night, magic money elves spread out across the entire economy. They sneak into every wallet, every purse, every bank account, every cash drawer, every paycheck, everyplace where money is, and they double it, everywhere.
2. The next morning, everyone rushes out to spend their new money, but prices soon double, and everyone goes home.
3. The lesson is that if all prices and wages rose at the same time, and everyone knew it was going to happen, it wouldn't make any difference to the real economy.

B. In the real world, inflation isn't evenly distributed and fully predictable. It offers surprising benefits to some and costs to others.
1. The clearest losers from unexpected inflation are those who lend money at a fixed rate of interest or those who

have invested their money in a bond that promises to pay only a fixed rate of interest.

    2. Conversely, someone who borrowed at a fixed rate will gain from unexpected inflation.

C. Indexing refers to the practice of having adjustments made for inflation automatically, such as when the interest rate on a home mortgage rises or falls with the rate of inflation.

D. When inflation rates get high, they can make it difficult for markets to work well and for firms to focus on long-term productivity growth.

    1. With significant inflation, price signals in the market become unclear; does a higher price mean something is actually more expensive, or is the increase just part of the overall inflation?

    2. Businesses have to spend time worrying about vulnerability to inflation, not about competing with higher productivity, and end up with a short-term focus.

IV. Higher inflation can have many different starting points, but ultimately, it is always a matter of too much money chasing too few goods.

A. The policy tools to fight inflation all involve holding down the overall level of demand to ensure that there are fewer dollars chasing goods; possibilities include raising taxes, cutting government spending, and raising interest rates.

B. Fighting moderate inflation will always be controversial, because the costs of slowing down demand are obvious, but the benefits of reducing a fairly low rate of inflation are less clear.

    1. Inflation hawks argue that an economy works best if inflation is close to zero and that inflation should be nipped in the bud.

    2. Inflation doves argue that a little inflation maybe isn't such a terrible thing; for example, maybe it helps the economy in carrying out wage cuts or price cuts where needed.

Essential Reading:

U.S. Department of Labor, Bureau of Labor Statistics, *Consumer Price Indexes*, bls.gov/cpi/home.htm.

Supplementary Reading:

Advisory Commission to Study the Consumer Price Index, *Toward a More Accurate Measure of the Cost of Living: Final Report to the Senate Finance Committee*, December 4, 1996, www.ssa.gov/history/reports/boskinrpt.html.

V. S. Naipaul, "The End of Peronism?" *New York Review of Books*, February 13, 1992, pp. 47–53.

Questions to Consider:

1. How might a rapid rise in inflation harm you? Consider your role as a consumer and a borrower. How might a rapid rise in inflation help you? Consider the likely effect on your wages, any interest you receive as a saver, and how you would react as a homeowner. Overall, and assuming for the moment that the inflation doesn't do drastic harm to the overall economy, do you think you would personally be better or worse off?

2. Discuss which problem seems the most important to you: economic growth, unemployment, or inflation. Does your answer depend, at least in part, on the current levels of these variables?

Lecture Twenty-Two—Transcript
Inflation

Our third major goal of macroeconomics is to have an economy with low inflation. Inflation represents an overall increase in the price level, measured over some combination of goods and services. This point is worth exploring. Inflation doesn't necessarily happen just because the price of gasoline goes up 30 cents a gallon, or because a movie ticket costs $1 or $2 more than it did a few years ago. At any given time in a market economy, some prices are going up and other prices are going down. For example, in recent years, the prices of a personal computer and a lot of home electronic appliances has been steadily dropping. So, in order to measure inflation, inflation has to be defined as a rise in the overall price levels, not just a few prices here and there.

How do you measure an overall rise in price level? Well, it's necessary to blend together price changes for many different goods and find some way to calculate sort of an average. The way this is done is by defining a basket of goods—a basket used in a metaphorical sense here—where the quantity of each good in the basket is chosen to represent typical consumption levels for a household. Then you can say, "How would the price of buying that basket of goods—not each individual good, but the overall basket of goods—change over time?"

This idea of using a basket of goods as a way to measure inflation goes back a long, long time. One of my favorite historical examples—and one of the first—is that, in the U.S. Revolutionary War, the State of Massachusetts faced a question of how it would pay its soldiers. The Continental Congress was issuing dollars, but it was hard to say what those dollars were actually worth or what they would actually buy by the time soldiers got home from the war. So the State of Massachusetts said, "We'll pay whatever amount of money will buy the following basket of goods." The basket of goods was: five bushels of corn; 68 and four-sevenths pounds of beef; 10 pounds of wood; and 16 pounds of leather. Your pay was whatever would buy that group of goods.

Now, when we think about the cost of a basket of goods, it's cumbersome and not always especially useful to refer to that cost of the basket of goods by the total dollar amount. Let me give you an example. Let's say that we added up the typical consumer's basket of goods one year and it cost $36,287.51. Then the next year, we added up that same basket of goods and it cost $37,376.13. Now, unless you are pretty much of a wizard with calculations, it won't be obvious to you that that increase was exactly three percent. Rather than using those dollar figures that can be somewhat complicated, what government statisticians do, instead, is to pick a base year, and they call the spending, what the price level was that year, 100. Then all other years are expressed in relation to that base year. The previous example of the base year was 100, then the next year would be 103.

With that kind of base year at 100, it's a lot easier to see what changes are at a glance, and it's also easier to compare across countries or across different measures of inflation at different times. That base year, the year that's equal to 100, gets updated every couple of decades. At the time these lectures are given, the most common base period is usually the average for the years 1982 to 1984, but I'm sure in a few years, they'll update it.

This idea of taking a base period and setting it equal to 100 is what's called an index number, just setting everything proportional to 100. There are a variety of different measures of inflation, depending on what basket of goods is used. The Consumer Price Index, for example, is a very common measure, sometimes called the CPI. The U.S. Bureau of Labor Statistics carries out something called the Consumer Expenditure Survey, and that provides detailed information on what people are actually buying. They can get information on the basket of goods, and then set the basket and see what people would buy over time.

Another common measure of inflation is called the Producer Price Index. The difference there is that, instead of looking at a basket of goods consumers buy, it would be a basket of goods that producers buy, like steel, and oil, and those sorts of things that producers are going to buy instead. There's also something called the Wholesaler's Price Index, or WPI, which looks at wholesale prices of things that retailers might buy.

Finally, there's something called the GDP Deflator. The GDP Deflator, the basket of goods, is everything in GDP. Remember, everything in GDP includes not only consumption, C, but GDP is C plus I plus G plus X minus N—consumption plus investment, plus government spending, plus exports, minus imports.

Probably the two most common measures of inflation that you'll see are the Consumer Price Index and the GDP Deflator. But you can make up a price index for any group. You can make up a basket of goods that shows what the elderly buy, or what the poor buy, or what people in a certain state buy. All you need to do is figure out the representative basket of goods and then figure out what it would cost at different time periods.

There's a longstanding concern that, when you calculate the inflation rate using the basket of goods, you might be overstating the true rate of inflation, if the true rate of inflation is the true increase in the cost of living, in a broad sense. The real problem here—the fundamental problem—with a fixed-basket approach is that, of course, the basket of goods in the real world doesn't actually stay fixed. People aren't buying identical goods one year and another year. There are two important ways in which it doesn't stay fixed.

Here's the first problem: imagine that the price of coffee goes way, way up, and coffee is part of the basket of goods. But when the price of coffee goes way, way up, people don't buy the same quantity of coffee. They substitute to tea, or hot chocolate, or other drinks. So the basket of goods shifts between the two time periods. Now, you're trying to measure inflation and you say, "Well, what basket of goods should I use here? Should I use the basket of goods where the quantity of coffee is what it was before the price increased? Should I use a basket of goods representing the quantity of coffee after the price increased? Should I use a basket of goods representing some average of the quantity before and after?" The answer is not at all obvious. You can do it any of those ways. But if you just assume that everyone is going to go right on buying just as much coffee as before, regardless of how much the price goes up, you're not taking substitution into account. You're not taking into account that people can shift to things that would give them almost as much pleasure as coffee, and so you're going to be overstating the rise in the cost of living.

More generally, how can you have a formula which allows for the fact that there's a constant pattern of shifting demand in the economy, away from goods that are becoming more expensive, and toward goods that are becoming relatively less expensive? So that's one big problem with a fixed basket of goods.

What's the second problem? Imagine that, for example, you have phone service in your basket of goods, but then cell phones come into the market. Now, the price of cell phones looks pretty high, but obviously, it's a new kind of service, a more flexible kind of service. Then picture phones come on the market. Then portable pocket devices to access the Internet, and do e-mail, and provide other services come on the market. Well, if all you're looking at is the price of basic phone service over time, over time, over time, then your basket of goods is not taking these quality improvements and these new goods into account. It's not taking the benefits of improved technology into account. As a result, you're going to be missing a way in which people are actually doing better in terms of their cost of living, in the sense that they have more options available to them than they did before.

So, how can we think about these two issues, of the problem of substitution within the basket and the problem of new goods and evolution of goods? Well, back in 1996, a prominent group of economists headed by Michael Boskin of Stanford University put out a report on these two biases. They did their best to look at the evidence on how much substitution between goods occurred; how that substitution would affect the rise in the cost of living; how many new goods are being invented; how that would affect the new cost of living, the true cost of living. Their bottom line, as they looked at this all, was that the true inflation rate was overstated by about one percent a year. In other words, the inflation rate the government was announcing was about one percent higher than the actual increase in the cost of living, if you took these other things into account.

One percent a year may not seem like much, but actually, the implications are huge. Let's say the nominal economy, nominal GDP, grows five percent, and inflation is three percent, so the real growth is two percent. But inflation was overstated by one percent, so then real growth was actually three percent a year, instead of two percent. As we know, one percent a year, year after year after year, is going to accumulate over time to have an enormous impact on how we think of real GDP and changes in the standard of living.

There's a fair amount of controversy about the Boskin report and what they were proposing, and whether they had things right. But what's happened over time is that the Bureau of Labor Statistics, when they're calculating inflation, now uses statistical methods that allow some substitution between goods when prices go up. So the basket of goods is an average of what was consumed at the beginning and the end of the period. Moreover, they rotate the basket of goods and update it over time, so there are always old goods rotating out and new goods rotating in. So in that way, they can take a lot of the quality adjustments and new goods into account.

When the quality adjustments are really, really large—like, say, in computers and information processing—the Bureau of Labor Statistics actually tries to take them into account explicitly, estimate how big the change is, and then plug that right into the formula.

So, there have been a lot of changes in how inflation is calculated since that Boskin report in 1996. You can certainly make a case that the measure of inflation is overstated, but as you look back at that report, it seems clear that any bias that did exist in 1996 has been substantially reduced in the following decade. Maybe there's still some, but it's not as high as one percent, certainly.

What's the historical record with actual U.S. inflation rates? Well, if you go back a long way—say back to 1900—from 1900 up until about 1965, U.S. inflation averaged about one percent a year. However, the inflation rate did have a few periods of extreme fluctuation. In the years right after World War I and right after World War II, the price level, the inflation rate, went way up into double digits for a few years. The standard reason for that, the standard argument that's given, is that, inflation at some fundamental level is when there's a lot of buying power in the economy and not quite enough goods. So right after a war, you've got a whole lot of people coming home, you've got people who have been saving up during the war and they all want to buy goods all at once. Soldiers have back-pay and so on, so you see an increase in the price level.

The one converse time was in the Great Depression. There was actually deflation. The average level of prices fell by about one-third over the period 1929 to 1933. Now, why that happened would be just the reverse of what happened after the war. During the Great Depression, nobody had any money, banks weren't lending—banks were all going broke—and the result was that, instead of having too much money chasing too few goods, there was hardly any money chasing goods. So the overall price level dropped and dropped.

Inflation on average—with the exception of the Great Depression and the post-war years—had been fairly low up through the mid-'60s. But in the late 1960s, inflation began to climb. In 1971, for example, inflation hit 4.4 percent in that year. That was considered, in 1971, to be such a dreadfully, awfully, terribly destructive rate of inflation that a conservative Republican president named Richard Nixon imposed national wage and price controls to try and hold down inflation. I still find it just frankly incredible that the U.S. economy tried to impose wage and price controls as recently as the early 1970s. They didn't work any better than you would expect a whole bunch of price floors and ceilings to do. By 1974, when they pulled off the wage and price controls, inflation kept going up. It was 11 percent by 1974; it was again in double digits by the late 1970s.

In the early 1980s, inflation came way back down, for reasons we'll talk about in later lectures. It was typically in the range of about two to five percent during the 1980s. In the 1990s, inflation came down a little bit further and it was typically maybe two to four percent or one to four percent.

So in recent years, inflation has not been a severe problem, but it's still trickling along at a rate where you worry that in the early 1970s, we would have sometimes thought it was bad enough to think about wage and price controls.

Why is inflation bad? Why are we worrying about it in the first place? This may seem, again, a question that's so obvious, only an economist could ever ask it, but bear with me. Let's start off with this thought: inflation isn't necessarily bad, at least in theory. Imagine that one night, for example, magic money elves came through the entire economy, and the magic money elves sneak into every wallet, every purse, every bank account, every cash drawer, every pay check, every place where money is, and they double the money everywhere in the economy. What happens the next morning? In the morning, everyone wakes up and they notice that their money has doubled and everyone says, "Yippee!" and everyone goes out shopping. But all the storekeepers know what's happened, too, and very quickly, they double all the prices on everything. So after the original burst of excitement, when everyone wanted to rush out and go shopping, everyone has twice as much money, but all the prices are double. No one is better off, no one is worse off, and everybody goes home.

The general lesson I'm trying to draw out of this perhaps slightly silly metaphor is that, if all the prices, and wages, and interest rates, and everything else went up at the same rate of inflation, and that rate was known to everybody, then nobody would care. It wouldn't make any difference to anyone. You could work the same, consume the same—no one is better off; no one is worse off—as long as everything is adjusted. The problem is that, in the real world, inflation is not evenly distributed and is not fully predictable. It's not going to be adjusted for everyone. Sometimes it'll offer surprising benefits to some groups and costs to others.

For example, if you're someone whose pay doesn't rise with inflation and inflation goes up, you're going to fall behind. If you borrowed money to buy a house and you borrowed at a fixed interest rate—say you borrowed at a five percent rate—and inflation goes up to 10 percent, you come out way ahead because when you're repaying that mortgage, you can repay in inflated dollars. You're, in effect, paying a negative real interest rate.

It's worth remembering: who is the biggest single borrower at a fixed rate in the U.S. economy? It's, by far, the U.S. government with its large budget deficits in the mid-2000s. It's worth remembering that inflation, if there was a big burst of inflation, would reduce the real value of all the government debt that's been accumulating.

If you borrowed to buy a house at a fixed rate and the inflation rate falls, on the other side—if you borrowed at, say, six percent or seven percent and the inflation rate went down to one or two percent—then the bank's going to come out ahead and you're going to suffer, unless you go ahead and refinance your loan at a lower interest rate. Of course, there are costs of doing that.

If, for some reason, you're the sort of person who holds a lot of cash, maybe buried in a jelly jar in the backyard or, if you're a big retail operation that just gathers a lot of cash in the process of sales, inflation always has you falling somewhat behind. Even relatively low rates of inflation can make a big difference when you're thinking about long-run decisions. Remember, if it's just one percent or two percent, that doesn't seem like much in one or two years; but if you think about it in terms of the money you're saving for your retirement several decades off in the future, or if you think about it in terms of a firm that's thinking about building a new factory that it hopes will last for a while, over 10 or 20 or 30 years, even low rates of inflation really matter a lot. You need to take them into account.

Indexing is the word that economists use to refer to the process of having adjustments automatically made for inflation. For example, if you have an adjustable rate mortgage on your house, which goes up and down with the interest rates, the nominal interest rates, those nominal interest rates are going up and down with inflation. So an adjustable interest rate, an adjustable rate mortgage loan, is really indexed for inflation. The U.S. Treasury issues index bonds where the payout of the bond changes automatically with the rate of inflation. Some union contracts specify that union wages will rise automatically with inflation. This was sometimes called a COLA, or a cost of living adjustment. Social Security payments have a COLA, a cost of living adjustment. They rise automatically with the Consumer Price Index. Indexing is protection against inflation. If you don't have indexing, you are vulnerable to inflation. Again, indexing means adjusting a price, a wage, or an interest rate automatically for the changes in inflation that might occur.

When inflation rates get really high, they can make it difficult for markets to work well, because they make it difficult for firms to focus on long-term productivity growth. When inflation gets to the rate of maybe 20 percent a month or 40 percent a month, we refer to that as hyperinflation. Hyperinflations have occurred most famously, perhaps, in Germany in the 1920s, but also in countries like Argentina, and Israel, and Bolivia in the 1980s. These countries offer some examples of the costs of letting inflation get completely out of control.

When inflation is high, price signals in the market become unclear. Does a higher price mean something is actually more expensive or, does it mean that there's just overall inflation? How can you tell a relative price increase from an absolute price increase? Businesses have to spend a lot of time worrying about their vulnerability to inflation. They can't spend their time worrying about productivity.

Instead, they have to worry, "Are we somehow vulnerable? Are we holding a lot of cash? Is our money invested in some way that we're going to be suffering because of high inflation?" They end up with a very short-term focus, a very financial focus.

Let me give you a couple of examples of what's happened in countries with very high inflation rates. Here's an example from a fellow who was working for the Bank of Israel in the 1980s as a deputy governor, and he's describing the problems of inflation at that time in Israel. He said:

> Inflation destroys the measuring rod of the economy. When inflation proceeds at, say, 400 percent annually, the average monthly rate is over 14 percent. A dollar received for sales at the end of the month is worth about 13 cents less than a dollar spent for productive inputs at the beginning of the month.

Consumers face problems too. Ordinarily, when people shop, they use a databank stored in their memory to assess the prices they're asked to pay; but when prices change continuously, people find themselves in the dark. I remember situations during the inflationary years when people could not decide on the reasonableness of prices by up to a factor of 10.

I remember when products at the supermarket had four price stickers, each with a different price attached to the product, one on top of the other. In the end, the cost of constantly changing the prices became so substantial, retailers abandoned price stickers. Instead, a code sticker was attached to each product and the cash register was programmed daily to associate prices with codes. Shoppers had no idea of the price of anything they pulled off the shelves until they reached the checkout counter. This makes the task of executing a household budget rather difficult. The government budget process was rendered useless for similar reasons. So that world of high inflation is just extremely difficult to live in.

Let me give you another example of Argentina's high inflation in the 1980s. V. S. Naipaul—the wonderful writer—went to Argentina, and here he's quoting a businessman from Argentina about what it was like living in that high rate of inflation. The businessman says:

Another negative aspect of inflation is that you cease to worry about productivity and even technology. Now, that is the secret of all progress—productivity—but you really can get no more than three percent or four percent per annum improvement in productivity anywhere in the world. With inflation like ours, you can get 10 percent in one day if you know when and where to invest. It is much more important to protect your working capital than to think about long-term things like technology and productivity, although you try to do both. This is the inevitable result of inflation, which is the monetary disease. Your money is disintegrating; it's like a cancer. You live day to day. That's all you can do when you have inflation more than one percent a day. You cease to plan. You're just happy to make it to the weekend.

An economy with really high inflation becomes, at some level, a truly dysfunctional economy. With the U.S. economy, we've never had that kind of hyperinflation, but we did have those high inflation rates in the 1970s. Is it really just a coincidence that the great productivity slowdown of the early 1970s coincided with the great burst of inflation? Or is it just a coincidence that, after inflation had been back under control for about a decade, then productivity growth recovered?

Prominent economists like John Taylor of Stanford University—who's no relation to me—have argued that there is a connection between these two, and that one of the causes of the U.S. low productivity period was inflation getting out of control.

To understand fully the policy tools for fighting inflation, we'll need to wait for the later lectures on fiscal and monetary policy, but we can offer a preview and a lead-in here.

Higher inflation can have many different starting points, but ultimately, inflation is always a matter of too much money chasing too few goods for the economy as a whole. There's consistently too much demand for everything across the board of the economy, and so prices of everything are moving up. You can think of the example of the magical money elves. When there was extra money out there, when they doubled the amount of money out there, then that's what caused everyone to rush out and all the prices to double.

The policy tools for challenging this situation, changing this situation, all involve holding down the overall level of demand, so that there are fewer dollars chasing goods. None of these policies are especially popular or attractive.

One possibility, for example, is raising taxes; then there would be less money chasing goods. Or cutting government spending; less money chasing goods. Or using higher interest rates. Higher interest rates would discourage borrowing; less borrowing would mean less buying houses and cars. Again, there would be less money, less cash, fewer dollars chasing goods.

Slowing down the economy in any of those ways—so that there's less money chasing goods to fight inflation—is never going to be a popular thing. When an economy is in hyperinflation, there's often a broad social consensus that the cure for inflation is better than the disease. When inflation is 400 percent a year, it's easy to get agreement that it needs to come way down. But is it really worth closing down the economy—maybe getting higher unemployment—to fight inflation if the inflation rate is five percent? Four percent? Three percent? There's a big argument around this point, between what we might call inflation hawks and inflation doves.

The empirical evidence—at least as I read it—on whether or not an economy does a lot better if five percent inflation is cut down to three percent inflation, it just doesn't show an enormous difference. In fact, there are some people out there, looking at international evidence around the world, who would argue that a lot of economies have been able to function pretty well around the world, in the sense of having fairly rapid economic growth with inflation rates that might be as high as 10 percent, or 20 percent, or 30 percent a year. I think there's a fairly broad consensus that once you get above about 40 percent a year, even the inflation doves would say, "There's a real problem there you need to work at."

What are the arguments here between the inflation hawks and the inflation doves? The inflation hawks—those who really want to chop down inflation extremely low all the time—tend to argue, look, an economy is going to work best if inflation is close to zero; so whenever you see inflation beginning to take off, you need to nip it in the bud. You need to try and get close to stable prices, the inflation hawks argue, because that's really the only long-term stability. You want people to be making their long-term plans—and maybe more important, businesses to be making their long-term plans—about how to get real rates of return, how to increase real productivity, how to see real gains. You don't want people trying to play games with how to make money off of inflation, by borrowing and then having a fixed rate and repaying in inflated dollars. You don't want those sorts of games in the economy. So the idea they have is to nip inflation in the bud, to fight even low rates of inflation, because you don't want anyone to start getting that mindset that inflation is coming, so I can start playing games; or, I need to think and focus my attention on inflation.

Inflation doves, on the other hand, argue that maybe a little bit of inflation—like two, three, or four percent—maybe isn't such a terrible thing. Remember, for example, that in the previous lecture, we talked about the problem of sticky wages; and that wages could get stuck above the equilibrium level and that employers didn't like to reduce those wages for a variety of reasons having to do with hurting the morale of employees, more or less. If that's true, what does inflation do? Inflation of maybe two percent, or three percent, or four percent means that you could give your workers a two percent increase and really, that's no increase at all because inflation eats it up. It's not a real increase. Or if inflation is four percent, you give your workers a two percent increase and actually, there's a little bit of a wage cut. So the argument is that, if there's a little bit of inflation, it can actually help wages to be less sticky, and can help them to come down a little bit.

There's also an argument that we don't want to have deflation. We don't want to have price levels actually falling. The big problem with deflation is that, when people are trying to repay loans, the value of what they're trying to repay is going up, because dollars over time are not becoming less valuable, but are becoming more valuable.

If we want to avoid deflation and make sure it doesn't happen, maybe we should hold inflation at about two or four percent, just to leave us a little margin for error so we know we're not going to go down into negative deflation numbers. The inflation doves would also say that there's no strong evidence that a country with two, three, four, or five percent inflation is likely to zoom up to 20 percent or 30 percent. At low rates of inflation, people can protect themselves from that in various ways.

There's no real consensus in this argument, but a common goal seems to be, across many countries of the world, that an inflation rate of about two percent is safe. It helps keep prices low and provides a steady basis for growth, but also doesn't try to push all the way down to zero.

Lecture Twenty-Three
The Balance of Trade

Scope:

The trade deficit is perhaps the most misunderstood statistic in all of economics. The single most comprehensive measure of the trade balance is called the *current account balance*, which includes trade in goods and services, returns paid on overseas investments, and unilateral financial transfers. The U.S. economy ran extremely large trade deficits in the late 1990s and into the 2000s. Conceptually, a current account deficit is always equal to the net flow of foreign investment into a country; a current account surplus is equal to a net flow of foreign investment leaving a country. The string of large U.S. trade deficits has turned the United States into the world's largest debtor economy. Trade deficits are not about "unfair" trade but, instead, result from national levels of saving and investment.

Outline

I. What is the balance of trade?
    A. The *merchandise trade balance* refers to the gap between exports and imports of goods.
        1. If imports are higher than exports, there's a trade deficit. If exports are higher than imports, there's a trade surplus.
        2. But in recent decades, imports and exports of services have become more important; for this reason, the merchandise trade deficit alone is a limited description of the overall trade picture.
    B. The *current account balance* is the single statistic that captures a comprehensive picture of a nation's trade.
        1. The current account balance includes trade in goods, services, investment income, and unilateral transfers.
        2. For the United States, the trade in goods has typically been in deficit; trade in services has been in surplus; trade in investment income was in surplus up to about 1996 but is now in deficit; and unilateral transfers are in deficit.

Current Account Balance for 2003

	Exports	Imports	Balance
Merchandise trade	$713 billion	$1,261 billion	− $548 billion
Services trade	$307 billion	$256 billion	+ $ 51 billion
Investment income	$294 billion	$261 billion	+ $ 33 billion
Unilateral transfers	—	—	− $ 67 billion
TOTAL			− $531 billion

Source: U.S. Bureau of Economic Analysis

3. Overall, the U.S. current account deficit has been fairly large for most of the 1980s, 1990s, and early 2000s.

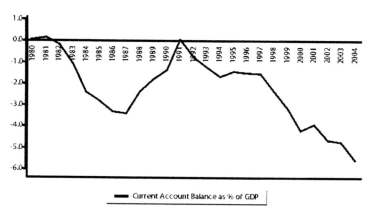

Current Account Balance as % of GDP (1980 - 2004)

II. From the late 1940s to about 1970, the U.S. trade deficit was near balance most years and typically ran a small surplus. In the 1970s, the United States ran some small trade deficits. But starting in the early 1980s, the U.S. trade deficit exploded, then declined in the late 1980s and early 1990s, before exploding again in the mid- and late 1990s and on into the 2000s

III. From a macroeconomic point of view, the balance of trade is intimately related to national savings and investment.

   A. The balance of trade always involves flows of financial capital going back and forth across national borders.

1. In macroeconomics, a trade deficit literally means the same thing as a nation that on net borrows from abroad.
2. Conversely, an economy with a trade surplus must be on net lending or investing abroad.

B. The national savings and investment identity is: Domestic Savings + Inflows of Foreign Capital = Domestic Investment + Government Borrowing.
1. An *identity* is something true by definition. In this case, the quantity actually supplied of financial capital must equal the quantity actually demanded of financial capital
2. Because an identity must always hold true, a change in one part of the identity must lead to changes in at least one other part. For example, if the U.S. government borrows more, one of three things *must* happen: more private-sector saving, more foreign borrowing, or less domestic investment.

C. The result of having an inflow of capital each year is that the U.S. economy becomes a net debtor to the rest of the world.
1. Relying on foreign capital investment is not necessarily a negative and probably better than not having that capital and the corresponding domestic investment.
2. However, in the long term, it would probably be better still if the United States could rely more heavily on domestic sources of capital, because then, the gains from investment would all flow to inside the United States.

IV. Thinking about the trade deficit in macroeconomic terms presents some unexpected implications.

A. Trade deficits are caused by patterns of national savings and investment: For example, the very large budget deficits of the mid-1980s and early 2000s were accompanied by large trade deficits. But the other two parts of the national savings and investment identity—investment and private saving—play a role in shaping the trade deficit, too.

B. From a macroeconomic perspective, unfair foreign trade practices, contrary to the argument one often hears, have nothing to do with U.S. trade deficits. For example, the pattern of U.S. trade deficits since the 1980s—rapid growth, near disappearance, and rapid growth again—has certainly *not* been caused by enormous fluctuations in foreign trade barriers.

C. Trade deficits are not primarily determined by a higher level of trade or by greater exposure to the world economy. Both Japan with its pattern of large trade surpluses and the United States with its pattern of large trade deficits have relatively low levels of trade by world standards.

D. Bilateral trade deficits—that is, trade deficit with one other country—have no macroeconomic importance. There are reasons to worry about a nation's overall trade balance, but that can easily be made up of surpluses with some countries and deficits with others.

E. High-income countries tend to run trade surpluses and, thus, be net investors abroad, investing in low-income countries. But in recent decades, the rest of the world is investing in the United States, on net. There is no precedent for this situation, and it seems unlikely to continue in the long run.

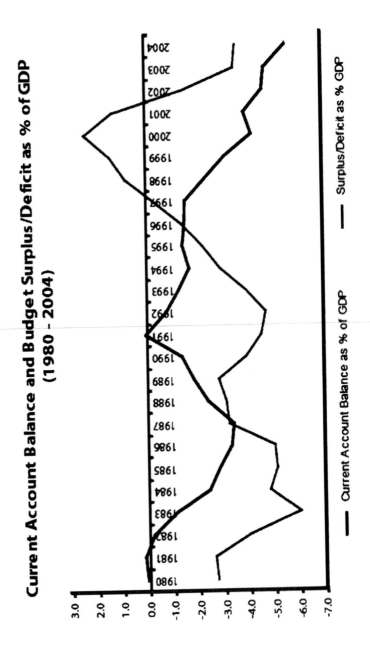

Current Account Balance and Budget Surplus/Deficit as % of GDP (1980 - 2004)

——— Surplus/Deficit as % GDP

——— Current Account Balance as % of GDP

Essential Reading:

Council of Economic Advisers, "Chapter 14: The Link Between Trade and Capital Flows," in *Economic Report of the President*, February 2004, www.gpoaccess.gov/eop.

Timothy Taylor, "Untangling the Trade Deficit," *The Public Interest*, Winter 1999, pp. 82–104.

U.S. Department of Commerce, Bureau of Economic Analysis, *International Economic Accounts: Balance of Payments*, bea.gov/bea/di/home/bop.htm.

Supplementary Reading:

Catherine L. Mann, *Is the U.S. Trade Deficit Sustainable?* bookstore.iie.com/merchant.mvc?Screen=PROD&Product_Code=47 (Institute for International Economics Web site).

Questions to Consider:

1. Draw up a specific list of how you are personally affected by international markets. Think about items you buy every day, such as food and clothing. Think about local companies that depend on export sales. Think about where your pension money is invested. Think about music and culture, travel and long-distance friends.

2. You are working as a staff assistant to an economically illiterate member of Congress. Explain why the trade deficit is the same as the amount of borrowing from abroad and why a trade surplus is the same as the amount of lending abroad. Also explain the connection between the foreign borrowing of the United States and the enormous trade deficits in the 1980s.

Lecture Twenty-Three—Transcript
The Balance of Trade

It's a tough contest to determine what economic statistic is most misunderstood—there are a lot of deep misunderstandings out there. But I think there's a clear winner for the most misunderstood economic statistic, and it's the balance of trade. Our fourth macroeconomic goal is going to be to talk about what's meant by a sustainable balance of trade.

A useful starting point here—most people's starting point—is to talk about what economists call the merchandise trade balance. The merchandise trade balance refers to the gap between exports and imports of goods, but goods only—not services, not other payments between countries. Most people see the trade balance and they think about goods; they think about cars, and computers, and those kinds of imports and exports. If exports are bigger than imports, then a country has a trade surplus. If imports are bigger than exports, then a country has a trade deficit.

In the good old days—which might mean 20 years ago—international trade really was ships and planes filled with cargo, filled with goods. But now telephone call centers and software design can happen in India or Ireland, just as if the person was down the hall, or in the next building, or in the next town. The same can happen with medical and legal transcription services; and lots of back-office records, like those relating to accounting, finance, health, insurance, personnel. Of course, we know that movies, and music, and software can be shipped around the world on the Internet at almost zero cost.

In that kind of a world, the merchandise trade deficit alone is a pretty limited description of the overall balance of international trade. The current account balance is the single statistic that captures the most comprehensive picture of a nation's balance of trade. The current account balance builds upon the merchandise trade deficit, and it captures a more comprehensive picture of what happens in a nation's trade. It includes trading goods; it includes trading services; it also includes investment income received from past investments in other countries, and unilateral transfers of resources between countries. I'll say that all the data here is easily available—updated as you like—at the website of the U.S. Bureau of Economic Analysis.

Let me walk through the four parts of the U.S. current account balance. The first part is merchandise trade—the merchandise trade balance we talked about a moment ago—which is trade in goods. So in 2003, for example, the U.S. exported $713 billion in goods and imported $1.2 trillion in goods. So the overall trade balance in merchandise trade was a deficit, a negative number, of $548 billion.

In services trade, which is the second big part of the current account balance, the U.S. exported $307 billion worth of goods in 2003, and imported $256 billion of goods, for an overall balance of positive $51 billion. The U.S. ran a trade surplus in trade with services.

In terms of investment income, investment income is the category where a country or a firm has made an investment in some other country. Having made an investment in some other country, now it's receiving a rate of return on that investment. That also represents a flow of money that's being passed back and forth. In terms of exports—that is, money which was sent out of the country by the U.S.—the U.S. exported $294 billion in investment income and imported $261 billion. So the U.S. actually had a surplus of $33 billion in investment income.

A final category called unilateral transfers refers to money that is sent overseas for any particular reason. It could be foreign aid money. It could be that there's a guest worker in the United States who is earning something in the United States and then sending it back overseas. So when they do that, that counts as a unilateral transfer. Unilateral transfers in 2003 ran about negative $67 billion. That is, it was money flowing out of the country, going out to other countries from the United States.

So, you take these four categories together: the deficit in merchandise trade; the surpluses in services trade; the surplus in investment income; and the deficit in unilateral transfers. For 2003, the overall current account balance for the U.S. economy was a deficit of $531 billion. That number seems to be going up and up. By 2004, it looked certain that the U.S. would have a current account trade deficit of over $600 billion, which is really a pretty large number, even relative to the enormous U.S. economy.

Let's think a little bit about U.S. experience with trade deficits—and when I say trade deficits, I'm really going to mean current account deficits—since World War II. If you look at a graph that shows U.S. trade deficits and trade surpluses going back to about 1950, what you see is, from the late 1940s up until about 1970, the U.S. trade deficit is really close to balance in most years. The surplus or the deficit is usually less than one percent of GDP; and typically, it's a small surplus rather than a small deficit.

In the 1970s, the trade balance remained small, typically less than one percent of GDP. But instead of usually being surpluses, in the 1970s, usually it's small trade deficits. But starting in the early 1980s, the U.S. trade deficit explodes. It goes up to over three percent of GDP, much higher than it's been at any time in the preceding years. Then, after a little bit of a sag in the late 1980s and early 1990s, the trade deficit begins exploding again in the late 1990s and into the first decade of the 2000s. By the mid-2000s, the annual trade deficits—like the ones for 2003 and 2004 I mentioned before—are running at something like four percent and five percent of GDP—really very large numbers for the size of an economy.

There is something you should notice here: something happened in both the mid-1980s, and again in the early or mid-2000s, that made U.S. trade deficits really large. Now, stick that thought in the back of your mind so we can call back on it later.

From a macroeconomic point of view, the balance of trade is intimately related to national saving and national investment. To understand how economists look at the trade balance as a macroeconomic fact, you need to notice this key relationship: everything on the surplus side of the trade balance involves money flowing into a country. For example, on the surplus side of the trade balance is when the U.S. economy exports goods or services. When we export goods or services, the U.S. economy gets money from abroad. The surplus involves money from aboard coming to the U.S. With investment income, it involves money coming from aboard to the U.S. With services trade—exports of services—money is coming from aboard to the U.S. Everything on the negative side of the trade balance represents money flowing out of the U.S. economy.

For example, if the U.S. economy imports goods or services, then that's U.S. spending power being sent to producers somewhere else.

With investment income, we're talking about foreign owners of assets in the U.S. sending money somewhere else. With unilateral transfers, we're talking about U.S. aid or payments from workers in the U.S. being sent somewhere else.

So, when we think about trade, and we think about trade surpluses and deficits, when there's trade balance—the flow of funds coming into the country, from all the goods and services that we export, and the flow of funds going out of the country, from all the imports and other parts of the current account balance—those two things balance out if the trade deficit is zero. The flows of funds balance out. When there's a trade deficit—like what the United States has—the trade deficit means that, on balance, dollars were flowing out of the United States. For example, we were importing lots and lots of things. The imports money was flowing out of the United States and there wasn't a corresponding flow coming back.

What happened to these extra dollars? What happens to the extra dollars flowing out of the U.S. economy that are not coming back? Well, we know what's not happening to them. We know those dollars were not used to purchase U.S. goods and services. We know they were not used as payment of investment income to U.S. owners who own foreign assets. We know they didn't come back as unilateral transfers—those are already counted in the current account balance.

So what happened, for example, to a dollar that was earned by a Japanese automobile manufacturer when they sold something in the United States? What happened to that money? It's possible that the money went into a bank somewhere in Japan, was deposited as dollars, but there's a really important thing here to remember.

An old professor of mine used to make a big point of saying, "You got to remember U.S. dollars are only legal tender in the United States." That's, of course, not literally true; there are a few little Caribbean countries where you can spend dollars pretty easily. But basically, it's true. U.S. dollars are not legal tender in Japan. If a Japanese firm earns U.S. dollars by exporting to the United States, it usually doesn't put those U.S. dollars in a bank in Japan because it doesn't want U.S. dollars. The Japanese firm wants yen. It wants yen to pay its workers, and its suppliers and to pay its shareholders. The

Japanese firm is in the Japanese economy, so it wants to trade the dollars to someone who has yen in the foreign exchange market.

When the Japanese firm trades those dollars, what happens to them? In one way or another, they end up invested in U.S. assets. Either it goes to someone who buys stocks and bonds directly, or property, or who somehow puts it in a bank account. And if you put it in a bank account, of course, then the bank will loan out the money to a borrower who wants to buy or invest in the United States. These extra dollars that flow overseas are not coming back as goods or services, but they're coming back as a flow of investment. They're coming back in terms of the U.S. economy as a whole borrowing from foreigners who have earned dollars in the United States and, in one way or another, are investing them back in the U.S. economy.

To economists, a trade deficit literally means the same thing as a nation that, on net, is borrowing from aboard and receiving an inflow of investment from abroad. For exactly the same reasons, a trade surplus literally means the same thing as saying that a nation, on balance, is lending money abroad or having an outflow of foreign investment.

A trade surplus and a trade deficit aren't just about the flow of goods. In fact, to most economists, they aren't primarily about the flow of goods. They're about this flow of money, and whether the flow is bigger going one direction or another.

How do we think about this flow of money across international borders and put it in some kind of an overall macroeconomic context? I'm going to introduce a tool here, a tool that's useful to thinking about these flows and that we'll be using throughout many of these macroeconomic lectures. This is, in mathematical terms, an identity. All an identity means is that this is a statement which is true by definition. This is the national savings and investment identity: if you take domestic savings of capital plus all the inflows of foreign capital, those have to equal domestic investment plus government borrowing.

Why must those be equal to each other? Well, the left-hand side of that equation—that is to say, the domestic saving and the inflow of foreign money—represents sources of a supply of financial capital. People's savings are a supply of financial capital. The investment coming in from foreign investors is a supply of financial capital. On the other part of the equation—investment in the government deficit—those both represent demand for financial capital. Business investment demands financial capital so they can build new plant and equipment, and the federal government is borrowing—that's what government budget deficits tell you—and that represents a demand for financial capital as well.

We know that in the market for financial capital, at any point, the quantity actually supplied must equal the quantity actually demanded. All this identity, all this statement is telling us is that a macroeconomy—the U.S. economy right now—has two big sources of capital: its own savings and foreign investment. And those two big sources of capital have to equal the two big demands for capital, which are from private firms and from the government. So, what a trade deficit ends up meaning, is that it's an extra source of money flowing into the economy. It's an extra source of capital, which can, in turn, be borrowed by firms or by the U.S. government.

An identity is true by definition. This one is true because quantity supplied of financial capital has to equal quantity demanded. As a result, since it always has to hold true, by definition, a change in one part of the equation must lead to changes in at least one other part of the equation. For example, let's say the U.S. government borrows more money. So, the quantity demanded of financial capital goes up. Somehow, this needs to balance out. So where's the extra money coming from when the U.S. government borrows more? Well, there are three possibilities, based on this national savings and investment identity. It could be, for example, that the U.S. government borrows more and domestic firms have less money available for private investment. It could be that the U.S. government borrows more and people save more, and so that extra savings means there's more money available for the government to borrow. Or it could be that, as the U.S. government borrows more, there's more inflow of capital from other countries, more borrowing and investment from abroad. My point is that is has to be some combination of these three factors. Exactly which one happens can vary, but it has to be some combination.

The result of having an inflow of financial capital each year into the economy is that the U.S. economy, taken as a whole, becomes a net debtor to the rest of the world. Now, what exactly do I mean by net debtor? At the end of 2003, if you took U.S. individuals, and firms, and the government, they owned—if you add it all up—$7.9 trillion in foreign assets. But if you take foreign firms, foreign investors, and foreign governments, at the end of 2003, they owned $10.5 trillion in U.S. assets in the United States.

Do the subtraction. The U.S. economy owns $2.6 trillion less of the rest of the world than the rest of the world owns of the U.S. economy. Now, whenever you own assets—stocks, bonds, property, whatever—you own those expecting to get some kind of a rate of return. In the current account balance, that investment income category tells you what the rates of return are, the actual flows of money going back and forth across national borders.

Relying on foreign capital to come in for investment purposes, may be better in some ways than not having that capital at all. I don't want to say that borrowing from abroad and having an inflow of international capital is always bad by any means.

For example, the U.S. economy in the 19th century ran trade deficits year, after year, after year. It experienced very large inflows of international financial capital. In fact, a lot of that international financial capital financed the railroads and a lot of U.S. industry, in a way that really helped the U.S. economy to grow in the 19th century.

Similarly, if you look at Korea's economy in the 1960s and 1970s, it was running big trade deficits year after year, having a big inflow of capital from abroad and investing that money wisely, helping Korea's very rapid economic growth rate. So, sometimes, borrowing from aboard can make perfect sense, as long as there's sufficient growth to pay back the loan.

Of course, there are other examples where borrowing from abroad can go very bad. In recent years, looking back through the 1990s and into the 2000s, countries like Argentina and Russia have found themselves in situations where they were running very large trade deficits, having very large inflows of capital, and then finding they couldn't repay; the money wasn't being invested in some way that was generating enough productivity to repay.

With any borrowing, whether it's on the national level or the individual level, the challenge is to borrow in a way that generates sufficient benefits or returns, so you can pay back the borrowing over time. For example, when you borrow for education, you're borrowing for education with the thought that you'll earn higher wages, and you can pay back over time, and still come out ahead. Or if a firm borrows money to build a factory, they're hoping to borrow money over time, pay back, and come out ahead. The problem with borrowing is, if you borrow a large sum of money to go on vacation or buy groceries that can be a real problem because you're not going to be able to get some gain in income that will allow you to repay that borrowing in the future. When you think about whether borrowing is out of control, or too high, or too low, a useful way to think about it is: is the borrowing generating some future stream of income, which is going to help in the future to pay it back; or is it not?

My own view, at least, is that U.S. trade deficits are large enough by the mid-2000s that it would be better if the U.S. could rely more heavily on domestic sources of capital, on its own private savings. Then the gains from investment are going to be flowing to inside the U.S. economy instead of outside. If you become a debtor nation—as the U.S. economy has—and you owe several trillion dollars to the rest of the world, that means that in the future, we need to be generating pretty good returns so that we can provide rates of return to the rest of the world that those investors are going to expect.

When we think about the trade deficit in these macroeconomic terms that I'm using here, I think there are some interesting and somewhat unexpected implications. We can turn around the national savings and investment identity to ask ourselves: what are the possible causes of a large trade deficit? Remember, this equation has to balance at all times.

For example, if the trade deficit goes way, way up, it must be that something else went up as well. If trade deficits went way, way up, and there's a lot more money flowing into the U.S. economy, what could be going on? Well, one possibility is that the U.S. economy would be running large budget deficits and, in effect, the large amount of money flowing in with the big trade deficit is being sucked into the economy by very large government borrowing.

Another possibility is that there's a big surge of investment in the U.S. economy, and foreign investment is being pulled into the U.S. economy by a surge of domestic investment. Another possibility is that there's a sharp drop in private savings rates. And if private saving goes way down, then foreign saving comes flooding in to fill the gap. Any of those three are possible; any of those three could happen. Again, at least one of the three has to happen for the national savings and investment identity to hold.

Remember, trade deficits got very large in the 1980s and in the early 2000s. These are also times—as we'll discuss in more detail later on—when U.S. federal budget deficits are very, very large. In some cases, the federal government was borrowing from aboard directly. In other cases, what was happening was that the federal government was soaking up the available U.S. financial capital, and so when firms wanted money, they were turning to foreign investors.

But trade deficits are not always caused by budget deficits. In the late 1990s, for example, the U.S. budget deficits were small and, in fact, the U.S. economy had budget surpluses for a few years. But at that point, private investment was booming during the dot-com years and private saving was low. In effect, the U.S. economy financed that boom in investment in the late 1990s with a large inflow of foreign financial capital and with large trade deficits. This pattern suggests some commonality between the agenda for fixing trade deficits and the agenda for helping long-term economic growth. After all, reducing the trade deficit—if we're going to try and keep domestic investment high—is going to require higher domestic savings. Raising the U.S. growth rate, as discussed earlier, also wants to keep investment high by having higher savings. Thus, the policy response to addressing two of these main macroeconomic goals is actually going to be somewhat similar. It's going to relate to encouraging national saving. We'll come back to that thought in a later lecture.

If the trade deficits are macroeconomic in nature, and they're about national savings rates, national investment rates, government budget deficits, and the like, then many of the most common arguments you hear about trade deficits are just flatly misguided.

For example, it's common to hear people say, "The U.S. trade deficit happens because of unfair foreign trade practices, shutting out U.S. products, unfair exports to the U.S." But from this perspective, those kinds of unfair trade practices have literally nothing to do with U.S. trade deficits. Again, think about the pattern of U.S. trade deficits in the last few decades. They were small in the 1970s, up in the mid-'80s, down in the early '90s, and then expanding in the mid-'90s and very large in the first half of the 2000s.

If unfair foreign trade practices are the cause of trade deficits, you need to believe foreign trade was really fair in the 1970s, then got really unfair in the mid-1980s, then got pretty fair in the early '90s, then got unfair in the late 1990s, and even more unfair in the 2000s. Some foreign trade practices are pretty unfair, but there's absolutely no evidence that the unfairness is fluctuating up and down according to this kind of a pattern. The general pattern is probably that foreign trade has become slightly less unfair in a gradual kind of way since the 1970s. Again, it's macroeconomic factors driving the trade deficit, not these unfair trade rules or complaints.

Similarly, the whole idea of protectionism—that is, restricting imports from abroad—isn't going to either cause or fix trade deficits. Yes, you can restrict imports from aboard; but if there's a big gap between national saving and national investment, it's going to show up somehow in a trade imbalance. Protectionism is also viewed by most economists as a poor idea because it deprives a nation of the benefits of international trade. This argument is discussed in more detail in Lecture 33 and Lecture 34. My point here is just that protectionism is not likely to solve the trade deficit either because it doesn't deal with these macroeconomic imbalances.

In addition, trade deficits are not primarily determined by a higher level of trade or by greater exposure to the world economy. In the world economy as a whole, world exports are about 25 percent of world GDP. So, question: do countries that export a lot more than 25 percent of GDP have bigger trade deficits and surpluses; and do countries that export less than 25 percent of GDP, and are less exposed to the global economy, have smaller trade deficits or surpluses?

Well, there's no such pattern observed in the data. The trade deficit is not about the level of trade. As I keep saying, it's about an imbalance between domestic saving and domestic investment. Think about the U.S. economy, for example. In the U.S. economy, exports are actually a fairly low share of the U.S. economy by global standards. U.S. exports in recent years are about 10 or 12 percent of GDP. But nonetheless, despite the fact the U.S. economy is somewhat less exposed to the global economy, it still has humongous trade deficits.

Or take Japan. Exports are actually a fairly low share of the huge Japanese economy, by world standards. They're about eight to 10 percent of Japan's GDP. But Japan has extremely large trade surpluses because it has an astonishingly high private savings rate and somewhat lower levels of domestic investment. That money has to flow somewhere, and it flows out of the country in the form of trade surpluses.

Yet another thought. You hear a lot about bilateral trade deficits, that is, the trade deficit the U.S. has with one other country, like China or Japan. But bilateral trade deficits have literally no macroeconomic importance. In economic terms, you would expect the U.S. to have trade surpluses with some countries and trade deficits with some other countries. You would expect those two to more or less balance out. You don't necessarily expect them to balance out with each individual country, though. There are a lot of reasons to worry about an overall trade balance that a nation has, but that overall trade balance can easily have surpluses with some countries and deficits with other countries. There's just no economic reason to strive for balance with every single separate country.

High-income countries, over time, have tended to run trade surpluses, and thus been net investors abroad, investing in low-income countries. But in recent decades, the rest of the world is investing in the U.S. economy, on net. There is no precedent for a situation of the rest of the world investing in the richest economy in the world, on net, and it just doesn't seem likely to continue in the long run.

The historical pattern makes sense. After all, it's usually rich countries and rich people who have money to lend, and they're the ones who then can lend to the poor. So that historical pattern of rich countries lending to poor ones makes perfect sense. The U.S. economy is like a rich person. It can certainly afford to loan to the rest of the world, but at some point, it's not doing so. Instead, it's borrowing money and at some point, those bills are going to need to be paid.

The key question is whether enough domestic investment is happening to produce the economic growth that will let the U.S. pay off all the foreign investors without having to reduce its own standard of consumption. But since the late 1990s, the U.S. has been drawing in enormous volumes of foreign investment from aboard, and it just doesn't seem likely that that's going to last forever.

Ultimately, the question for the rest of the world is: how much in U.S. assets are you willing to hold? At some point, when the rest of the world isn't willing to keep adding and adding to how many U.S. assets it's holding in its financial portfolio, something is going to adjust. Either there will have to be a lower budget deficit—and lower budget deficits, remember, mean higher taxes or less spending; or there will have to be higher domestic savings, which means less consumption; or there will have to be lower investment by firms in plant and equipment. None of these options are attractive ones. Some of them don't even seem very likely, like a much lower budget deficit. But if the U.S. keeps running a high trade deficit, one of those options, at least—and maybe all three—are going to have to come to pass.

Lecture Twenty-Four
Aggregate Supply and Aggregate Demand

Scope:

Economists commonly organize their thinking about the macroeconomy with the model of aggregate demand and aggregate supply. *Aggregate supply* shows the output of the economy given the price level prevailing for inputs. *Potential GDP* refers to the maximum that an economy can produce at a given time, given the labor, capital equipment, and technology available. At any given time, *aggregate demand* may not be sufficient to reach potential output, which leads to a recession, or aggregate demand may exceed potential GDP, which leads to inflation. The model of aggregate supply and aggregate demand helps in understanding how the goals of growth, inflation, unemployment, and the trade balance are related to one another and why certain goals sometimes involve tradeoffs with others. The model also helps in determining appropriate macroeconomic policies.

Outline

I. Trying to accomplish the four goals of macroeconomics at the same time may be tricky. The aggregate supply-aggregate demand model is a macroeconomic framework for thinking about how these goals relate to each other and what tradeoffs may arise. Or is it possible for an economy to attain several or all of its macroeconomic goals at the same time?

II. *Aggregate supply* describes the productive ability of the macroeconomy, while *aggregate demand* is made up of the five components of consumption, investment, government, exports, and imports.

A. Aggregate supply is limited by potential GDP, which is the amount that the economy can produce if all resources are fully employed. At potential GDP, cyclical unemployment is zero and any remaining unemployment is accounted for by the natural rate of unemployment.

B. Aggregate supply shifts for two main reasons: technological growth and sharp changes in conditions of production.

1. The process of productivity growth over time means that the productive potential of the economy is expanding gradually over time.
2. At certain times, there are sharp changes in conditions of production that can reduce what an economy is able to produce. A classic example is the sharp increases in oil prices in the 1970s.

C. Aggregate demand is determined by its five components: consumption, investment, government, exports, and imports. Shifts in these factors will lead to changes in aggregate demand.

III. Aggregate supply in the economy must equal aggregate demand. But one theory argues that aggregate supply creates aggregate demand, while another theory argues that aggregate demand creates aggregate supply.

A. Say's Law is: "Supply creates its own demand." After all, each time a good or service is produced and sold, it represents income that is earned for someone. Neoclassical economists emphasize this view today.

B. The main challenge for Say's Law and neoclassical economics is the existence of recessions. If supply creates its own demand, then it's hard to explain why an economy ever shrinks in size.

C. Keynes's Law is: "Demand creates its own supply." This perspective holds that the economy will often find itself in situations with unemployed workers and unused productive capacity, but it needs a surge of aggregate demand to put that capacity to use. Keynesian economists emphasize this view today.

D. The main conceptual challenge for Keynes's Law is that if demand were all that mattered at the macroeconomic level, then the government could make the economy as large as it wanted just by pumping up total demand through a large increase in government spending or by legislating large tax cuts. But clearly, economies do face genuine limits on how much they can produce at a point in time.

E. In the short run, aggregate demand may not increase smoothly with aggregate supply for two main reasons:

fluctuations in investor or consumer sentiment and price and wage stickiness.

    1. Fluctuations in investor and consumer sentiment can cause firms and consumers to bunch their aggregate demand at certain time periods, which can cause the level of aggregate demand to fall short of potential GDP or to exceed it in the short run.

    2. If wages and prices in markets throughout the economy are often "sticky" and do not adjust immediately to changes in the economy, then unemployment and periods of shortage and surplus can occur.

  F. In the long run, aggregate supply determines the size of the economy. But in the short run, aggregate demand may run behind or ahead of aggregate supply, which can lead to recession or inflation.

IV. The aggregate demand and aggregate supply model can be related to each of the four goals of macroeconomic policy: economic growth, low unemployment, low inflation, and the sustainable balance of trade.

  A. Economic growth is captured by the way in which aggregate supply and potential GDP gradually increase over time. Recessions occur when aggregate demand falls short of potential GDP.

  B. When aggregate demand and aggregate supply meet at potential GDP, there is a low rate of cyclical unemployment. The natural rate of unemployment is embodied in the concept of potential GDP.

  C. If aggregate demand exceeds potential GDP, then the economy faces a situation of too many dollars chasing too few goods, and inflation will result. Also, if the aggregate supply experiences a negative shock, such as higher oil prices, inflation can result.

  D. Exports, imports, and the balance of trade influence both aggregate demand and aggregate supply in various ways.

Essential Reading:

Council of Economic Advisers, "Chapter 1: The Year in Review and the Years Ahead," in *Economic Report of the President*, February 2005, www.gpoaccess.gov/eop.

"Oil in Troubled Waters: A Survey of Oil," *The Economist*, April 30, 2005.

Supplementary Reading:

Douglas A. Ruby, *The Components of Aggregate Demand*, revised January 15, 2003, www.digitaleconomist.com/ad_4020.html.

————, *Long Run Aggregate Supply and Price Level Determination*, revised January 18, 2003, www.digitaleconomist.com/as_4020.html.

Questions to Consider:

1. How would you expect an increase in aggregate demand to affect inflation? Output? Under what conditions would you expect it to have a bigger effect on inflation? On output?

2. Discuss which is more important in the long run in shaping national output: aggregate demand or aggregate supply. Which is more important in the short run?

Lecture Twenty-Four—Transcript
Aggregate Supply and Aggregate Demand

At this point, I'm hoping you feel comfortable with some of the basic concepts and measurements that are often tossed around in discussions of macroeconomics. I'm hoping you feel comfortable with how GDP is measured, and also with the four macroeconomic goals of economic growth, low unemployment, low inflation, and a sustainable balance of trade. But it is a hard fact that having four separate goals can cause confusion because it raises a question about whether it's possible to reach all of the goals at roughly the same time, or if there are inevitable trade-offs between the goals.

For example, it is impossible to accomplish simultaneously the four goals of being in Los Angeles, London, Beijing, and Rio de Janeiro. But if your four goals are to visit the Statue of Liberty, the Empire State Building, the New York Stock Exchange, and a Broadway show, then all four goals can be accomplished with a single trip to New York City.

Are the four goals of macroeconomics—economic growth, low unemployment, low inflation, and a sustainable balance of trade—like trying to visit four completely different cities in the sense that it's impossible to achieve all four at the same time? Or is it possible for an economy to attain several or all of its macroeconomic goals at more or less the same time?

To think about this issue, we need an organizing framework for how to think about the macroeconomy. The basic framework most commonly used is the aggregate demand/aggregate supply model. So what I want to do in this lecture is to lay out the ideas of aggregate supply and aggregate demand.

Let's start with aggregate supply. Aggregate supply is limited by potential GDP, where potential GDP is the amount that the economy can produce if all resources in the economy are fully employed. At potential GDP, cyclical unemployment would be zero, and so any remaining unemployment would be accounted for by the natural rate of unemployment.

Sometimes, potential GDP is referred to as full employment GDP because it refers to the notion that everyone is employed, and also that the machinery and the capital equipment in the economy is fully employed as well. When we think about the aggregate supply of the economy—that is, the total amount that an economy can produce—it's going to be limited. The most it can do is potential GDP.

Let's think about why aggregate supply might shift. What will change what an economy is capable of producing? There are really two main reasons: one is technological growth, and the other would be a sharp change in the conditions of production that affected many firms across the economy. So let's think about each of these in turn.

The process of productivity growth over time means greater output per hour. In essence, it means the productive potential of an economy is expanding over time. Remember from our earlier lecture that the fundamental determinants of economic growth are: increases in human capital, in physical capital, and in technology, over time. With gradual increases in all three of these, you could imagine potential GDP and aggregate supply slowly rising steadily over time—for a high-income country like the U.S., maybe rising two percent or three percent a year.

But at certain times, there are going to be sharp changes in the conditions of production, and those might reduce what an economy is able to produce. The classic example here is the sharp increases in oil prices that the U.S. economy experienced in the 1970s. Oil is very widely used in the U.S. economy and, of course, energy, including natural gas and other things, are even more widely used. So when the cost of energy rose, it drove up the costs of production for many, many industries all at the same time. This was a negative shock to aggregate supply. While the economy went through a period of adjustment, a period of transition, for some period of time, the economy was able to produce less than it had been before all the costs of energy rose so dramatically.

There we have an idea of aggregate supply. Let's now switch over and think about the idea of aggregate demand. Aggregate demand is determined by its five components. As I've said several times now, its components are: C plus I, plus G, plus X, minus M; that is, consumption plus investment, plus government spending, plus exports, minus imports.

Back in Lecture 19, the discussion of what GDP was and how it's measured, I pointed out that GDP could be measured either by what the economy produced or equivalently, by the main sources of demand in the economy. In terms of the framework we're using here, you can think of aggregate supply as, of course, what the economy produces, and then you can think of aggregate demand in terms of those main ingredients of aggregate demand that we talked about when we were measuring GDP.

Remember that, of the components of aggregate demand, consumption is the biggest one, at two-thirds or more of GDP most years. Investment is smaller, but it's the most volatile, bouncing up and down. Government spending is perhaps under the most direct policy control at any given time. With exports and imports, the demand components there, are heavily shaped by what's happening in other countries. But as these factors shift—that is, consumption, investment, government spending on goods and services, and exports and imports—shifts in those factors will lead to corresponding changes in aggregate demand, and make it go up or down.

For the economy as a whole, the quantity of aggregate supply must equal the quantity of aggregate demand. But, there are competing theories of macroeconomics. One theory argues or emphasizes that aggregate supply really creates or drives aggregate demand. The opposing theory puts aggregate demand first, and suggests that aggregate demand creates or drives the quantity of aggregate supply. So let's run through these two theories in turn.

A famous French economist of the early 19th century named Jean-Baptiste Say is credited with Say's Law: "Supply creates its own demand." Now, as a matter of historical accuracy, it seems clear that Jean-Baptiste Say never actually wrote down this law. It, moreover, seems clear that the law oversimplifies his beliefs. Indeed, there's sort of a running joke among academic economists that every so-called law of economics is named after someone who didn't quite believe it. But Say's Law lives on as useful shorthand for summarizing a certain point of view.

How does supply create demand at the macroeconomic level? Well, each time a good or service is produced and sold, it represents income that is earned for someone. It might represent income for a worker, or a manager, or an owner; or those who are workers, and managers, and owners at firms that supply the inputs down the chain of production to the firm that did the actual selling. Of course, in individual markets, prices and wages will rise and fall depending upon microeconomic supply and demand in each market. But the bottom line, from a macroeconomic point of view, is that every sale represents income to someone. Therefore, Say's Law argues, a given value of supply in a macroeconomic sense must create an equivalent value of income and demand somewhere else in the economy.

Because Jean-Baptiste Say and Adam Smith, and other economists writing around the turn of the 19th century, who discussed this point of view, were called the classical economists, modern economists who subscribe to a version of Say's Law, that supply creates its own demand, are typically called neoclassical economists.

The main challenge for Say's Law and neoclassical economics is recessions. After all, if aggregate supply always creates exactly enough aggregate demand at the macroeconomic level, then why should a recession ever happen? Why should there ever be high unemployment? Why should the economy ever contract? Just for the record, to be fair to good old Jean-Baptiste Say, he was perfectly aware of this problem, and it's one of the reasons he didn't completely believe what we now call Say's Law.

Even if total supply—aggregate supply in the economy, always creates an equal amount of aggregate demand—the economy could still experience a situation where some firms are earning profits and other firms are earning losses. But a recession, remember, is not a situation where business failures are being counterbalanced by an off-setting number of successes. A recession is a situation in which the whole economy is shrinking in size; business failures heavily are outnumbering the few remaining success stories; many firms are suffering losses and laying off workers. So if supply always creates its own demand, it's difficult to explain how an economy can get into that situation.

The alternative to Say's Law, with its emphasis on aggregate supply, can be named Keynes' Law, after the great 20th-century British economist John Maynard Keynes. It says, "Demand creates its own supply." Now, as a matter of historical accuracy, just as Jean-Baptiste Say never wrote down anything as simply-minded as Say's Law, John Maynard Keynes never wrote down anything as simple as what I'm calling Keynes' Law. But the law is still a useful simplification that conveys a certain point of view.

When John Maynard Keynes was writing his great work *The General Theory of Employment, Interest, and Money* during the Great Depression of the 1930s, he pointed out that during the Depression, the capacity of the economy to supply goods and services really had not changed by much. U.S. unemployment rates were higher than 20 percent between 1933 and 1935, but the number of possible workers, the number of potential workers, had not increased or decreased much. In that time period, factories are closed and shuttered, but the machinery and the equipment, and the potential supply from that machinery and equipment, hadn't disappeared. Technologies that had been invented in the 1920s were not "dis-invented" and forgotten in the 1930s.

Thus, Keynes argued that the Great Depression—and many ordinary recessions as well—are not caused by a drop in the ability of the economy to supply goods—at least as measured by the ability to supply, as measured by labor, and physical capital, and technology. But instead, Keynes argued, economies went into a recession because of a lack of demand in the economy as a whole. A lack of aggregate demand led to inadequate incentives for firms to produce.

Keynes argued that the level of GDP in the economy was, thus, not primarily determined by the potential of what the economy could supply, but rather by whether there was enough total demand to encourage firms to take advantage of that potential supply. In his mind, a greater amount of aggregate demand could, thus, call forth an increase in supply and move an economy out of a recession.

What's the main conceptual challenge for Keynes' Law? Well, if aggregate demand is all that matters at the macroeconomic level, then the government could make the economy as large as it wanted, just by pumping up total demand, through a large increase in government spending or by enormous tax cuts to push up consumption. After all, just push up demand as high as you possibly can, and if demand creates its own supply, then the result should be that you can make the economy infinitely large with infinitely large tax cuts.

But economies do face genuine limits on how much they can produce at a point in time. Those genuine limits are determined by the quantity of labor, and physical capital, and technology, as well as by the market structures and the institutions of the economy that bring these factors of production together. These constraints on what an economy can supply at the macroeconomic level don't disappear just because there was some increase in demand.

The fundamental problem is: why don't aggregate supply and aggregate demand match up? In the short run, aggregate demand might not increase smoothly with aggregate supply, for at least two reasons. One reason is that there can be fluctuations in business and consumer confidence, and that can cause firms and consumers to bunch their aggregate demand at certain time periods. That could cause the level of aggregate demand in the economy to fall short of potential GDP or sometimes even to exceed potential GDP, at least in the short run.

When firms are thinking about whether it's a good time to invest, they look out at the economy as a whole and they think to themselves, "Does this look like a time when, if we put in the costs of an investment, we'll get a relatively quick future payoff? Or does it look like a time when the future payoff might be deferred quite a few years, and so we should wait and do it at some point in the future?"

When firms are pessimistic or uncertain about the economic future, they put off their investment projects—or at least some of them; they postpone some into the future. Then, when businesses think the economy's doing well, and they become more optimistic, they often have a backlog of projects that they have all ready to go, and all ready to start up all at once. This is, of course, one reason why the investment component of aggregate demand is likely to surge and decline so rapidly.

An example: in the second half of the 1990s, the U.S. economy experienced a wave of new information and communications technologies, including the Internet, technologies that involved computing, and vastly improved mobile phones. So U.S. investment levels surged at this time, from about 18 percent of GDP in 1994, up to 21 percent of GDP by the year 2000. However, a recession starts in the U.S. economy in 2000, and many firms came to believe that the returns from investing in new computers and new equipment—at least for any additional investment—were not as high as they had been thinking. So, U.S. investment levels quickly sank back to 18 percent of GDP by 2002. This fluctuation in investment can create a situation where, instead of having aggregate demand growing step by step in a smooth way with aggregate supply, aggregate demand sometimes surges and sometimes falls back.

Another reason for big fluctuations in investment patterns can be tied to a nation's financial system. In the Great Depression, for example, many businesses and households were unable to repay their loans, and banks went bankrupt as a result. In fact, of 24,000 U.S. banks that were in operation in 1929, only about 14,400 banks remained in operation in 1933. When so many banks went out of business, the availability of loans diminished for firms that were seeking to invest, and the availability of loans diminished for households that were seeking to buy a home or a car. When households and firms weren't able to borrow as much, aggregate demand dropped off sharply. This combination of financial market pressures and lack of demand helped create a situation where aggregate demand fluctuated in an extreme way rather than keeping up with aggregate supply and its slow, long-term growth.

If wages and prices in markets throughout the economy are often sticky, and don't adjust immediately to changes in the economy, then that's another reason why periods of shortage, and surplus, and unemployment can occur. We talked about some of this back in the lecture on unemployment. Remember, wages are often what economists call "sticky." That is, wages adjust to market conditions, but slowly, and businesses tend to avoid wage cuts because such cuts may depress morale, and hurt the productivity of existing workers, and can even cause all the best workers to leave a firm.

So when demand for product diminishes—when there's a recession, when demand diminishes, perhaps, because consumers are deciding not to buy; or the financial market isn't making a lot of loans—firms don't immediately cut workers' pay. Instead, they try and hold onto workers for a time and pay the same amount. Maybe they lay some workers off temporarily. The result is unemployment, and a pattern of aggregate demand that doesn't match this slow, long-term growth of aggregate supply.

©2005 The Teaching Company Limited Partnership

Some modern economists have taken that theory of sticky wages and extended it to argue that it's not just wages that might be sticky in an economy, but prices as well. For example, think about many companies that publish sales catalogs; they publish them every six months or every year, instead of saying, "Well, the price might change any given day." Clearly, their prices are sticky; they're not bouncing up and down on a daily basis.

The underlying issue here is that when a firm considers changing its price, it has to analyze the competition and the market demand, and decide what it thinks the new price should be. It also has a lot of costs. It might need to update sales materials, update billing records, change product labels and price labels. Also, particularly if prices are going up, it might make some important customers angry or confused. So, the firm has to think about when it is a good time to incur those costs of substantial price changes. Economists call these costs of changing prices the *menu costs*. They call them menu costs because it's like if a restaurant wants to change its prices, it has to print up a new set of menus.

Prices do respond to forces of demand and supply. All the microeconomic stuff we learned about markets holds true. But from a macroeconomic perspective, the process of changing all the prices throughout the economy—when they're going up, when they're going down—just takes time. It doesn't always happen instantaneously; it doesn't happen overnight.

If the prices in a number of markets do not adjust quickly to equilibrium, then you're going to have periods when the price is out of equilibrium. You're going to have periods of surpluses, when things are piling up on shelves throughout the economy. You're going to have other periods when people might have to wait six months if they want to buy a certain kind of car. You're going to have these surges of aggregate demand and declines of aggregate demand in a way where, at least in the short run, aggregate supply and aggregate demand don't match up with each other.

In the long run, aggregate supply does determine the size of the economy. In the long run, productive capacity is what determines how much an economy can make, and that does shape the course of the economy over time. Sure, the U.S. economy has a recession now and then, but if you look at the basic determinants—human capital, physical capital, technology—and the size of its population, the U.S. economy doesn't suddenly plummet down to, say, Mexico's standard of living and then suddenly plummet back.

Instead, Say's Law is roughly right in the long run. It is true that in the long run, potential GDP and aggregate supply do create the necessary demand for the economy to run at that level. But in short run, in contrast to the long run, aggregate demand can run a little behind or a little ahead of aggregate supply, which can lead to situations of recession or inflation. The basic argument here is that Keynes' Law is probably right in the short run, but perhaps not in the long run.

In one of the most famous quotations in economics, John Maynard Keynes recognized this fact. He talked about how it was true that aggregate supply ruled the long run, but aggregate demand perhaps ruled the short run. In an essay he wrote in 1920–21, well before the Great Depression, Keynes wrote, "Now, in the long run, this is probably true." And, "in the long run," he's referring to how aggregate supply determines the output in an economy. So, "in the long run," Keynes wrote, "this is probably true. But this long run is a misleading guide to current affairs. In the long run, we are all dead. Economists set themselves too easy, too useless a task if, in tempestuous seasons, they can only tell us that when the storm is long past, the ocean is flat again." That's a lovely metaphor, I think. It's not useful in the middle of a recession to say, "Well, in the long run, potential supply will make it all work out." When you're in the middle of the storm, when you're in the middle of the Depression, when you're in the middle of a recession, you need to do something about it at that time, even if it involves aggregate demand.

Overall, if we look at the macroeconomy, we think about how this combination of surges and drop-offs in investment, surges and drop-offs in consumption, combined together with ways in which labor markets and goods markets have sticky wages, and sticky prices, and are slow to adjust; and the combination of those together means, from a macroeconomic view, aggregate demand is not always going to easily match aggregate supply in the short run. Aggregate demand may be moving up and down, and shifting away and toward potential GDP.

Some economists take a neoclassical point of view; some economists take the Keynesian view. Probably the mainstream view for the economics profession as a whole is that Keynesian statements about the importance of aggregate demand are more relevant for short-run policy, and neoclassical statements about the importance of aggregate supply are more important in the long run. This, of course, leaves us at some level riding two horses, an aggregate supply horse and an aggregate demand horse, and trying to make them work together, without a clear sense of exactly how we're supposed to bridge the gap. There's a lot of modern work in macroeconomics, which is trying to piece together a model that would include both the short run and the long run; but I think it's fair to say that no widely accepted model like that has yet gained sway over the economics profession.

The aggregate demand and aggregate supply model that we've been talking about can be related to each of the four goals of macroeconomic policy: economic growth, low unemployment, low inflation, and sustainable balance of trade. Let's run through how each of these different things is taken into account.

For example, how is growth is GDP and recession taken into account in the aggregate demand/aggregate supply model? Well, economic growth is captured by the way in which aggregate supply and potential GDP gradually increase over time in the long run. On the other side, recessions occur in the aggregate demand/aggregate supply model when aggregate demand falls short of potential GDP in the short run. So, the model can help us think about both the long-run growth pattern and why the economy might not live up to potential GDP in the short run.

How is unemployment taken into account in the aggregate demand/aggregate supply model? Well, if aggregate demand and aggregate supply are meeting at potential GDP, so that the economy is producing at its potential, then there's going to be a low rate or zero cyclical unemployment—no cyclical unemployment at all. However, the natural rate of unemployment will continue, even if the economy is producing at potential GDP.

If you're thinking about how to fix unemployment that is happening during a recession, the logical answer is to think like a Keynesian, at least for the short term, and figure out a way to increase aggregate demand, so there's enough aggregate demand in the economy to have a derived demand for labor that will reduce cyclical unemployment down to zero. But if you're at potential GDP, and the economy's producing at potential GDP, and you want to reduce unemployment, then you need to think about the natural rate of unemployment, and how you might find ways to reduce that.

How is inflation taken into account in the aggregate supply/aggregate demand model? Well, you can get into a situation, in some cases, where aggregate demand exceeds potential GDP. What does that exactly mean? Well, there's a certain amount the economy can produce. And if the government really, really pumped a lot of demand into the economy, through enormous tax cuts, or through very, very low interest rates, or just by printing money and disturbing it—like the case of the magical money elves we talked about in the inflation chapter—then you can have a situation of too many dollars chasing too few goods, and inflation will result. The implication is that, if a country has inflation, it needs to reduce, or at least restrain, the growth of aggregate demand, so that you don't have a situation where there's so much being demanded in the economy that it can't conceivably produce it all.

Also, if aggregate supply experiences a negative shock, like the higher oil prices we talked about before, this can lead to a situation of inflation as well. Higher oil prices, or higher energy prices, mean that across the economy, many firms are facing higher prices for inputs, and those firms will want to get a higher price for their outputs, too. As they try and pass that higher cost along, you can end up with higher inflation for the economy as a whole.

What about exports and imports? They don't show up directly in this model, but they come up in a lot of different ways. In terms of aggregate demand, remember that exports and imports are two of the components of aggregate demand. Exports to other countries add to aggregate demand; imports to other countries decrease aggregate demand. Sharp movements in exports and imports are going to move aggregate demand. When we think about the balance of trade, it's clearly going to have implications for whether aggregate demand is going up or down.

On the other side, in terms of aggregate supply, the balance of trade is closely linked to the national savings and investment identity that we talked about back in Lecture 23. Remember, that inflow of foreign investment capital because of trade deficits is one key element that determines U.S. levels of investment—the investment capital that's available for firms—and thus, helps to determine what the U.S. rate of economic growth is going to be.

Ideally, in the perfect macroeconomy, aggregate supply would steadily grow with productivity; so there would be more investment in human capital, physical capital and technology; and aggregate supply would steadily grow. In the meantime, aggregate demand would steadily grow, based on the income being produced by that aggregate supply. The two would march together in locked step; so the economy was always producing at potential GDP and steadily growing, with fairly low levels of inflation and fairly low levels of unemployment. But in the real world, economic growth is not a given, nor is coordination between aggregate supply and aggregate demand. That's, of course, with makes macroeconomics intellectually interesting and a real policy challenge.

Glossary

absolute advantage: one nation can produce a certain good with higher productivity (or fewer inputs)

adverse selection: the problem that relatively safe risks will not desire to buy insurance, while relatively unsafe risks will, which unless dealt with, will make it impossible to offer insurance

appropriability: the ability of a producer to reap the benefits of an investment or an invention

automatic stabilizers: the property of taxes and certain government spending that they help stimulate aggregate demand when the economy is declining and hold down aggregate demand as the economy is expanding

balanced budget: when government taxes are equal to spending; see also **budget deficit** and **budget surplus**

barter: exchanging one good or service directly for another, without the use of money

bilateral trade balance: the balance of trade between two specific countries, as opposed to the trade balance between one nation's economy and the rest of the world economy

bond: a way for a government or private firm to borrow money from private investors, then to repay the money with interest

budget deficit: when annual government spending exceeds taxes

budget surplus: when annual government taxes exceed spending

business cycle: the rise and fall of the economy from troughs of recessions to peaks in periods of growth and back again

capital market: the exchanges between lenders of capital, those who have money to save, and borrowers of capital, who will pay interest for the use of that money

cartel: a group of producers who agree to act together in setting prices and output

central bank: the agency in any country that conducts monetary policy; the U.S. Federal Reserve, the Bank of Japan, and the European Central Bank are examples

certificate of deposit: a certificate where the investor agrees to leave the money with a bank for a preset time, and the bank, in exchange, pays a higher interest rate

command-and-control regulations: regulations that specify the quantities and/or prices of what will be produced

comparative advantage: when a nation has either the largest productivity advantage in producing a certain good or service, compared to other nations, or if it has no area of productivity advantage, the smallest productivity disadvantage in producing a certain good or service

compound interest: interest paid both on the original amount saved and on other interest that has accumulated over time

concentration ratio: adding up the market share of the largest firms in an industry, typically the largest four firms

contractionary policy: when fiscal or monetary policy is used to reduce aggregate demand; also called *tight* policy

copyright: a form of legal protection against copying original works of authorship, including literary, musical, and other works

cost-plus regulation: setting a regulated price that a firm is allowed to charge by first calculating its costs of production (allowing for a low normal level of profit), then setting the price to cover that amount

countercyclical policy: going against the cycle of the economy; that is, increasing aggregate demand when the economy is producing below potential GDP and holding down on aggregate demand if the economy threatens to exceed potential GDP

current account balance: the broadest measure of the trade balance, looking at imports and exports of goods, services, investment income, and unilateral transfers

cyclical unemployment: unemployment caused because the economy is in a recession

demand: the relationship between market price and the quantity demanded; it is a line, not a single quantity

discount rate: the interest rate charged by the central bank on loans to individual banks

diversification: buying a number of investments to reduce risk, so that those investments that do unexpectedly poorly will be offset to some extent by those doing unexpectedly well

division of labor: dividing the production of a certain good or service into a related group of smaller tasks, with each worker focusing on a limited part of the overall process

double coincidence of wants: a situation in which two people each want some good or service that the other person can provide, thus making it possible for them to trade without the use of money

dumping: the practice of selling at below cost to drive out the competition, then being able to charge higher prices; also called *predatory pricing*

economies of scale: when a larger firm can produce at a lower average cost of production than a smaller firm, at least up to some level of output

efficiency: when a market operates without wasted effort; that is, no excess quantity supplied and no excess quantity demanded at the prevailing price

elastic: elasticity (in absolute value) greater than 1

elasticity of demand: (% change in quantity demanded)/(% change in price)

elasticity of supply: (% change in quantity supplied)/(% change in price)

equilibrium: the price at which quantity supplied is equal to quantity demanded

equity: part ownership of a firm; also called *stock*

exchange rate: the rate at which one currency can be traded for another

expansionary policy: when fiscal or monetary policy is used to increase aggregate demand; also called *loose* policy

externality: when a party outside of the buyer and seller is directly affected by the transaction

Federal Reserve: the somewhat public, somewhat private agency that conducts monetary policy

fiscal policy: government tax and spending policy

free-rider problem: when some people can receive benefits from public goods without a need to pay their fair share of the costs

frictional unemployment: unemployment caused by the ebb and flow of some companies losing money in a dynamic market economy

goods market: the exchanges between sellers of goods and services (which are usually businesses) and buyers of goods and services (usually consumers)

gross domestic product (GDP): the total value of final goods and services produced in an economy in a year

Herfindahl-Hirschman index: a measure of the concentration of a market, calculated by summing the square of the market share of each firm

Hyperinflation: very rapid inflation; say, 40% per *month* or more

import quota: a quantitative limit on how much of a certain good can be imported

indexing: adjusting a price, wage, or interest rate automatically for changes in inflation

inelastic: elasticity (in absolute value) less than 1

infant industry: an industry that, it is argued, needs temporary government subsidies so that it can expand and be able to compete effectively

inflation: a rise in the overall level of prices

inflation-targeting: when the central bank is legally required to focus only on keeping inflation low

in-kind: when payment is made in the form of goods or services, not in the form of cash

labor market: the exchanges between sellers of labor, workers, and buyers of labor, which are firms and other employers

liquidity: whether an investment is easy to sell (that is, to liquidate)

log-rolling: when two politicians agree to each support provisions that are especially important to the other, with the result that many bills important to individual legislators but perhaps not important to the broad social welfare become law

macroeconomics: the aggregated top-down view of the economy, focused on such issues as unemployment, inflation, economic growth, and the balance of trade

marketable permits: a right to produce a certain amount of something; if not used or desired, this right can be sold to others; often applied to pollution control, as a right to produce a certain amount of pollution

medium of exchange: the property of money that it can be traded for almost all goods, services, and debts

merchandise trade balance: the balance between imports and exports of goods only; for contrast, see **current account balance**

microeconomics: the study of how individual households and firms make decisions in markets

monetary policy: policies of the Federal Reserve that affect interest rates and credit

money market mutual fund: a mutual fund that invests in very liquid, low-risk bonds

monopolistic competition: when many firms compete by selling differentiated products

monopoly: when a single seller has all or most of the sales in a given market

moral hazard: the problem that when insurance is provided against a risk, the incentives to prevent the danger from happening are diminished

mutual fund: an investment fund that makes a number of different investments; investors receive returns according to how the fund performs as a whole

natural monopoly: when a monopoly exists because the industry has economies of scale, giving a large, established firm an advantage over any new entrants

natural rate of unemployment: the level of unemployment generated by the institutional structures in an economy that encourage hiring and firing

negative externality: when a party outside the transaction between buyer and seller is negatively affected, as in the case of pollution

negative income tax: when the government reduces welfare benefits as the recipient earns additional income

nominal interest rate: the actual interest rate charged or paid

nonexcludable: when a seller cannot exclude those who did not pay from using the good; for example, clean air

nonrivalrous: the good itself is not diminished as more people use it; for example, national defense

non-tariff barriers (NTBs): bureaucratic and regulatory steps that have the effect of restricting imports

oligopoly: when a small number of large firms have most or all of the revenues in a given market

open-market operations: when a central bank buys or sells bonds with the goal of decreasing or increasing the money supply

opportunity costs: true cost is measured by the opportunities given up, including possible alternative purchases and uses of time

patent: an exclusive legal right granted by the government to make, use, or sell an invention for a specific and limited time

per capita: divided by the population

perfect competition: small firms making identical products that must act as price-takers in their market

Phillips curve: a diagram showing the tradeoff (or lack of a tradeoff) between inflation and unemployment

pollution taxes: a tax added to the price of products, according to the social cost of the pollution produced by that product

pork-barrel spending: spending in which the benefits are focused on one politician's district, while the costs are spread across the country

portfolio: a group of investments

positive externality: when a party outside the transaction between buyer and seller is positively affected, as in the case in which new technology is developed but others benefit from it

potential GDP: the economic output that is achievable with full employment of labor and other productive resources

predatory pricing: the practice of selling at below cost to drive out the competition, then being able to charge higher prices; also called *dumping*

present discounted value (or present value): the amount that future payments are worth in the present if they were to be received immediately and could then be invested at the prevailing interest rate

price-cap regulation: the regulator sets a price that the regulated firm can charge over the next few years, and if the firm can cut costs by more than expected, it can earn additional profits

price ceiling: when government sets a price above which more cannot be charged

price floor: when government sets a price below which less cannot be charged

price index: a way of showing how the overall price level changes over time, which involves setting the price level in a base year equal to 100, then calculating all other years respective to the base year

progressive tax: a tax requiring the rich to pay a higher share of income than the poor; opposite of **regressive tax**

protectionism: laws or rule that reduce or shut out imports

public goods: goods that are nonexcludable and nonrivalrous, so that a seller cannot exclude people from using the good, and the good itself is not diminished as people use it

public utility: a firm that is privately owned but regulated by the government and that provides a commodity used by almost every home, such as water, electricity, or communication

purchasing power parity: the exchange rate that equalizes the prices of internationally traded goods across countries

quantity demanded: the actual amount demanded at a specific price

quantity supplied: the actual amount supplied at a specific price

random walk: the mathematical name for a pattern in which the direction of the previous movement doesn't tell you anything about the direction of the next movement

real: adjusted for inflation

real gross domestic product: gross domestic product adjusted for inflation

real interest rate: the nominal interest minus the rate of inflation

recession: a significant and lasting downturn in GDP

regressive tax: a tax requiring the poor to pay a higher share of income than the rich; opposite of **progressive tax**

reserve requirement: a percentage of its deposits that a bank is not allowed to lend out

Ricardian equivalence: the theory that a rise (or fall) in government borrowing will cause an offsetting rise (or fall) in private saving

risk: the probability and extent by which the actual result may differ from the expected result

stock: part ownership of a firm; also called *equity*

store of value: the property of money that it retains most or all of its value over a period of time

structural unemployment: unemployment caused by the taxes and regulations in the economy that discourage working and/or hiring

supply: the relationship between market price and the quantity supplied; it is a line, not a single quantity

tariff: another word for tax, commonly applied to a tax on imported goods

trade balance: a measure comparing total imports and exports; see also **merchandise trade balance** and **current account balance**

trade deficit: when imports exceed exports

trade secret: a formula, process, device, or item of information that gives a business an advantage over competitors, that is not generally known or easily discovered, and that the business makes reasonable efforts to keep secret

trade surplus: when exports exceed imports

trademark: a word, name, symbol, or device that indicates the source of the goods

unemployment: when people who are willing to work at the prevailing wage level can't find jobs

unit of account: the property of money that is used as a yardstick for measuring all economic values across the economy

unitary elasticity: elasticity (in absolute value) equal to 1

voluntary export restraints (VERs): when a nation agrees, usually under diplomatic pressure, to reduce its exports to another nation

Biographical Notes

Kenneth Arrow (1921–) spent most of his academic career at Stanford University, although he was on the Harvard faculty for an interlude in the late 1960s and 1970s. Arrow is known for pathbreaking theoretical work in several areas of economics, such as identifying the precise mathematical conditions under which markets will reach equilibrium, exploring when political institutions will make choices that benefit social welfare, and analyzing the economics of situations where uncertainty and imperfect information exist. In 1972, he was a co-winner of the fourth Nobel Prize in economics ever given. For a concise biography of Arrow, see www.econlib.org/library/CEEBiographies. The Web page at nobelprize.org/economics/laureates/ 1972/index.html offers an autobiography that was updated by Arrow in 2005, along with the (somewhat technical) text of his Nobel Prize address and links to his Web page at Stanford University. For an illuminating 1995 interview with Arrow, see www.minneapolisfed.org/pubs/region/95-12/int9512.cfm.

Frederic Bastiat (1801–1850) was not a professional economist but, rather, one of the most skilled polemicists who has ever written for a popular audience in favor of free trade and free markets. He specialized in satirical anecdotes with a sharp point, such as his proposal that sunlight should be banned because of the unfair competition it provided to candle makers. For a brief biography of Bastiat, see www.econlib.org/library/CEEBiographies.html.

Adolf Berle (1895–1971) was born in Boston, Massachusetts. His undergraduate and law degrees were from Harvard University. In 1927, he became a professor of corporate law at Columbia. In 1933, he wrote (with Gardiner Means) the classic book *The Modern Corporation and Private Property*, which emphasized how large corporations had developed a separation between their ownership by shareholders and their day-to-day control by corporate managers. Berle was also involved in politics and diplomacy for much of his life. He was a member of the Versailles peace delegation at the end of World War I (and he strongly opposed the outcome as being too punitive toward Germany). He had close links to the Franklin Roosevelt administration and the New Deal. He was assistant secretary of state for Latin American affairs from 1938–1944 and ambassador to Brazil from 1945–1946, after which he returned to his academic position at Columbia.

Alan Blinder (1945–) has been a professor of economics at Princeton University since 1971. He is especially well-known for his work on fiscal policy, monetary policy, and the distribution of income. He served as a member of President Clinton's Council of Economic Advisers in 1993–1994 and as vice chairman of the Board of Governors of the Federal Reserve System from June 1994 until January 1996. More recently, he acted as an economic adviser to Al Gore in 2000 and John Kerry in 2004. Blinder is one of the best writers and expositors among top-notch professional economists. He is a co-author, along with William Baumol, of one of the leading economics textbooks, *Economics: Principles and Policy.* He also wrote one of the best books for describing to the general public how economists think (although the specific policy examples in the book have become dated over time), *Hard Heads, Soft Hearts: Tough-Minded Economics for a Just Society.* For an interview with Blinder, see minneapolisfed.org/pubs/region/94-12/int9412.cfm.

Anthony Downs (19XX–) has been a senior fellow at the Brookings Institution in Washington, D.C., since 1977. For 18 years before that, he worked for the Real Estate Research Corporation, a consulting firm specializing in real estate and urban affairs. His most famous academic work is the 1957 book *An Economic Theory of Democracy.* In recent years, Downs has often written about traffic congestion issues, including a book called *Stuck in Traffic,* originally written in 1992 but updated and revised as *Still Stuck in Traffic* in 2004. His personal Web site with additional information is at www.anthonydowns.com.

Milton Friedman (1912–) was a professor of economics at the University of Chicago for 33 years, from 1940–1973. He then moved to the Hoover Institution at Stanford University, where he has remained intellectually active as of this writing (in mid-2005). He won a Nobel Prize for economics in 1976. Among the general public, he is well known for his advocacy of free-market views, including support for school vouchers and for an all-volunteer military force. Among professional economists, he is especially well known for his work on monetary economics. One of his major works, *A Monetary History of the United States, 1867–1960,* appeared in 1963 and tells the history of the U.S. economy through its monetary policy. For a short biography, see www.econlib.org/library/ CEEBiographies.html. The Nobel Prize Web site offers a nice autobiography by Friedman, updated in 2005, as well as other resources about his career, at nobelprize.org/economics/laureates/1976/index.html.

Alan Greenspan (1926–) was appointed as chairman of the Federal Reserve in 1987, and his term is scheduled to expire in 2006. He has held other high-profile government positions, including chairman of the President's Council of Economic Advisers under President Ford from 1974–1977 and chairman of the National Commission on Social Security Reform from 1981–1983. He has never been an academic professor of economics. From 1954–1974 and again from 1977–1987, Greenspan ran his own economic consulting firm in New York City.

Michael Harrington (1928–1989) was perhaps the most prominent socialist in the United States from the 1960s through the 1980s. His 1962 book, *The Other America: Poverty in the United States*, galvanized politicians toward the set of programs that became known as the War on Poverty of the 1960s. This volume of statistics, straightforward analysis, and simply told narratives attracted an extraordinary amount of attention. In 1972, Harrington became a professor of political science at Queens College of the City University of New York.

Robert Heilbroner (1919–2005) spent his professional career at the New School for Social Research, where he taught from the early 1960s into the late 1990s. His most well known work is *The Worldly Philosophers*, a beautifully written and highly accessible history of economic thought. In his other work, Heilbroner was a highly unconventional economist who avoided economic jargon and mathematical and statistical modeling and often criticized the field of economics for a lack of concern with social and political issues.

John Maynard Keynes (1883–1946) worked in the British Civil Service in India in the early part of the 20th century, taught economics at Cambridge, and then took a position in government. After attending the World War I peace conference at Versailles, Keynes resigned in protest over the economic terms of the treaty and wrote *Economic Consequences of the Peace*, which predicted that the requirements for economic reparations from Germany in the treaty would bring financial and political disasters to Europe. Keynes believed that market forces worked fairly well in microeconomic markets, but in his most famous work, *The General Theory of Employment, Interest and Money*, published in 1936, he laid out the then-novel case that the government had a role to play in reducing the length and depth of recessions. He was also a key participant in the Bretton Woods Conference, from which emerged the International Monetary Fund and the International Bank for Reconstruction and Development (the World Bank). For a short biography, see www.econlib.org/library/ Enc/bios/Keynes.html. For a quick survey of his professional writings with some useful links, see cepa.newschool.edu/het/profiles/keynes.htm.

Robert E. Lucas (1937–) began his career at Carnegie Mellon University but has been at the University of Chicago since 1980. His most prominent early work examined how people's expectations about government policy could affect or even offset the desired effects of that policy. Much of his later work has focused on understanding causes and patterns of global economic growth. He won the Nobel Prize in economics in 1995. For an autobiography and other resources, see the Nobel Prize Web site at nobelprize.org/economics/laureates/ 1995/index.html.

Burton Malkiel (1932–) has spent most of his academic career at Princeton University, with an interlude on President Ford's Council of Economic Advisers from 1975–1977. Malkiel is well known as a defender of the *random walk hypothesis* of stock market prices, which is the theory that the prices of individual stocks are fundamentally unpredictable because they take all past information into account and change only in response to new information. Malkiel's highly readable book, *A Random Walk Down Wall Street*, explains the evidence behind this theory to a popular audience. His home page at Princeton is www.princeton.edu/~bmalkiel/.

Karl Marx (1818–1883) is the preeminent economist and philosopher of communism. His best-known work is probably *The Communist Manifesto*, with its famous closing lines: "The proletarians have nothing to lose but their chains. They have a world to win. Working Men of All Countries, Unite!" Among economists, however, Marx is better known for his analyses and predictions of how the 19th-century economy was evolving, especially in the conflicting relationship between workers and owners of capital.

Although most of his specific economic predictions did not, in fact, come true, his view of the economy as involving an ongoing conflict between owners and workers has had a powerful resonance. For background information about Marx and many links to his writing, two useful Web sites are homepage.newschool.edu/het/profiles/marx.htm and www.marxists.org.

Gardiner Means (1896–1998) is well known among academic economists for his classic 1932 book, *The Modern Corporation and Private Property*, co-authored with Adolf Berle, which discussed how the large corporations that had become eminent in preceding decades suffered from a separation of ownership (nominally by their shareholders) and their day-to-day control (by their managers). Means also prominently argued in the 1940s–1960s that large corporations and some large unions do not face much competition and, thus, have considerable discretion to adjust their quantity of output and the prices they charge to maintain high profits.

John Stuart Mill (1806–1873) was one of the great economists and political philosophers of the 19th century. In one famous essay, "On Liberty," he explained and defended the idea that society should avoid interfering in people's decisions. In another famous essay, "On the Subjection of Women," he argued for the equality of men and women. Among economists, Mill's most famous work was his *Principles of Political Economy*. The first edition was published in 1848, and the book became the standard textbook for learning economics over the following 40 years. This comprehensive work offered detailed explanations of supply and demand, money, the merits of free trade, taxation, and many other principles. Overall, Mill argued that society could separate decisions about the production of goods, which was best done through markets, and decisions about the distribution of goods, where government taxes and spending programs might play a useful role. For a short biography of Mill with links to some of his writings, see www.econlib.org/library/CEEBiographies.html. Mill also wrote one of the greatest of all intellectual autobiographies, describing how he was raised by his father to be a utilitarian genius, how he rebelled against this training as a teenager, and how his career developed. His autobiography is available on-line at www.utilitarianism.com/jsmill.htm.

Mollie Orshansky (1915–) was not an academic economist but, instead, worked in government agencies, including the U.S. Children's Bureau, the U.S. Department of Agriculture, and the Social Security Administration. In the early 1960s, she was given the task of defining a poverty line. Her insight was to link the poverty line to the cost of purchasing a basic necessary diet, which in turn, allowed a poverty line that varied according to the number of people in a household. Her poverty line was officially adopted by the U.S. government in the late 1960s and, with minor changes and adjustments for inflation, has been used ever since.

Vilfredo Pareto (1848–1923) was not especially famous during his lifetime, although he did hold a position at the University of Lausanne in Switzerland. His work was rediscovered and given higher prominence during the 1930s. Pareto is perhaps best known today for enunciating the *Pareto principle*, that is, that a society is better off in situation A than in situation B if at least one person is better off in situation A than in B and no one is worse off. This principle is not uncontroversial, but it has proven a useful starting point for theories of social choice ever since. Pareto was also one of the first to demonstrate that for the purposes of economic theory, people did not need to measure utility in any numerical way but needed to decide only whether they preferred one set of goods and services to another. For a personal and intellectual biography with many links to his works, see homepage.newschool.edu/het/profiles/pareto.htm.

Alban W. Phillips (1914–1975) is known as the originator of the *Phillips curve*, which plotted data on unemployment and inflation and showed that there was a tradeoff between them; that is, higher unemployment tended to mean lower inflation and vice versa. More recent thinking commonly holds that the Phillips curve represents a short-run tradeoff, but that in the long run, unemployment reverts to a level determined by the laws and regulations that establish incentives to work and to hire in an economy. For a short biography and links, see cepa.newschool.edu/het/profiles/phillips.htm.

David Ricardo (1772–1823) made an immense personal fortune, estimated at more than $100 million in current dollars, in finance. He didn't become interested in economics until middle age, then focused on the subject for the rest of his life. He is best known among modern economists for the first clear demonstration of the principle of comparative advantage as applied to international trade, which shows that even if one nation has better productivity in all goods than another, both countries can still benefit from trading with each other if they focus on the goods where their relative productivity advantage is greatest or their relative productivity disadvantage is least. Ricardo is highly respected among economists in part for his rigorous, point-by-point explanations of his arguments, but this also makes for a prose style that can be dry and difficult to read. For short biographies and links, see homepage.newschool.edu/het/profiles/ricardo.htm and www.econlib.org/library/Enc/bios/Ricardo.html.

Joan Robinson (1903–1983) taught at Cambridge University from 1928 until retiring in 1971. She was probably the most prominent female economist of the 20th century—which also means, perhaps, ever. Her most prominent work involved developing a theory of imperfect competition, that is, a theory of firms that were not monopolies but still had some power to raise prices without losing all their sales to competitors. For a useful biography and links, see homepage.newschool.edu/het and www.econlib.org/library/Enc/bios/Robinson.html.

Jean-Baptiste Say (1767–1832) discovered economics by reading Adam Smith and became one of the most well known expositors of Smith's views. His eventful career included editing a publication that encouraged free-market thinking in the late 1700s, writing a *Treatise on Political Economy* that got him into trouble with Napoleon, making a private fortune running a cotton factory, and eventually holding some of the first academic appointments in the subject of economics in France. He is remembered among modern economists for *Say's Law*, which holds that for the macroeconomy as a whole, supply creates its own demand. Say did argue for something like Say's Law, but he always argued the theme with a host of sensible qualifications and concerns that are often ignored today. For short biographies with links to some of his work, see homepage.newschool.edu/het/profiles/say.htm or www.econlib.org/library/ Enc/bios/Say.html.

Adam Smith (1723–1790) is viewed as the originator of the field economics. Of course, many others had written on economic issues at earlier times, but in his pathbreaking book *The Wealth of Nations*, Smith provided a comprehensive overview of how economies worked, ranging from the division of labor in factories to issues of foreign trade, money, taxation, and public education. Smith saw economics within a larger context of ethics and justice. He was originally a professor of logic and, later, of moral philosophy at Glasgow University. His first major work was *The Theory of the Moral Sentiments* and his third major work, which we know only from notes because he never completed it, was to be about jurisprudence. For a biography and links, see www.econlib.org/library/ CEEBiographies.html and for more links to Smith's work and writings about him, see cepa.newschool.edu/het/profiles/smith.htm.

Robert Solow (1924–) has spent his academic career at the Massachusetts Institute of Technology. He won the Nobel Prize in 1987 for work exploring the determinants of economic growth, which came to the then-surprising conclusion that the main source of economic growth in an advanced economy is not more investment in physical capital nor more investment in education but, rather, new technology and new methods of production. He is also known as one of the most lucid and graceful writers and speakers in the economics profession. For an example, see his autobiography and other links at the Nobel Prize Web site at nobelprize.org/economics/laureates/1987/index.html.

Herb Stein (1916–1999) worked in a wide array of government economist jobs, culminating in serving as chairman of the Council of Economic Advisers under Presidents Nixon and Ford. As an economist, he was known as a pragmatist and a problem-solver, rather than someone who created new theories. He also blossomed into one of the most lucid and lively writers in the economics profession. For a sample of his writings, see the columns he wrote for Slate magazine toward the end of his life, which are collected at slate.msn.com/?id=3944&cp=2553&nav=navom. A particular favorite of mine is a reflection on the meaning of marriage—from a man who was married for 61 years before the death of his wife—at slate.msn.com/id/2562.

John Taylor (1946–) bounced between Columbia and Princeton Universities early in his career before settling at Stanford. From 2001–2005, he served as undersecretary of treasury for international affairs. He has made a number of important contributions to macroeconomics, including models that seek to explain the stickiness of prices in terms of contractual relations in the economy and a so-called "Taylor rule" for describing and predicting how central banks adjust interest rates. His Stanford Web page has biographical information and links to much of his work at www.stanford.edu/~johntayl.

Paul Volcker (1927–) was chairman of the Federal Reserve from 1979–1987; that is, he was the chairman who broke the back of the double-digit inflation of the 1970s and early 1980s. Volcker did so by being willing to raise interest rates, which brought on a severe recession in the early 1980s but has left a legacy of low inflation in the decades since. He has held a variety of other roles, including undersecretary of the U.S. Treasury in the early 1970s, president of the New York Federal Reserve Bank in the early 1970s, and head of a commission to investigate possible corruption in the United Nations' Oil-for-Food program with Iraq in the 2000s.

Bibliography

Essential Reading:

"American Productivity: The New 'New Economy.'" *The Economist*, September 11, 2003. This article discusses whether the U.S. gains in productivity in the early 2000s are likely to be sustained and argues that ultimately, the information technology revolution may have as big an impact on productivity as did electricity—a previous mega-innovation.

Asch, Peter, and Gigliotti, Gary A. "The Free Rider Paradox—Theory, Evidence, and Teaching." *Journal of Economic Education*, 22:1, Winter 1991. An interesting article that points out that people don't free ride in many situations, at least not completely.

"Asset Management: Other People's Money." *The Economist*, July 3, 2003. *The Economist* regularly runs excellent surveys. This one focuses on the evolution of the industry of managing other people's money.

Bastiat, Frederic. *Economic Sophisms*. Arthur Goddard, trans. and ed. Irvington-on-Hudson, NY: The Foundation for Economic Education, 1996 (1845). Available at www.econlib.org/library/Bastiat/basSoph.html. Bastiat was a talented polemicist, with a gift for showing the absurdity in certain points of view. This book is a series of short essays, good for dipping in and out. For example, I recommend Bastiat's essay on the "negative railway."

Bebchuk, Lucien, and Jesse Fried. "Pay Without Performance: The Unfulfilled Promise of Executive Compensation." *Milken Institute Review*, 2nd quarter 2005. The authors lay out the difficulties that shareholders face in monitoring corporate executives and suggest that something along the lines of a revolution in shareholder power is needed. Available at www.milkeninstitute.org. Click on "Publications" and follow the links.

Bhagwati, Jagdish. "Protectionism." *The Concise Encyclopedia of Economics*. Library of Economics and Liberty. Available at www.econlib.org/library/Enc/ Protectionism.html. Bhagwati is one of the most fierce and able defenders of free trade. This short essay will give you a taste of his arguments and style.

Cohen, Linda, and Roger Noll. "Privatizing Public Research: The New Competitiveness Strategy." In *The Mosaic of Economic Growth*. Ralph Landau, Timothy Taylor, and Gavin Wright, eds. Stanford, CA: Stanford University Press, 1996. More and more, politicians of both parties are attempting to push R&D into the private sector. The results may be good for certain companies that receive government support for their research, but this "privatized" research is not widely available, making it hard for it to have an impact throughout the economy.

Congressional Budget Office. *Baby Boomers' Retirement Prospects: An Overview*. November 2003. Available at www.cbo.gov. The nonpartisan research agency for Congress examines how well prepared the baby-boom generation is for retirement. Most will live far better than their parents did in retirement—but perhaps not as well as they are currently expecting.

―――. *The Economic Costs of Fuel Economy Standards versus a Gasoline Tax*. December 2003. Available at www.cbo.gov. The nonpartisan research agency of Congress evaluates the choice between tougher fuel economy standards and a tax on gasoline as ways of reducing gasoline consumption.

―――. "The Effect of Price Changes on Gasoline Consumption." In *Reducing Gasoline Consumption—Three Policy Options*. November 2002. Available at www.cbo.gov. This report discusses how to reduce gasoline consumption—with some discussion of elasticities along the way.

―――. *The Budget and Economic Outlook: Fiscal Years 2006 to 2015*. January 2005. The nonpartisan research arm of Congress publishes this report each year, along with updates at several points through the year. These CBO projections assume that all current laws remain in force, and they provide a baseline for the policy-makers' discussion of fiscal policy. Available at www.cbo.gov.

―――. *The Long-Term Budget Outlook*. December 2003. Available at www.cbo.gov. The nonpartisan research arm of Congress offers a number of budget scenarios out to 2050, with a particular emphasis on Social Security, health-care costs, and revenue options.

Council of Economic Advisers. *Economic Report of the President*. Each year (usually in February), the Council of Economic Advisers, an agency of academic economists appointed by the president, publishes this report. It typically includes a couple of chapters that offer an overview of macroeconomic developments in the last year or two, then has a set of chapters on specific topics in economic policy. In the back are 120 pages or so of convenient tables with different breakdowns of GDP, employment, inflation, international trade, government taxes and spending, financial markets, and more—usually going back to about 1960. The most recent year and the past few years are available at www.gpoaccess.gov/eop.

————. "Chapter 3: Policies for Dynamic Labor Markets." In *Economic Report of the President*. February 2003. Available at www.gpoaccess.gov/eop. Discussions of movement in and out of the labor force, skill development, and other issues.

————. "Chapter 1: Lessons from the Recent Business Cycle." In *Economic Report of the President*. February 2004. This chapter draws out five lessons of the recession of 2001 and its aftermath, including lessons about why recessions happen and about countercyclical macroeconomic policy. Available at www.gpoaccess.gov/eop.

————. "Chapter 8: Regulating Energy Markets." In *Economic Report of the President*. February 2004. Available at www.gpoaccess.gov/eop. An accessible discussion of some of the ways flexible prices and markets work well in encouraging sensible consumption and production decisions and how a combination of market forces and misguided regulation can sometimes go very wrong, as in the market for electricity.

————. "Chapter 9: Protecting the Environment." In *Economic Report of the President*. February 2004. This chapter offers an introduction to market-oriented perspectives on protecting the environment, along with some discussion of current environmental issues.

————. "Chapter 14: The Link Between Trade and Capital Flows." In *Economic Report of the President*. February 2004. Available at www.gpoaccess.gov/eop. This chapter offers some basic background and trends on the trade deficit, along with a nice explanation couched in terms of the national savings and investment identity.

————. "Chapter 1: The Year in Review and the Years Ahead." In *Economic Report of the President*. February 2005. A chapter similar to this one appears at the start of the ERP each year. It runs through each of the main categories of aggregate demand—C, I, G, X, and

M—and explores how they have behaved in the past few years. Available at www.gpoaccess.gov/eop.

————. "Chapter 2: Expansions Past and Present." In *Economic Report of the President*. February 2005. This chapter discusses patterns of economic expansions over the last few decades and points out what is different in the expansion that started in late 2001. The end of the chapter focuses on countercyclical fiscal policy. Available at www.gpoaccess.gov/eop.

————. "Chapter 6: Innovation and the Information Economy." In *Economic Report of the President*. February 2005. Available at www.gpoaccess.gov/eop. This chapter discusses the revolution in telecommunications and information technology, with some focus on the issues of natural monopoly, appropriate regulation, and how to achieve universal access to broadband Internet service.

————. "Chapter 8: Modern International Trade." In *Economic Report of the President*. February 2005. Available at www.gpoaccess.gov/eop. This chapter discusses various current issues in international trade, including trade in services, the growth of global supply chains, and trade negotiations with China.

"Cracking Down on the Cartels." *The Economist*, April 3, 2003. This three-page survey discusses how many oligopolistic cartels have been investigated and brought down in recent years.

Cross, Sam Y. *All About...The Foreign Exchange Market in the United States*. Federal Reserve Bank of New York, 1998. Available at www.ny.frb.org/ education/addpub/usfxm. The author offers a clear and lucid description of how the foreign exchange market works behind the scenes—that is, through a network of dealers and brokers, together with their customers and the occasional participation of central banks.

Danziger, Sheldon, and Rucker C. Johnson. "Trends: Welfare Reform Update." *Milken Institute Review*, 1st quarter 2005. This even-handed review shows how the welfare reform act of 1996 succeeded in reducing the number of welfare recipients and encouraging work effort among single mothers. It also discusses how issues of health insurance for low-income mothers and their children, along with a growing number of mothers who lack welfare and work, pose ongoing problems. Available at www.milkeninstitute.org. Click on "Publications" and follow the links.

"The Diamond Cartel: The Cartel Isn't Forever." *The Economist*, July 15, 2004. De Beers has long been a dominant force in the market for diamonds, but under competitive pressure from other producers, its position is weakening.

"The Economics of Saving: The Shift away from Thrift." *The Economist*, April 7, 2005. This three-page survey discusses the trends in national and personal saving, the potential explanations behind them, and how much to worry about them.

Federal Reserve System. *Purposes and Functions*. 1994. A public information booklet that describes the structure of the Fed and the goals and implementation of monetary policy and has some discussion of other functions, such as bank oversight and consumer protection. Available at www.federalreserve.gov/ pf/pf.htm.

————. *Monetary Policymaking: Federal Open Market Committee*. This Web site gives a quick overview of open market operations as a tool of monetary policy. But perhaps more interesting, it offers links to the announcements of the Federal Open Market Committee and to minutes from its meetings. Available at www.federalreserve.gov/FOMC/default.htm.

Federal Reserve Bank of Chicago. *Modern Money Mechanics*. 1994. This useful booklet walks through the steps of how banks work and how banks create money. It's apparently not in print from the Chicago Fed any more, but typing the title and Federal Reserve Bank of Chicago into an Internet search engine will result in a number of hits on the Web. For example, at the time of this writing, it is at www.worldnewsstand.net/money/mmm2.html.

Federal Reserve Bank of New York. *The Basics of Foreign Trade and Exchange*. Available at www.ny.frb.org/education/fx/index.html. The early chapters of this useful report review the reasons why international trade provides economic benefits and the arguments against protectionism. Then, there is a step-by-step discussion of how the foreign exchange market works and the arguments over fixed and floating interest rates.

Federal Trade Commission. *Promoting Competition, Protecting Consumers: A Plain English Guide to Antitrust Laws*. Undated. Available at ftc.gov/bc/ compguide/index.htm. A nice introduction to public policy with regard to antitrust, monopoly, mergers, and competition.

Friedman, Benjamin M. "Why the Federal Reserve Should Not Adopt Inflation Targeting." *International Finance*, 7:1, 2004. This article can be read in tandem with the article by Frederick Mishkin in the same issue.

Friedman, Milton, and Rose Friedman. "Chapter 1: The Power of the Market." In *Free to Choose*. New York: Harcourt Brace Jovanovich, 1980. Milton Friedman is one of the great economists of the 20th century. In this book aimed at a generalist readership, he describes and defends how market forces work.

Friedman, Milton, and George J. Stigler. "Roofs or Ceilings? The Current Housing Problem." Originally published in *Popular Essays on Current Problems*, 1:2. New York: The Foundation for Economic Education, 1946. Reprinted with revisions, along with many other articles on rent control, in *Rent Control: A Popular Paradox*. Vancouver: The Fraser Institute, 1975.

"The Global Environment: The Great Race." *The Economist*, July 4, 2002. This survey discusses the ongoing race between economic development and environmental dangers and how market-oriented environmental tools can help to ease the tension between the two.

Gruben, William C. *Yesterday's Crisis Countries: Where Are They Now?* Federal Reserve Bank of Dallas, January 2001. Available at www.dallasfed.org/ research/indepth/2001/id0101.pdf. The author discusses the international financial crashes in Mexico, Thailand, Indonesia, Korea, Russia, and Brazil, looking for points of similarity and difference and considering possible policy options.

Hardin, Russell. "The Free Rider Problem." *The Stanford Encyclopedia of Philosophy*, Summer 2003. Edward N. Zalta, ed. Available at plato.stanford.edu/ archives/sum2003/entries/free-rider. This useful entry walks through the topics of public goods, free-riding, collective action, and the role of democracy.

"Health-Care Finance: The Health of Nations." *The Economist*, July 15, 2004. A thoughtful survey that asks whether the health-care industry is providing value commensurate with the money spent. It offers a useful discussion of how health care is financed in countries around the world and the consequences of these different choices.

International Monetary Fund. *World Economic Outlook.* The IMF publishes this volume twice a year. The first chapter goes through the regions of the world, discussing current economic issues facing them. Later chapters then examine particular issues. For example, the

April 2005 issue has chapters on the world oil market and on the role of remittances from workers abroad in the economic development of low-income countries. Current and past issues of the journal are available on the IMF Web site at www.imf.org/external/pubs/ft/weo/weorepts.htm.

Irwin, Douglas. *Free Trade under Fire*. 2nd ed. Princeton: Princeton University Press, 2005. Irwin walks carefully through the many arguments that have been made against free trade, using his skills both as an economist and a historian. He offers a fair-minded review of the strengths and weaknesses of these arguments—but is ultimately a strong supporter of free trade.

Kerr, Steven. "On the Folly of Rewarding A, While Hoping for B." *Academy of Management Journal*, 18, 1975. This classic essay gives a series of examples and arguments concerning situations in which various organizations hoped for outcome B, rewarded outcome A—and then were surprised when they got outcome A. Incentives matter!

Krugman, Paul. "Technology's Revenge." *Wilson Quarterly*, Autumn 1994. An eminent economist argues that technology is the most likely cause of growing income inequality. He then offers a provocative historical twist: Even if technology is bringing greater inequality just now, technological waves of the past have sometimes brought greater equality, as when the assembly line helped millions of workers reach upper-middle-class status during their careers. He predicts that information technology will also, eventually, bring about a wave of greater equality.

"The Lender's Long Lament." *The Economist*, December 25, 1993. Those who charge interest have been unpopular for centuries. Yet as this article shows, the history of public attitudes toward moneylenders over the last few centuries has been filled with ambiguity. The reader might consider a person's likely attitudes toward a bank when his or her loan for a home mortgage has been approved and the likely attitude if the bank foreclosed on the loan and sells off the property because the mortgage payments weren't made.

Leonard, George. "Competition." *Esquire*, May 1984. This little essay explores the adverse reaction that some people have to the concept of competition and some ways of thinking about competition that cast it in a more positive light.

"Low-Cost Airlines: Turbulent Skies." *The Economist*, July 8, 2004. A discussion of how low-cost airlines are challenging the established firms in both the United States and Europe, thus creating both additional competition and occasional calls for re-regulation of the airline industry.

Mishkin, Frederick S. "Why the Federal Reserve Should Adopt Inflation Targeting." *International Finance*, 2004, 7:1. This article can be read in tandem with the article by Benjamin Friedman in the same issue.

Office of Management and Budget. "Part III: The Long Run Budget Outlook." In *Analytical Perspectives: Budget of the United States Government, Fiscal Year 2006*. February 2005. Available at www.gpoaccess.gov/usbudget. This discussion from the proposed 2006 budget shows long-term spending and tax trends and emphasizes how Social Security and Medicare are due to drive up government spending under current law.

"Oil in Troubled Waters: A Survey of Oil." *The Economist*, April 30, 2005. Sharp increases in oil prices are often given as a reason for negative shocks to aggregate supply. However, sharp increases in oil prices in 2004 didn't cause a recession that year. This survey explores why and discusses the future of the oil industry.

"Open Skies and Flights of Fancy." *The Economist*, October 2, 2003. This article gives a nice overview of what could be the next big step in airline competition: that is, letting all airlines, whatever their country of origin, compete all around the world. Along the way, it discusses the history of airline regulation and deregulation around the world.

Ortiz, Guillermo. *Recent Emerging Market Crises: What Have We Learned?* Per Jacobsson Foundation, 2002. Available at www.perjacobsson.org/lectures/2002-ortiz.pdf. Ortiz was the head of the central bank of Mexico at the time of giving this lecture; thus, he had a front-row seat for many of the financial crises of the 1990s and early 2000s. This thoughtful overview proceeds step-by-step, looking for common elements of the crises and possible policy solutions.

"Paper Money: Crisp and Even." *The Economist*, December 20, 2001. The single biggest introduction of a new currency in history occurred at the start of 2002, when most of the countries of the European Union agreed to give up their national currencies for the euro. This article discusses the practical difficulties of introducing the euro—along with some cautionary lessons from history about failed currencies of the past.

Penner, Rudolph G., Isabel V. Sawhill, and Timothy Taylor. "Chapter 3: Inequality and Opportunity: Winners and Losers in the New Economy." In *Updating America's Social Contract: Economic Growth and Opportunity in the New Century*. New York: W. W. Norton, 2000. We discuss the trends in inequality, the possible explanations behind the trends, and the range of policy options for addressing them.

Read, Leonard E. "I, Pencil." *The Freeman*, December 1958. Available at www.econlib.org/library/Essays/rdPncl1.html. The essay that describes how the components of a pencil are made, with far-reaching economic connections all around the world.

Ritter, Joseph A. "Feeding the National Accounts." In *Review: Federal Reserve Bank of St. Louis*. 2000. Ritter offers a step-by-step and survey-by-survey account of the sources for the data behind the GDP estimates.

Robbins, Lionel. *An Essay on the Nature and Significance of Economic Science*. London: Macmillan, 1935. The short, classic philosophical essay that, especially in its opening chapters, defines how many economists see their field as the study of choices in a world of scarcity.

Rockoff, Hugh. "Price Controls." *The Concise Encyclopedia of Economics*. Library of Economics and Liberty. Available at www.econlib.org/library/ Enc/PriceControls.html. Rockoff uses a variety of historical examples to point out how government attempts to prevent prices from adjusting to their equilibrium level, through either price floors or price ceilings, run into a predictable set of unintended consequences.

Rowen, Harry. "World Wealth Expanding: Why a Rich, Democratic, and (Perhaps) Peaceful Era Is Ahead." In *The Mosaic of Economic Growth*. Ralph Landau, Timothy Taylor, and Gavin Wright, eds. Stanford, CA: Stanford University Press, 1996. In this thoughtful article, Rowen reviews the economic and political prospects of the largest developing countries around the world and explains why economic prospects for the next couple of decades are reasonably rosy. In reading, you might pay special attention to the factors that could derail this rosy scenario. Do you find yourself in agreement with Rowen that these aren't especially likely to happen?

Shaw, Jane W. "Public Choice Theory." *The Concise Encyclopedia of Economics*. Library of Economics and Liberty. Available at www.econlib.org/ library/Enc/PublicChoiceTheory.html. The public choice field of economics applies the idea that people act in their own self-interest to the actions of voters, lobbyists, and politicians and points out conditions under which governments can fail to act in the broader public interest.

Smith, Adam. *An Inquiry into the Nature and Causes of the Wealth of Nations*. 5th ed. Edwin Cannan, ed. London: Methuen and Co., 1904 (1776). Available at www.econlib.org/library/Smith/smWN.html. This book is usually credited as the first systematic work of economic analysis, and Adam Smith is usually named as the founder of the systematic study of economics. The book is generally very lucid and readable, and the table of contents is quite helpful in locating topics.

Spence, A. Michael. "Science and Technology Investment and Policy in the Global Economy." In *The Mosaic of Economic Growth*. Ralph Landau, Timothy Taylor, and Gavin Wright, eds. Stanford, CA: Stanford University Press, 1996. Spence offers one possible solution to increase R&D funding that is sure to be controversial: international arrangements for sharing the funding of science and technology.

Statistical Abstract of the United States. Annual. This desk reference pulls together government statistics, economic and otherwise, from a wide range of sources. It's the first place to look for information; if you want more detail, follow the footnotes.

Stone, Deborah A. "Making the Poor Count." *The American Prospect*, Spring 1994. This is the story of Mollie Orshansky, the woman who designed the official poverty line. The author talked with Orshansky and offers an interesting view of what Orshansky was thinking about when she designed the poverty line.

Taylor, Timothy. "Department of Misunderstandings." *Milken Institute Review*, 3rd quarter 2004. This article discusses the history of the "lump-of-labor" fallacy that the economy has a fixed number of jobs that need to be protected from women, immigrants, new technology, and long working hours. In the early 2000s, the fallacy manifested itself as the claim that high productivity was reducing the number of jobs.

―――. "The Economy in Perspective." *The Public Interest*, Fall 2004. I review the macroeconomic performance of the U.S. economy from 2001 to 2004, along with how the spending and tax policies of the first George W. Bush administration affected the economy and were affected by the economy.

―――. "Thinking about a New Economy." *The Public Interest*, Spring 2001. I put the current surge in productivity in some historical context and discuss what makes it different and likely to continue.

―――. "The Truth about Globalization." *The Public Interest*, Spring 2002. I discuss how to measure globalization and how far globalization has proceeded, along with evaluating the arguments on how globalization brings economic gains.

―――. "Untangling the Trade Deficit." *The Public Interest*, Winter 1999. I explain why a trade deficit has macroeconomic underpinnings and is not related to unfair trade barriers.

U.S. Census Bureau. "Poverty." Available at www.census.gov/hhes/ www/poverty.html. This Web site covers such issues as the definition of poverty and how it has changed over time. It also provides an annual report on the poverty rate among different groups, as well as historical data.

U.S. Department of Commerce, Bureau of Economic Analysis. *International Economic Accounts: Balance of Payments*. This Web site is the official starting point for data on the current account balance and its components. Check the most recent news release and look at some historical data. Available at bea.gov/bea/di/home/bop.htm.

―――. *National Economic Accounts: Gross Domestic Product*. Available at bea.gov/bea/dn/home/gdp.htm. This Web site lists the most recent news announcements about GDP, as well as providing historical data.

U.S. Department of Justice. *Antitrust Enforcement and the Consumer*. Available at www.usdoj.gov/atr/overview.html. The DOJ, along with the FTC, is responsible for enforcing antitrust laws. Here is a brief, accessible explanation of what laws the DOJ enforces and how such enforcement benefits the consumer.

————. *Timeline of Antitrust Enforcement Highlights at the U.S. Department of Justice*. Available at www.usdoj.gov/atr/timeline.pdf. This timeline, best viewed on the Web, is a compact three-page summary of major antitrust actions going back through the 20th century.

U.S. Department of Labor, Bureau of Labor Statistics. *Consumer Price Indexes*. Available at bls.gov/cpi/home.htm. This is the official Web site for the Consumer Price Index, with current data, historical data, answers to frequently asked questions, and a wealth of background material.

————. *Labor Force Statistics from the Current Population Survey*. Available at bls.gov/cps/home.htm. This Web site is the official starting point for unemployment rates, current or historical, broken down in many different ways.

————. *Working in the 21st Century*. Available at bls.gov/opub/working/ home.htm. This Web-based presentation is a series of charts and discussion about the evolution of the U.S. labor force, covering issues from education to retirement, often with information from 1950 and projections several decades into the future.

Wirtz, Ronald A. "Will That Be Cash, Check or Debtor's Hell?" "Buyer Beware." "A Helping Hand, or New Age Loan Sharking?" *FedGazette: Federal Reserve Bank of Minneapolis*, October 2000. Available at minneapolisfed.org/ pubs/fedgaz/ffeature.cfm. These three articles explore how borrowers, especially low-income borrowers, can become trapped in a world of high-interest credit-card overruns and payday loans.

World Bank. *Global Economic Prospects*. The World Bank publishes this volume annually. Each year, it begins with a global outlook focused on the developing countries of the world, then turns to a particular theme. For example, the 2005 report focuses on how regional efforts at developing trade and markets can affect economic development. An appendix at the back of the volume goes through the regions of the world one at a time. The report is available free at the World Bank Web site, www.worldbank.org, although you will need to look in the "Publications" area or type the title into the "search" command to find it.

World Bank. World Development Indicators. Annual. This book is the place to look for tables of economic statistics that compare all countries and regions of the world.

"The World Economy: A New Economy for the New World?" *The Economist*, September 23, 1999. In the late 1990s, with the U.S. economy booming and no inflation in sight, some economists wondered if the Phillips curve tradeoff between inflation and unemployment was truly dead. This article reviews the evidence and arguments on the tradeoff and concludes that inflation is not nearly dead.

Zeckhauser, Richard. "Insurance." *The Concise Encyclopedia of Economics*. Library of Economics and Liberty. Available at: www.econlib.org/library/Enc/ Insurance.html. A solid basic explanation of insurance markets, moral hazards, and adverse selection.

Supplementary Reading:

Abraham, Katharine, and Christopher Mackie, eds. *Beyond the Market: Designing Non-Market Accounts for the United States.* Washington, DC: National Research Council of the National Academies, National Academies Press, 2005. Available on the Web at www.nap.edu, although it's in a format that isn't easy to read. This report examines the possibilities for expanding the concept of GDP to include leisure, health, education, environmental concerns, and other values—to make it a more complete measure of society's output broadly understood.

Advisory Commission to Study the Consumer Price Index. *Toward a More Accurate Measure of the Cost of Living: Final Report to the Senate Finance Committee.* December 4, 1996. Available at www.ssa.gov/history/ reports/boskinrpt.html. In this report, done for the Senate Finance Committee, five economists evaluate potential biases in the Consumer Price Index. Although these biases have been partially addressed over time, the background and conceptual discussion remain relevant.

Bastiat, Frederic. "Reciprocity" and "A Petition." In *Economic Sophisms*. Arthur Goddard, trans. and ed. Irvington-on-Hudson, NY: Foundation for Economic Education, 1996 (1845). Bastiat was a formidable polemicist, and these are two of his most famous satirical essays against protectionism. In "Reciprocity" (First Series, chapter

10), two countries compete to make it harder and harder to trade with each other—because they both believe that fewer imports will make them wealthier. "A Petition" (First Series, chapter 7) is an impassioned argument from the candlestick makers for government protection from the unfair and job-killing competition posed by sunlight. Available at www.econlib.org/library/ Bastiat/basSoph.html.

Bordo, Michael D., and David C. Wheelock. "Monetary Policy and Asset Prices: A Look Back at Past U.S. Stock Market Booms." In *Review: Federal Reserve Bank of Saint Louis*. November/December 2004. The authors present an in-depth historical overview of the connections between monetary policy and asset booms. They find little evidence that monetary policy has played a major role in causing asset booms and caution hesitancy before using monetary policy to deflate an asset boom.

Bridges, William. "The End of the Job." *Fortune*, September 19, 1994. Back in the 19th century, when the bulk of the population worked on farms, the idea of a "job," in which you worked a fixed number of hours in a factory owned by someone else, was viewed with grave discontent. Today, as more and more people become independent contractors, providing services by telecommuting from a distance, the notion of a "job" is changing dramatically again. The author makes a provocative argument that the "job" as we have known it this last century "is vanishing like a species that has outlived its evolutionary time."

Buchanan, James, and Herbert Stein. "Should the Senate Pass a Balanced Budget Constitutional Amendment?" *Congressional Digest*, February 1995. See the "pro" article from James Buchanan on p. 50 and the "con" article from Herbert Stein on p. 53. Early in 1995, the U.S. Congress debated a plan for a constitutional amendment to require balancing the budget. The plan passed the House of Representatives but did not receive the two-thirds vote required in the Senate. This magazine contains a number of pro-and-con arguments. The two recommended here are from prominent economists: Buchanan is a Nobel laureate; Stein was a policy economist in Washington for decades.

Centers for Medicare and Medicaid Services. *2005 Annual Report of the Boards of Trustees of the Hospital Insurance and Supplementary Medical Insurance Trust Funds*. March 23, 2005. Each year around the end of March, the trustees of Medicare publish this readable report. The facts and analysis in this report provide the baseline for policymakers' discussion of Medicare. The current report and reports for the last few years are available at www.cms.hhs.gov/publications/trusteesreport.

Citro, Constance F., and Robert T. Michael. *Measuring Poverty: A New Approach*. Washington, DC: National Academy Press, 1995. This report, from a group of social scientists, offers a new definition of the poverty line. This involves both a comprehensive critique of the current definition of poverty, how it might be redefined, how the new definition would change the poverty rate, and who is below the poverty line.

Clement, Douglas. "Inflation and the Phillips Curve: The Magic Is Gone." In *The Region: Federal Reserve Bank of Minneapolis*. September 2001. This article reviews several decades of evidence and argues that the short-run Phillips curve tradeoff was never as reliable as it looked and is now unsupported by evidence. The argument is the case that the economy has a fixed natural rate of unemployment, not an unemployment-inflation tradeoff. Thus, it takes the other intellectual side from the article by Jeffrey Fuhrer.

Coase, R. H. "The Lighthouse of Economics." *Journal of Law and Economics*, 17:2, October 1974. Lighthouses have often been used by economists as an example of a public good. In this classic article, Nobel laureate Coase presented evidence that many lighthouses were privately built—and that apparently the free-rider problem wasn't as severe as many economists have assumed.

Congressional Budget Office. *Budget Options*. February 2005. This report is produced annually by the CBO, the nonpartisan research arm of the Congress. It lists literally hundreds of possible spending cuts and tax increases, with projections for how they would affect the deficit over the next few years. It also offers a few paragraphs of explanation about each one. Many teachers of economics use this book as a framework for letting students design their own plan for reducing the budget deficit. Available at www.cbo.gov.

———. *Historical Effective Federal Tax Rates: 1979 to 2002*. March 2005. The nonpartisan research agency for Congress regularly publishes different breakdowns of the tax rates paid by different income groups over time. Other CBO publications also include forecasts of the rates by income group over the next decade or so.

These reports are available at www.cbo.gov. Click on "Publications" and follow the links.

————. *Federal Terrorism Reinsurance: An Update.* January 2005. Can private insurance markets provide insurance against terrorism? What are the moral hazards and adverse selection problems likely to arise? In fact, most governments around the world help to provide terrorism insurance. This report summarizes the situation in the United States. Available at www.cbo.gov.

Council of Economic Advisers. "Chapter 6: A Pro-Growth Agenda for the Global Economy." In *Economic Report of the President.* February 2003. This chapter offers some discussion of growth patterns in the world economy and emphasizes the importance of investment in people and a rule of law to economic development. Available at www.gpoaccess.gov/eop.

"Counting the Jobless." *The Economist,* July 22, 1995. Unemployment rates can be adjusted to include "discouraged" workers or "underemployed" workers. This one-page article describes a recent report that carries out such a calculation for the industrialized nations of the world. In the end, the conclusion is that the old-fashioned unemployment rate may remain the best single measure of pressure in the labor market.

"Debating the Minimum Wage." *The Economist,* February 1, 2001. This brief article sums up the state of the academic research about whether minimum wages cause job loss.

Environmental Protection Agency. *Draft Report on the Environment.* 2003. Available at www.epa.gov/indicators/roe/index.htm. This report provides a useful summary of environmental conditions and trends affecting air, water, land, pollutants, and ecology. As with many government reports, it's better at summarizing facts than at offering solutions.

Farrell, Paul B. *The Lazy Person's Guide to Investing: A Book for Procrastinators, the Financially Challenged, and Everyone Who Worries About Dealing with Their Money.* New York: Warner Business Books, 2004. A well-known columnist for CBS *MarketWatch,* Farrell does a nice job of describing for a popular readership how saving in a well-diversified portfolio with long-term horizons lets the power of compound interest increase your wealth.

Federal Reserve. "Chapter 4: The Federal Reserve in the International Sphere." In *Purposes and Functions.* 1994. Available at www.federalreserve.gov/pf/ pdf/frspf4.pdf. This chapter focuses in particular on the role of the Federal Reserve in foreign exchange markets.

Federal Reserve Bank of Atlanta. *The Story of Money*. A Web exhibit devoted to the history of money, with a number of examples. Available at www.frbatlanta.org/atlantafed/visitors_center/tour/story.cfm.

Federal Reserve Bank of New York. *The Foreign Exchange and Interest Rate Derivatives Markets: Turnover in the United States.* April 2004. Available at www.ny.frb.org/markets/triennial/fx_survey.pdf. Once every three years, the New York Fed and 51 other central banks around the world do a survey of the large participants in foreign exchange markets. The survey results are a little dry, but if you want to get a real image of how foreign exchange markets work, the triennial survey is the place to start.

Fieleke, Norman S. "International Capital Transactions: Should They Be Restricted?" *New England Economic Review*, March/April 1994. One common suggestion for addressing international financial crises is to slow down the flow of international finance through some sort of tax or other restrictions. The author evaluates these proposals and finds that they are in some ways appealing but ultimately unpersuasive.

Flamme, Karen. "A Brief History of Our Nation's Paper Money." *Annual Report: Federal Reserve Bank of San Francisco*. 1995. Available at www.frbsf.org/publications/federalreserve/annual/1995/history.html. A description of the evolution of U.S. currency from the American Revolution to the present.

Fuhrer, Jeffrey C. "The Phillips Curve Is Alive and Well." *New England Economic Review of the Federal Reserve Bank of Boston*, March/April 1995. This article reviews several decades of evidence. It argues that even after the macroeconomic experiences of the 1970s, 1980s, and early 1990s, the short-run Phillips curve properly understood is a strong empirical relationship. Thus, it takes the other intellectual side from the article by Douglas Clement.

Gibbons, Robert. "Incentives in Organizations." *Journal of Economic Perspectives*, 12:4, Fall 1998. A discussion of how economists think about solutions to the principal-agent problem, with a particular focus on how workers might be paid in different settings. Because this article is written for economists, it is likely to be a tough read for others. On the other hand, although it has a small bit of algebra, the text is otherwise nonmathematical, and the language is introduced as it is used.

Gottlieb, Bruce. "How Much Is That Kidney in the Window?" *New Republic*, May 22, 2000. This article offers a nice summary of the arguments for and against allowing the sale of kidneys.

International Financial Institutions Advisory Commission. *International Financial Institutions Reform.* May 2000. Available at. www.house.gov/jec/ imf/meltzer.pdf. In 1998, Congress appointed a commission headed by an economist named Allan Meltzer to consider the appropriate role of international financial institutions, such as the International Monetary Fund and the World Bank. Meltzer is a well-known skeptic about such institutions; thus, this report suggests various ways that the role of international institutions could be more tightly defined.

International Monetary Fund. *Finance and Development.* This journal offers an authoritative and honest description of many issues in the global economy based on current economic research. The journal is not always the liveliest reading one could find, but it is intended for the general-interest reader, and the articles are typically quite accessible. Subscriptions are free, and current and past issues are available at www.imf.org/external/pubs/ft/fandd/fda.htm.

Krugman, Paul. *Peddling Prosperity.* New York: W. W. Norton & Company, 1994. For our purposes, the relevant chapters are 9 and 10 and the appendix to 10, in which Krugman offers a splendid explanation of why the argument for a "strategic" trade policy, which would favor certain key industries, is so misguided. More broadly, Krugman suggests that the rhetoric of "competitiveness" (like the rhetoric of "fair trade") will often lead to misguided economic policy.

Kuran, Timur. "Islam and Mammon." *Milken Institute Review*, 3rd quarter 2004. An expert on Islamic economics considers the potential conflict between Islamic prohibitions on the payment of interest and a modern financial sector. Available at www.milkeninstitute.org; click on "Publications" and follow the links to the MIR.

Malkiel, Burton. *A Random Walk Down Wall Street.* Updated and revised 8th ed. New York: Norton, 2004 (1973). Malkiel is a high-powered academic who offers an accessible popular treatment of the economic logic and academic work behind the random walk theory of financial markets. If you want a thorough understanding of the random walk theory, the evidence behind it, and what it implies for personal investing, this classic book is the place to get it.

Mankiw, Gregory N. *Principles of Economics*. 3rd ed. Forth Worth, TX: Thomson South-Western, 2004. Some listeners may want to supplement these lectures with an introductory economics textbook. This book, written by a top Harvard economist who also served a stint as an economic adviser for George W. Bush, is a fairly recent, highly readable, and very popular textbook.

Mann, Catherine L. *Is the U.S. Trade Deficit Sustainable?* Washington, DC: Institute for International Economics, September 1999. Available at the IIE Web site: bookstore.iie.com/merchant.mvc?Screen=PROD&Product_Code=47. As trade deficits have gotten larger in the 2000s, the question posed in the title of Mann's 1999 book has only seemed more relevant. You can also look under her name at the IIE Web site and usually find some of her more recent analyses on this subject.

McConnell, Campbell R., and Stanley L. Brue. *Economics: Principles, Problems, and Policies*. 16th ed. New York: McGraw-Hill, 2004. Some listeners may want to supplement these lectures with an introductory economics textbook. This book has been the bestseller for several decades.

"Men and Machines: Technology and Economics Have Already Revolutionized Manufacturing. White-Collar Work Will Be Next." *The Economist*, November 11, 2004. This article discusses how technology is causing the division of labor to shift, first in manufacturing and now in service industries.

Moffatt, Mike. "A Beginner's Guide to Elasticity." Available at economics.about.com/cs/micfrohelp/a/elasticity.htm. This Web site contains articles on a wide range of subjects.

Naipaul, V. S. "The End of Peronism?" *New York Review of Books*, February 13, 1992. What is it like to live with hyperinflation? No one knows better than the people of Argentina, where inflation averaged more than 400% per year during most of the 1980s. In this article, the novelist and writer Naipaul travels to Argentina and discusses the shock of this experience with a number of people. This isn't exactly an article about economics, but it is a fascinating look into the human and economic impact of letting inflation roar out of control.

National Bureau of Economic Research. *Information on Recessions and Recoveries, the NBER Business Cycle Dating Committee, and Related Topics.* Available at nber.org/cycles/main.html. A panel of experts at the NBER determines the actual months when recessions start and end. This Web site offers dates of past business cycles, the memos the agency has released (on an irregular basis) about past business cycles, answers to frequently asked questions, and an opportunity to sign up to receive future memos.

National Science Foundation. *National Patterns of Research Development Resources: 2003.* Annual report, 2005. Available at www.nsf.gov/statistics/ nsf05308/pdfstart.htm. If you want to get down and dirty with the facts on U.S. R&D spending—trends over time, divided into categories, how funded, who carries it out—this annual report is the place to turn.

Office of Management and Budget. *Budget of the United States Government.* Available at www.gpoaccess.gov/usbudget/index.html. If you really want to develop a feel for the federal budget, you need to look at the budget itself. The presentation and format of the budget seems to be a little different every year, and most readers won't be deeply interested in the detailed budget, which is a *lot* of fine print. But I recommend browsing through the "Historical Tables" for the budget, which offer a breakdown of major categories of taxes and spending, expressed in many different ways, for the last few decades. I also recommend browsing through the "Analytical Perspectives" volume, which looks at the budget from a variety of different angles.

Oxfam International. *Food Aid or Hidden Dumping? Separating Wheat from Chaff.* Oxfam Briefing Paper 71, March 2005. Available at www.oxfam.org.uk/ what_we_do/issues/trade/bp71_foodaid.htm. Oxfam is an international aid organization that, in the last few years, has published a series of reports on how aid to farmers in high-income countries can injure farmers and living standards in low-income countries. This report points out the problems that arise when farm surpluses from high-income countries are donated or sold at low cost in low-income countries—thus making it difficult for farmers in those countries to earn a decent level of income.

Posner, Richard A. *Natural Monopoly and Its Regulation.* Washington, DC: Cato Institute, 1999. Posner is one of the gurus of the law-and-economics movement and a lovely, lucid writer. Back in 1969, he wrote a book questioning whether natural monopolies needed to be regulated by the government. In 1999, the book was reissued with new material on the lessons of regulation and deregulation over the intervening years.

President's Commission on the United States Postal Service. *Embracing the Future: Making the Tough Choices to Preserve Universal Mail Service.* 2003. Available at www.treas.gov/offices/domestic-finance/usps. This report offers a sound diagnosis of the financial problems facing the U.S. Postal Service in the Internet era and an overview of how other countries have deregulated their post offices. However, its ultimate recommendations are a little timid, as those of presidential commissions tend to be.

Radcliff-Richards, J., A. S. Daar, R. D. Guttmann, R. Hoffenberg, I. Kennedy, M. Lock, R. A.Sells, and N. Tilney. "The Case for Allowing Kidney Sales." *The Lancet*, June 27, 1998. A group of doctors and specialists in ethics make a case for why kidney sales should be allowed.

Radford, R. A. "The Economic Organization of a P.O.W. Camp." *Economica*. New Series, 12:48, November 1945. A classic article describing how markets worked in an unexpected place—in prisoner-of-war camps during World War II.

Resources for the Future. *Resources.* A Washington think-tank called Resources for the Future, which has often led the way in providing economic analyses of environmental problems, has a readable magazine called *Resources*. It's available on the Web at www.rff.org/rff/Publications/Resource_Articles.cfm. If you like it, you can also order a free subscription at the Web site.

Rosenberg, Nathan. "Uncertainty and Technological Change." In *The Mosaic of Economic Growth*. Ralph Landau, Timothy Taylor, and Gavin Wright, eds.. Stanford, CA: Stanford University Press, 1996. When Marconi invented the radio, he thought it would be used only for place-to-place "narrowcasting," not broadcasting to the public. When Bell's engineers invented the laser, they saw no point in seeking a patent for it, because lasers would never have anything to do with the telephone industry. In this delightful and provocative article, Rosenberg argues that examples like these are not the result of short-sightedness or stupidity, but simply occur because new technologies are extraordinarily unpredictable. As a result, he argues that government policy should steer away from trying to channel scientific effort in a way that attempts to predict the unpredictable and, instead, should focus on ensuring strength in a broad portfolio of technologies.

Ruby, Douglas A. *The Components of Aggregate Demand.* Revised January 15, 2003. www.digitaleconomist.com/ad_4020.html. This Web site offers a textbook-style explanation of aggregate demand and its components, together with some graphical analysis.

―――. *Long Run Aggregate Supply and Price Level Determination.* Revised January 18, 2003. Available at www.digitaleconomist.com/as_4020.html. This Web site offers a textbook-style explanation of aggregate supply in the long run, together with some graphical analysis.

Scheller, Hanspeter K. *The European Central Bank—History, Role and Functions.* 2004. Available at www.ecb.int/pub/pdf/other/ecbhistoryrolefunctions2004en.pdf. The European Central Bank and the euro are the greatest new experiments in money and central banking in at least the last few decades. This book offers a comprehensive overview of the ECB goals and operations.

Social Security Administration. *2005 Annual Report of the Board of Trustees of the Federal Old-Age and Survivors Insurance and Disability Insurance Trust Funds.* March 23, 2005. Each year around the end of March, the trustees of Social Security publish this report on the immediate, short-term, and long-term outlook for the system. The report is mostly quite readable, and the introductory chapter provides a nice overview. The most recent report and the past few reports are available at www.ssa.gov/OACT/TR.

Stewart, James B. "Whales and Sharks." *The New Yorker,* February 15, 1993. Two of the most famous antitrust cases in recent decades were the attempts by the government to break up IBM (a suit that was dropped) and to break up AT&T into separate local and long-distance companies (a suit that succeeded). Paradoxically, if IBM had allowed itself to be broken up, its various parts might be stronger competitors in the computer market today. After all, greater competition in telecommunications has invigorated that entire sector of the U.S. economy.

U.S. Census Bureau. *Historical Income Inequality Tables.* Available at www.census.gov/hhes/income/histinc/ineqtoc.html. For a variety of tables illustrating the extent of inequality and trends over time, check here.

U.S. Department of Labor, Bureau of Labor Statistics. *How the Government Measures Unemployment.* Available at www.bls.gov/cps/cps_htgm.htm. Last modified October 16, 2001. This 12-page report explains basic questions about how unemployment is measured. It is aimed at a general audience, but it includes a lot more detail than appeared in the lecture. This is a good starting point for those who want to know about "seasonally adjusted" unemployment, issues concerning the unemployment survey itself, and other topics.

U.S. House of Representatives, Ways and Means Committee. *2004 Green Book: Background Material and Data on the Programs within the Jurisdiction of the Committee on Ways And Means.* The *Green Book* is published every other year, and it offers an up-to-date if somewhat dry overview of many federal programs that affect the poor. For example, Temporary Assistance for Needy Families (TANF) is in Section 7, the Earned Income Tax Credit is in Section 13, and Food Stamps and Medicaid are in Section 15. Available at www.gpoaccess.gov/ wmprints/green/2004.html.

Wikipedia: en.wikipedia.org/wiki/Main_Page. Wikipedia is an interesting venture, because the quality of the entries depends on who wants to work on them.

Wolf, Charles, Jr. "The New Mercantilism." *The Public Interest,* Summer 1994. *Mercantilism* is the name given to a view of trade that was prevalent several centuries ago, before the writings of Adam Smith. In a nutshell, the mercantilists believed that exporting was good for a country and importing was bad. Modern economists believe that both sides of trade are interrelated, that trade as a whole is beneficial. Wolf accuses some opinion leaders and policymakers of succumbing to the mercantilist view.

World Trade Organization. *Understanding the WTO.* 2003. A short book that gives background on what the WTO actually is and how it operates and addresses many of the issues that arise about the WTO. The WTO Web site has a fair number of accessible publications, from pamphlets to short books, that discuss trade issues. Available at www.wto.org/english/thewto_e/ hatis_e/tif_e/tif_e.htm.